T0316803

THE GLOBAL MANAGEMENT SERIES

Project Management

Amos Haniff and Mohamed Salama

(G) Goodfellow Publishers Ltd

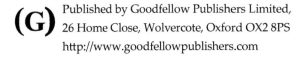 Published by Goodfellow Publishers Limited,
26 Home Close, Wolvercote, Oxford OX2 8PS
http://www.goodfellowpublishers.com

Published 2016

British Library Cataloguing in Publication Data: a catalogue record for this
title is available from the British Library.
Library of Congress Catalog Card Number: on file.

ISBN: 978-1-911396-03-1

Copyright © Amos Haniff and Mohamed Salama, 2016

All rights reserved. The text of this publication, or any part thereof, may not
be reproduced or transmitted in any form or by any means, electronic or
mechanical, including photocopying, recording, storage in an information
retrieval system, or otherwise, without prior permission of the publisher or
under licence from the Copyright Licensing Agency Limited. Further details
of such licences (for reprographic reproduction) may be obtained from the
Copyright Licensing Agency Limited, of Saffron House, 6–10 Kirby Street,
London EC1N 8TS.

All trademarks used herein are the property of their repective owners, The
use of trademarks or brand names in this text does not imply any affiliation
with or endorsement of this book by such owners.

 Design and typesetting by P.K. McBride, www.macbride.org.uk

Cover design by Cylinder

Printed by Baker & Taylor, www.baker-taylor.com

Contents

Dedications

To my beautiful wife Lisa and our gorgeous children Qasim and Safia. Love you xxx

AH

To my Mum & Dad, my lovely wife Zaza and our boys Omar and Ally. You are the most precious!

MS

Acknowledgments

The editors of this text book are grateful to the series editors Professors Robert Macintosh and Kevin O'Gorman who were the main drivers behind writing this book. We are also grateful to all our colleagues in the School of Management and Languages as well as the very professional team at Goodfellow publishers who contributed to and have helped in the production of this book. It has been a pleasure to work with you.

AH & MS

Biographies

Amal Abbas is a doctoral researcher in the school of Management and Languages at Heriot-Watt University. Drawing on the new institutional economics theory, her doctoral research investigates the effect of the individual, the firm and the environmental level factors on female entrepreneurial activity in Egypt. More widely she is interested in examining entrepreneurial behaviour and entrepreneurial ecosystems in both the developing and developed countries. Additionally, Amal works as an assistant professor in the Business Administration Department, Cairo University, Egypt

John Rudolph Raj, PhD is with the Faculty of Management, Multimedia University, Malaysia. He has more than 30 years of experience in corporate, industry, and academia. His research interests are in the disciplines of Project Management, Operations Management and Advanced Statistical Analysis.

Isla Kapasi, PhD is an early career researcher in the field of entrepreneurship. She has published several academic papers in well-respected peer-reviewed journals and presented at major national and international conferences. Isla is also experienced in the development of innovative teaching curricula, most recently with Team Entrepreneurship and has taught at all levels. Prior to developing her academic career, Isla was involved in public, private and third sector employment and self-employment.

Amos Haniff is Associate Professor of Project Management at Heriot Watt University and Deputy Head of the Department of Business Management within the School of Management and Languages. He teaches project management and strategic project management at postgraduate and executive levels, and delivers training courses in project management and strategic change to public and private sector organizations. His research interests is on project success and the strategic alignment of projects with organizational strategy. In particular, he has conducted research into the strategic behavior of temporary multi-organizations and project leadership. He has created a portfolio of MSc and Executive MSc programmes in project management, including European funded Erasmus Mundas courses. He is a member of the Court of the University, a fellow of the Higher Education Academy, a PRINCE2 Practitioner, and former Scottish representative for the Association of Project Management (APM) Education Network. He is also a frustrated blues guitarist.

Laura Galloway is a Professor of Business and Enterprise in the school of Management & Languages at Heriot-Watt University and Dean of the University for Arts, Humanities and Social Science. Based in the School of Management and Languages, her teaching focuses on leadership and entrepreneurship and her research interests are in these broad themes too. In particular, Professor Galloway's research involves the theory and practice relating to entrepreneurship amongst different groups, leadership, and the effects of entrepreneurship education on skills and business outcomes. Examples of her recent work include exploring the experiences of being a leader or an entrepreneur.

Robert Graham is Associate Professor of Organisational Behaviour in the School of Management and Languages, Heriot-Watt University. His research interest is in the emergence of Human Resource Management and organisational change. Robert teaches both Organisational Behaviour and Human Resource Management on the Post-Graduate Masters in International Business Management and Human Resource Management at undergraduate level. Robert is a member of both the Centre of Work and Wellbeing (CROWW) and the HR Research Group at Heriot-Watt University. Robert has delivered courses on organisational change to the Nigerian Securities and Exchange Commission, the Wood Group and Standard Life Investments, and he was a visiting lecturer in management at Shanghai University of Finance and Economics (SUFE). He has a background in trade union education, having been a tutor with the Trades Union Congress for fifteen years and then worked in management training and development for a number of years. Robert has worked with the Scottish Fire Service, the General Teaching Council for Scotland, Edinburgh University, the Faculty of Advocates and the Royal College of Surgeons (Edinburgh).

Reza Mohammadi is Course Director and Project Coordinator for the suite of MSC Engineering and Physical Programme at Heriot Watt University. He teaches courses in Project Management and Critical Analysis, and Research Preparation at postgraduate and undergraduate levels. He also delivers workshops in Project Management Concept and Project Soft Skills to public and private sector organizations. His research interests are in human factor and stakeholder management in programs and the project environment. He is an Information Technology Project Manager by background with extensive professional experience in the public and private sectors both national and international levels. He is also a PRINCE II, ITIL, Waterfall, Kanban, Scrum and Agile project management methodologies Practitioner and an active member of Association of Project Management (APM) and the Project Management Institute (PMI).

Mohamed Salama is currently the Director of Corporate Executive Relations and the former Acting Associate Head of the School of Management and Languages, Heriot Watt University, Dubai Campus. He has joined academia in 2002 and has been the Programme Director of MSc in Strategic Project Management since 2006 at Dubai Campus. Dr. Salama has 30 years of academic and industrial experience in Project Management, Marketing, Strategy and Mergers & Acquisitions. Mohamed has taken senior management posts in Construction Management, Marketing and Mergers & Acquisitions in ME, Italy and UK over the period 1990 – 2002. He holds BSc (Hons) in Civil Engineering from Cairo University, an MBA from Edinburgh Business School and a PhD in Construction Management from the School of Built Environment, Heriot Watt University. He has been delivering training workshops in project management and strategy for executives over the past decade in the UK, Middle East, and Denmark. He is a Fellow of the Higher Education Academy (HE) in Scotland and a member of the Project Management Institute PMI (USA), The Chartered Management Institute (CMI-UK), and The Association of Researchers in Construction Management (ARCOM) in the UK. He has publications in the areas of Project Performance, Green Buildings and Higher Education.

Mo Sherif is an Associate Professor of Finance. He received his PhD from the University of Manchester, Manchester Business School, UK. He is an interdisciplinary finance researcher whose initial contributions to the finance literature are in entrepreneurial and behavioural finance, stock trading strategies and asset pricing fields. He is a fellow of the Higher Education Academy in the UK and a member of American Finance Association in the USA. He is currently the Director of Postgraduate Taught Programmes in Finance (AEF) at SML at Heriot-Watt University.

Gowrie Vinayan, PhD is Assistant Professor in the School of Management and Languages, Heriot Watt University, Malaysia campus. Gowrie teaches International entrepreneurship and resources and talent management at undergraduate level and project management and demand and planning for the postgraduate masters in project management. Her scholarly efforts are devoted to areas of operations and production management, project management and supply chain management. Prior to joining the academia, she was with a multinational organization where she received extensive industry exposure in the area of project management, logistics, warehousing and procurement. Besides lecturing, she has also designed and conducted trainings related to project management and strategy execution to working adults.

Preface

Introduction

Project management has attracted significant attention over the past decades and in a world that continues to witness very dynamic business environments regardless of location, change is inevitable and project management tools and techniques become even more popular. During the early days of its evolution, project management was predominantly an engineering-led specialization. During that period, those who wrote about project management and who taught or conducted research about project management were mostly either engineers or looking at engineering related sectors such as construction.

Context

Now-a-days, project management tools and techniques have attracted the attention of almost all disciplines, as emphasized in the membership of the major professional bodies such as PMI, and indeed in the diversity of students attending the project management courses offered at undergraduate and postgraduate levels. This textbook aims to provide readers from different backgrounds with the essential knowledge that would help them acquire and furthermore develop basic project management skills.

In the past few decades, Higher Education, endorsed by the advancements in technology, has witnessed a notable shift from the traditional learning and teaching methods. Having taught project management in different contexts and for a wide range of audience for a combined total of more than 30 years, the editors have been motivated to introduce this textbook as a useful guide to facilitate the learning of students regardless of the mode of study. In addition, practitioners and independent learners who are seeking to enhance their knowledge base and develop their project management skills away from the classroom will benefit from the practical approach adopted in writing this textbook; simplifying some of the challenging concepts and numerical aspects.

In this pursuit, the authors of different chapters have attempted to gradually guide the readers in developing their knowledge, starting from first principles and working towards a relatively advanced stage, with the help of a range of case studies, practical examples and numerical worked examples. The end of chapter questions aim to provoke critical thinking, analysis and synthesis. In addition, the references listed at the end of each chapter and cited within the text offer the reader an additional set of resources that will provide further in-depth knowledge about some of the specific areas mentioned in the text.

Content and pedagogy

This textbook comprises 12 chapters covering the key areas in the context of managing projects that span both soft and hard skills. Each chapter starts with a list of learning outcomes that pinpoint the objectives of the chapter and should be used alongside the end of chapter questions as a benchmark for students to evaluate their erudition and learning. Chapter 1 provides a background to the development of modern project management and sets the scene for the following chapters. Key concepts are introduced, including the project life cycle, project constraints and project success criteria. Chapter 2 positions projects within the context of the organization and environment. Project stakeholders are identified, with guidance on how they should be managed. This is followed by presentation of three types of organizational structure that need to consider the organizational culture when implementing projects. This chapter also introduces the growing practice of the project management office.

Chapter 4 discusses the critical project management competency of leadership. This chapter explains the concept of project leadership, in detail, through the introduction of contemporary leadership theories. Following on from the discussion on leadership, Chapter 5 provides a comprehensive explanation of managing project teams. Key concepts include the stages in team development, team dynamics and the management of virtual teams.

A detailed discussion about the financial dimension, supported by simple numerical examples, is presented in Chapter 3 with emphasis on the impact of inflation and taxation on project appraisal and selection decisions. The areas of project scope management and communication management are detailed and debated in Chapter 6 with some useful templates, exercises and practical examples. The core areas of project cost estimating and budgeting, time scheduling and resource management are presented and discussed in depth with a range of examples, case studies and end of chapter multiple choice and numerical questions in Chapters 8, 9 and 10, respectively.

An introduction to cost modeling techniques and the factors affecting the accuracy of the different cost models is presented and discussed under cost estimating and cost forecasting. In addition, Chapter 8 includes a section on bidding strategies, with emphasis on the difference between front and back loading and the importance of considering the present value of the tender price whilst comparing different bids. In Chapter 9, the concept of project scheduling complemented by a detailed step-by-step guide that helps students to estimate activity duration then draw and analyze the network for a simple work package using the critical path method. In addition, the project evaluation and review technique (PERT) is introduced and explained.

Project Risk management is discussed in Chapter 7, with a range of practical examples covering the different types of risk, and also has a detailed section on risk clinic with useful templates. The important aspect of risk attitude has been presented and utilized to explain why managers may have different responses to the same risk event. In addition, the chapter concludes by comparing and contrasting the traditional project management methodology to the contemporary Agile Project Management methodology in the context of risk. In this pursuit, the discussion presents the basic concepts of Agile methodology which has proven to be quite popular within IT and software development projects over the past two decades.

Chapter 11 falls into two main parts. The first discusses change management and configuration management. The second part addresses the areas of project evaluation and control. The earned value analysis as a performance measurement technique, that can shed light on project cost performance as well as the progress of the project, is explained and discussed using numerical examples. The challenges of project closure and the key attributes of this, often neglected, stage of the project life cycle is presented and discussed in Chapter 12.

Project management is a practical discipline. No matter how many books one reads about managing projects, students can only get a feel of the real-life project themes, issues and challenges through interactive discussions, practice, critical thinking and analysis of the various exercises, and case studies provided within the different chapters. Hard skills such as the numerical techniques presented under project financial appraisal, project cost estimating, budgeting, time scheduling (CPM), crashing and project performance measurement (EVA) need to be well understood and practiced through numerical examples followed by a clear interpretation of the results. On the other hand, the soft skills such as leadership, communication, and team issues need more practical workshop based activities such as group activities and team work based projects.

In order to maximize the benefit of the resources provided within this text book, it is recommended that students should be assigned prior relevant reading utilizing the references provided at the end of chapters before being introduced to, and asked to engage in higher order discussions such as those pertaining to leadership theories, the different types and accuracy level of cost models or the debate about the pros and cons of the traditional project management methodology versus more contemporary approaches such as agile methodologies.

Mohamed Salama and Amos Haniff

1 Introduction to Project Management

Amos Haniff and Mohamed Salama

Learning objectives

By the time you have completed this chapter you should be able to:

- ☐ Identify the essential characteristics of a project
- ☐ Draw a distinction between projects and routine operations
- ☐ Describe the four phases of the project life cycle
- ☐ Evaluate the time, cost and quality constraints on the project.
- ☐ Evaluate the project success criteria
- ☐ Understand how the discipline of project management has evolved
- ☐ Summarise the project manager's knowledge areas

1.1 Introduction

Over the past thirty years, projects have changed the way we live and work. Through technology and new product development projects, we have seen changes in the way we communicate, the way we exchange knowledge and even how we spend our leisure time. Through capital projects, we have witnessed significant regeneration of major cities, faster transportation routes and new public spaces. Through drug development projects, we have witnessed mass immunisation, new medical treatments and an extension in the average life expectancy. Furthermore, through events projects we have been able to enjoy major, international sporting occasions, such as the Olympic Games, the FIFA World Cup and the American Super Bowl.

Within the world of business, organisations recognise that to remain competitive they need to develop project management methodologies. As a result of the World Wide Web, development in new technologies and globalisation, there are now fewer barriers to trade. With this increase in competition, powerful corporations are being threatened by small home businesses, across the globe. Changes in lifestyle have also led to a more demanding customer who wants new products and new technologies quicker and more advanced than before.

Through project management, organisations are able to bypass the traditional bureaucracies, inherent in large firms, and deliver products and services to customers faster and more efficiently. The project management methodology enables organisations to reduce costs, make better use of resources and improve quality. Significantly, the adoption of project management leads to a reduction in risk, which means fewer errors and improved success rates. This enables customer focus, improved customer service and increased customer satisfaction. It should, therefore, be of little surprise to find that 80% of global executives believe that having project management as a core competency within the organisation is critical to remaining competitive (Economist, 2009). It is for this reason that building a strong project management capability is a top priority for many firms as they plan for the future (PMI, 2010).

1.2   A brief history of project management

Before we begin to explore what a project is and how projects plans are developed and executed, it is worth considering how the discipline of project management has evolved over the past 50 years.

There has been the suggestion, within many project management textbooks, that that projects have been around since the pyramids of Giza. However, typical historical feats of engineering were not 'project managed' as we understand the term. In the first instance the architect or engineer responsible for the delivery of the 'project' did not have the same resource constraints as project managers do today. Rather, most ancient landmarks were built using slave labour, and failure to deliver often resulted in public execution of the project manager. Second, our ancestral 'project managers' did not plan within budget and deadline constraints. In fact, the majority of famous buildings were constructed at great costs, over many decades. The Great Wall of China took eleven centuries to complete, St. Peters Bascilia in Rome took 120 years to build, and Antoni Gaudi's Sagrada Familia, has been in construction since 1882.

Morris (1997) provides the most respected history of project management in which he makes the argument that *modern* project management did not emerge until the 1950s. This is when project management techniques started to be used in an organised process. At this time, the primary focus was on mathematical planning and control techniques to aid the management of large complex projects. These efforts resulted in the creation of two of the most important project management, planning tools. Firstly, in 1958 the US Department of Defence (DoD) developed Programme Evaluation and Review Technique (PERT) as a tool to support the POLARIS submarine and missile programme. Meanwhile in 1959, E.I du Pont de Nemours Company developed the Critical Path Method (CPM), to schedule the construction of major chemical plants in the US. As a result of the success of these planning methods, project management became very well publicised and other quantitative tools were developed. These included work breakdown structures (Chapter 6), earned value analysis (Chapter 11) and project crashing (Chapter 9).

Despite early success of project management, during the1960s it was recognised that managing projects requires more than a toolbox of planning and control techniques to be successful (Avots, 1962). Researchers, therefore, began to consider the human dimension of projects. Subsequently projects became concerned with organisational structures (Chapter 2), team development (Chapter 5) and project leadership (Chapter 4). However, the most significant impact to the recognition of project management as a distinct management discipline was in 1969, when the first project management professional body, the Project Management Institute (PMI), was formed.

The 1970s was a time of refinement of project management tools. This included attention to matrix organisational structures (Chapter 2), the introduction of responsibility assignment matrices (Chapter 5), risk management (Chapter 7) and the development of project teams (Chapter 5). During this decade there was also advancement in information technology and computing that led to the development of highly sophisticated project management software. Project managers were gaining access to software that would allow the creation of Gantt charts, PERT diagrams, control resource usage and manage costs. Indeed, the developments in project management techniques and the benefits of adoption saw the discipline move outside its traditional heartlands of construction and engineering into mainstream management. PMI also reacted to the unprecedented growth in project management and introduced the first edition of the *Project Management Body of Knowledge* (PMBOK) in 1987, which has underpinned project management professionalism and education for the past three decades.

As a result of developments, by the 1990s project management was no longer confined to the creation of products and services, but were being used as a tool for business transformation, continuous improvement, organisational change, value creation and strategy implementation. The concept of project management had become so widespread that commentators began to speak of the *"projectification of society"* (Midler, 1995, Haniff and Fernie, 2008), where life in general appears to be guided by project-related principles. It would appear that fifty years after its conception, 'projects' and 'project management' have not only become fashionable terms, but now play a significant role within all types of organisations.

1.3   What is a project?

A review of the abundant texts on the field project management will discover a number of similar definitions for the term *project:*

- A temporary endeavour, undertaken to create a unique product or result (PMI, 2013)

- A set of activities with a defined start point and a defined end state, which pursues a defined goal and uses a defined set of resources (Slack et al., 2007)

- A unique venture with a beginning and end, conducted by people to established goals within parameters of cost, schedule and quality (Buchanan and Boddy, 1992)

- A temporary organisation that is needed to produce a unique and predefined outcome or result at a pre-specified time using predetermined resources (OGC, 2005)

From these definitions it can be determined that a project has the following essential characteristics:

Predetermined goal: Every project has a predefined purpose to be achieved within specific limitations.

Temporary: Every project has a definite beginning and a definite end.

Unique: No two projects are the same in that the project outcome differs, in some form or another, from previous project outcomes

Organised resources: Every project requires a combination of human and non-human resources, directed by a project manager to achieve the project goal.

1.4 Projects and routine operations

Another way to define projects is to distinguish them from the routine operations that provide goods and services to customers on a daily basis. In project-based organisations such as construction and engineering or software development, normal work activities are performed as projects. However, in the modern business environment all types of organisations are required to perform activities that differ from the daily operations of the business. All businesses have repetitive, routine operations that they require to function. For example, an operations function of a finance department is to process and pay invoices, an operations function of a marketing department is to collate information on customer preferences and an operations function of a manufacturing department is to manage the continuous supply chain in the production of products.

Projects are the non-repetitive, non-routine activities that are required to achieve specific organisational goals. This may be in the form of implementing a new IT system to track payments and manage invoices more efficiently, or the design and launch of new marketing campaign, or the design and development of a new product for mass production. Table 1.1 summarises some the distinctions between projects and routine operations.

Projects	Routine operations
Creates a unique product or service	Creates repeat products or services
Temporary life-cycle	Ongoing
Has a single purpose	Has several purposes
High levels of uncertainty	Uncertainties managed before production
Has a primary customer	Has numerous customers
Managed as a separate organisation	Managed within the organisation
Requires multi-skilled resources	Requires dedicated resources

Table 1.1: Differences between projects and routine operations

It is the unique and temporary characteristics of projects that make them difficult to fit within normal organisational context, hence the need for a different way of managing them.

Exercise 1

From the definitions stated above, identify some projects that you are either familiar with or have been involved in. What made the project unique?

1.5   The project life cycle

Another way of defining the unique nature of projects is the way they are organised. Because projects are complex and have an element of uncertainty, project mangers prefer to split the project into phases. This is referred to as to the **project life cycle**. By dividing a project into a logical sequence of phases, the project manager is able to minimise risk.

The project life cycle typically consists of the four sequential phases that all projects pass through from beginning of the project to its end. Each phase consists of a number of activities that the project manager must achieve in order to realise the project objectives. These are referred to as the **project management deliverables,** illustrated in Figure 1.1.

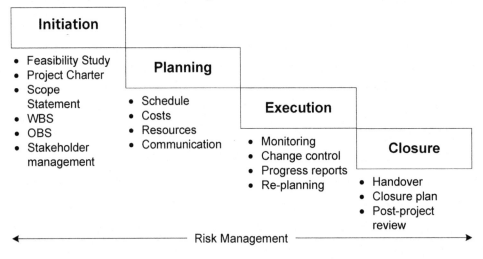

Figure 1.1: The project life-cycle with project management deliverables

1 **Initiation phase:** This is the inception phase where projects are defined in terms of the project requirements, deliverables, objectives, stakeholder needs, rationale for the project and production of the project charter. It is normally at this stage that the project manager is appointed, the project team is formed and the major responsibilities for delivery of the project are assigned.

2 **Planning phase:** In this phase plans are developed to meet the requirements of the specification by the project team. This includes identifying the projected activities, formulating the project schedule, calculating the project costs and assigning project resources.

3 **Execution phase:** It is only once the planning stage is complete that the project should be implemented. This is the execution phase. During this stage the

project needs to be monitored to ensure that the work meets the objectives of the project in accordance with the specification. The project also needs to be controlled to bring any deviation from the plans back in line with the requirements of the specification.

4   **Closure phase:** This final phase is when the project is complete. During this phase the project must be formally handed over to the customer with all appropriate documentation. All costs must be paid and project resources must be redeployed.

Throughout the project life cycle, the project is subject to internal and external risks. This is discussed further in Chapter 7

Exercise 2

Think about these phases in terms of doing a course assignment. What activities and deliverables are required to complete the assignment?

1   **Initiation Phase:** Clarify the assignment.
- ☐ What are the requirements?
- ☐ What does the lecturer expect from me?
- ☐ When is the deadline?

2   **Planning Phase:** Decide how it will be done
- ☐ How long will take to complete the assignment?
- ☐ What activities do I need to do to complete the assignment?
- ☐ What resources do I need?

3   **Execution Phase:** Execute the assignment.
- ☐ Acquire the resources from the library.
- ☐ Conduct the necessary research.
- ☐ Write a draft.
- ☐ Amend the draft and complete the finished assignment in line with the requirements.

4   **Closure Phase:** Hand-over
- ☐ Submit the assignment.
- ☐ Return resources to the library.
- ☐ Await results

Level of effort

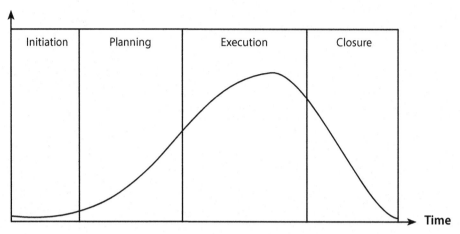

Figure 1.2: Level of effort required throughout the project life-cycle

As shown in Figure 1.2, the level of effort throughout the project life cycle varies between phases. Effort could also be expressed as man-hours or cost.

- At the **initiation phase** most of the effort required is by that of the project manager who is responsible for clarifying the project requirements. However, there may also be other team members and project support.

- During the **planning phase**, the level of effort and activity gradually increases, as the project team defines the specific activities that need to be complete in order to realise the project objectives. It is also at this phase that the project manager may identify the need for external specialists and consultants, to carry out some of the work packages that need to be complete as part of the project deliverable.

- During the **execution phase** the actual work on the project is performed. This is the highest point of financial commitment for the client organisation, as a result of the necessary expenditure on resources, materials and equipment required on the project. The main role of the project manager at this phase is to monitor and control the project in order to ensure that the schedule and costs of the project remain as planned through the execution.

- The final phase of the life cycle is **project closure**. This is when the project is complete and transferred to the client organisation for use. The project team disbands to begin assignment on their next project.

1.6   The project constraints

All projects are constrained by three key objectives; these are **time**, **cost** and **quality**. More often it is these three objectives that are used to define project success, which is discussed later in this chapter. Commonly referred to as the **'triple constraints'**, these define the primary measureable goals as articulated by the project client.

- **Time:** All projects have a specific time in which they should be completed. This should be reflected in the project schedule. For example, implementation of a new marketing campaign that must be launched in October to ensure Christmas sales; construction of new university accommodation that must be completed in time for the start of the academic year; or a new training programme that must be complete in time for legislative changes.

- **Cost:** All projects are constrained by a limited budget. This is the cost made available by the project sponsor to achieve the project requirements, and is reflected in the project cost estimates. For example, for a new a product launch the client organisation may have a marketing budget based on the expected return of profit from sales that cannot be exceeded without eroding profits. A university may have a budget for building new accommodation based on the time it would take the rental income from students to recover the expense. Organisations would have training budgets based on the number of people that need training over a set period.

- **Quality:** In general, clients expect projects to be delivered to specific level of quality. This includes adherence to the specification of project requirements, or standards that the project is expected to achieve. The expected level of quality should be clearly stated in the project specification and scope statement. For example, as part of an organisation's marketing campaign the quality of the brochure may be specified as "high gloss, full colour printing on heavy-weight paper" as opposed to double sided A4 photocopies. When building new university student accommodation, the Estates Department would specify built-in wardrobes, desk and carpets, but these items would not be expected to be to the same level of quality as a 4-star hotel. An organisation which embarks on a project of staff training would specify that the training organisation provides fully qualified trainers, appropriate facilities and suitable learning materials. These factors would determine the project sponsor's perception of quality.

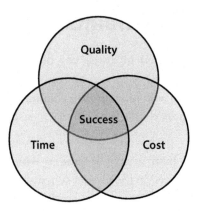

Figure 1.3: The project 'Iron Triangle'

Figure 1.3 demonstrates the relationship between time, cost and quality constraints on a project. This is commonly known as the 'iron-triangle'. The challenge for the project manager is to balance the competing constraints. Changes to any of the constraints will have an impact on, at least, one other. For example, a reduction in the project schedule will result in, either an increase in cost to pay for additional resources to meet the revised deadline, or a reduction in the quality of the project as there is less time to achieve the desired standards. Similarly, a reduction in budget often equates to a reduction in quality or the project taking longer to complete as a result of fewer resources being allocated for the project. Similarly, an increase in the quality standards will result in, either an increase in costs or an increase in the time required to achieve the project deliverables.

Recently, PMI (2013) have proposed that, at least three other competing constraints that need to be considered by the project manager when planning and executing the project.

- **Scope:** This is what is included within the project deliverable. The scope may be reduced to deliver the project deliverable in less time or at a lower cost.

- **Resources:** These are the people, materials and equipment required to deliver the scope of the project. The project team need to consider the level of resources required to deliver the project by the required time within the allocated budget.

- **Risk:** Changes in any of the project requirements or objectives may create additional risks that will need assessment by the project team.

1.7   Project success criteria

Traditionally, the dominant criteria on which to measure project success has long been on achieving the specific project objectives within the 'iron triangle' of time, cost and quality. More recently, the concept of project success has begun to consider the wider perception of the stakeholders, throughout the project life cycle. These include client satisfaction, satisfaction of the project team and end-user satisfaction.

However, it has been recognised that meeting the project within the schedule, budgetary and quality constraints does not necessarily mean that the project will be a success. For a project to be successful, it must also add value to the organisation in terms of the business benefits enabled as a result of implementation. Organisations invest in projects to enhance the business, and therefore the output of the project must align with the strategic aspirations established in the company vision. In recognising the strategic value of projects, Shenhar *et al* (2001) presents a model showing four dimensions of project success. Significantly, the model shown in Figure 1.4 demonstrates that the relative importance of each dimension is time dependent. The varied dimensions are more important at different times during and after completion of the project.

Importance

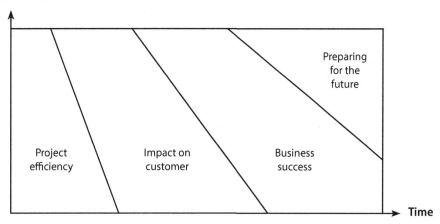

Figure 1.4: Relative importance of success dimensions. *Source: Shenhar et al (2001)*

- The first dimension considers the efficiency of the project team in delivering the project within the time, cost and quality objectives. This dimension can be assessed only in the very short-term during the execution of the project and immediately after its completion.

- The second dimension addresses the importance placed on client requirements and meeting the client needs. This includes end-users and end customers. This dimension can be assessed a short time after the project has been delivered to the client and the end-user has experienced the final deliverable.

■ The third dimension addresses the immediate impact the project has on the business, in terms of sales, income and profit, as a result of investment into the project. This dimension can only be assessed after a reasonable time to achieve sales, usually one or two years.

■ The fourth dimension considers the long-term strategic contribution of the project and how participation of the project has prepared the organization for future opportunities. These include exploration of new markets, ideas, innovations and products. This dimension can only be assessed after a period of at least three to five years.

The model of success dimensions is a useful tool to understand the varied perceptions of success and different timeframes in which success can be measured. However, it should be noted that varied projects have their own specific dimensions and their relevant importance will vary accordingly. This is yet another challenge for the project manager.

1.8   What is project management?

PMI define project management as "the application of knowledge, skills, tools, and techniques to project activities to meet project requirements" (PMI, 2013). Managing a project typically includes identification of the project requirements, defining the scope of the project and establishing the time, cost and quality project objectives. Besides managing the project objectives, the project manager also needs to address the varied needs, expectations and success the stakeholders. This includes the creation of efficient communication channels between stakeholders in order to meet the project requirements and ensure the project deliverables.

Indeed, the project manager is the person responsible for leading the project and therefore the person ultimately responsible for achieving the project goals. All projects must have a project manager, and for project success the project manager must be highly competent as a manager, have the appropriate analytical skills, have strategic skills, must be a good negotiator, a good listener and, above all, an effective leader. It is for these reasons that exceptional project managers are in high demand.

Whether exceptional or average, all project managers must have a core set of skills and competencies. These are referred to as the *project managers' knowledge areas*. In considering the role of the project manager, the Project managers knowledge areas must include project management tools, processes and other general management disciplines. The PMBok identifies nine specific project knowledge management areas, as shown in Figure 1.5.

Figure 1.5: The PMI project management knowledge areas

Project integration management

As no two projects are identical, project managers must decide on the appropriate methodology and tools required for project success. Project integration management involves selecting the appropriate project management processes and ensuring they are coordinated efficiently. This may include deciding on where to concentrate resources on a daily basis, and making trade-offs between competing objectives (such as time and cost) to meet stakeholder expectations.

Project scope management

Before a project can be planned the project scope must be defined. Project scope management is therefore primarily concerned about what is included and what is not included in the project. Project management tools for this knowledge area includes project scope statements, work break-down structures and change control processes.

Project time management

As already discussed in Section 1.5, time is a primary objective on all projects and one of three constraints. Project time management is therefore a critically important skill for any project manager. Project managers must be able to accurately estimate the completion date at any point in time on the project, must know what resources are required to achieve the new deadlines and calculate the impact when critical activities have not been implemented according to plan. Project management tools for this knowledge area includes network analysis, Gantt charts, resource scheduling and project crashing.

Project cost management

Far too often the success of projects is measured on whether they are completed within the project budget. The quality of estimates at the outset needs to be high as does the management of the costs throughout the project life cycle. It is therefore essential that project managers are skilled in project cost management. Project management tools for this knowledge area includes cost estimates, cost management plans and earned value analysis.

Project quality management

Projects must conform to the specification and satisfy the needs for which they are undertaken. It is the responsibility of the project manager to ensure that the quality standards, policies are objectives are strictly adhered to. This includes establishing levels of quality at the start of the project and ensuring the quality is maintained throughout the project life cycle. Project management tools for this knowledge area include the quality management plan, quality control measurements and change requests.

Project human resource management

No project will be successful without a well management project team. It is the responsibility of the project manager to guide and manage the team to successful completion of the project. This involves establishing the project team, assigning responsibilities, motivating the team, conflict management and developing the team to improve competencies and enhance performance. Project management tools for this knowledge area includes organisational breakdown structures, responsibility matrices and team building exercises.

Project communication management

Project managers must ensure the timely and efficient collection, distribution and storage of project information. Project managers spend a significant amount of time communicating with the project team, project sponsor and other stakeholders and therefore must have the competences to communicate project related matters as effectively as possible. Project management tools for this knowledge area includes communication plans, project plans, progress reports and web based communication skills.

Project risk management

As projects are unique they carry a significant element of risk. A key requirement of the project manager is to identify any risks that could have a negative impact on the project and prioritising these in terms of action to be taken. This could involve either proposing alternative courses of action to avoid risks or seeking ways to mitigate the impact on the project. Project management tools for this knowledge area include development of the risk management plan, risk analysis and risk registers.

Project procurement management

Nearly all projects require material, equipment, products or services from outside the project team. The project manger is the person responsible for requisitioning and purchasing these necessities from an outside organisation. This also includes managing the contractual relationship between the outside organisation and the project sponsor, and ensuring performance is met. Project management tools for this knowledge area include purchasing and acquisition, negotiation, contact administration and contract closure.

Exercise 3

Project management draws on a number of other management disciplines. From the knowledge areas above identify where in your course, you have already been made familiar with some of these concepts.

1.9   Agile project management

Over recent years, the concept of **agile project management** has been adopted within the technology as an alternative to the tradition project life-cycle model, discussed in Section 1.5. The traditional model makes the assumption that the scope of the project is developed at the initiation stage and is mostly fixed at the planning stage. Planning, therefore, requires a reasonable degree of predictability in order to successfully execute the project.

However, the concern in IT and technology projects is that the scope and end deliverable of the project can always be defined at the early stages. Quite often, in technology projects, the project manager is unaware of the scope until the project is mostly complete. As such, it is impossible to develop detailed plans to manage and execute the project at the early stages. Therefore, rather than progressing through the project in clearly defined phases, agile project management relies on incremental, iterative development cycles. This allows the scope of the project to evolve as the project progresses, which is more suited to exploratory projects and projects where new technologies need to be tested.

Although there are benefits to the agile methodology, in terms of minimizing risk in technology development, it does not allow for control of time and cost. Despite this, on IT or small projects where the outcome is not clearly defined, agile project management can be a very effective. We discuss agile project management in more detail in Chapter 7.

Chapter summary

- Projects are the non-routine activities performed by the organisation. All projects have a single predetermined goal, have a temporary life-cycle, deliver a unique product, service or result and require a project manager to direct and organise the required resources to realise the project.

- Projects are normally managed in four sequential phases of initiation, planning, execution and closure. This is referred to as the project life-cycle. Each phase consists of the deliverables the project management must complete in order to manage the project. As the project moves through the life-cycle the level of effort and investment will increase until it comes to project closure.

- Projects are constrained by three key objectives. These are the time it will take to complete the project, the total financial cost of the project and the level of quality specified in the project brief. If the scope of the project is to remain consistent, any changes to these constraints will have an impact on the other. If cost is reduced the level of quality will be reduced and/or the project duration will increase. If time is reduced, the cost will increase and/or the quality will be reduced. Finally if quality is increased the cost will increase and/or the time will increase.

- Project success is often measured by the delivery of the scope of the project within the time, cost and quality constraints. However, other measures should include end user satisfaction; impact on the customer and realisation of business benefits as a result of investment in the project.

■ Project management is the discipline of managing projects. The project manager is the person ultimately responsible for achieving the project objectives. The project managers' knowledge area includes project integration management, project scope management, project time management, project cost management, project quality management, project human resource management, project communication management, project risk management and project procurement management.

End of chapter questions

1 Define the typical characteristics of a project and evaluate how projects differ from routine operations.

2 Discuss the typical phases a project passes through, from initiation to closure. What are the key deliverables of the project management at each stage?

3 Using examples, discuss the criteria that deem a project to be successful.

4 Under what conditions would agile project management be effective?

5 What are the "project management knowledge areas" and why are these important for organisations embarking on a project?

References

Avots, I. 1962. The management side of PERT, *California Management Review,* **4,** 16-27.

Buchanan, D. & Boddy, D. 1992. *The Expertise of the Change Agent,* New York, Prentice Hall

Economist, T. 2009. Closing the gap: The link between project management excellence and long-term success. Economist Intelligence Unit.

Haniff, A. P. & Fernie, S. Projects: Where Strategies collide. *In:* Carter, K., Ogunlana, S. & Kaka, A., eds. *Transformation through Construction*. Joint 2008 CIB W065/W055, 2008 Dubia CIB, 130-131.

Midler, C. 1995. 'Projectification' of the firm: The Renault case. *Scandinavian Journal of Management,* **11,** 363-375.

Morris, P. W. G. 1997. *The Management of Projects,* London, Thomas Telford.

OGC 2005. *Managing Successful Projects with PRINCE2,* Norwich, The Stationary Office.

PMI 2010. *The Value of Project Management*, The Project Management Institute.

PMI 2013. *A Guide to the Project Management Body of Knowledge: PMBOK guide.* 5th ed. Pennsylvania Project Management Institute.

Shenhar, A. J., Dvir, D., Levy, O. & Maltz, A. C. 2001. Project success: A multidimensional strategic concept. *Long Range Planning,* **34,** 699-725.

Slack, N., Chambers, S. & Johnston, R. 2007. *Operations Management,* Harlow, UK, Pearson Education Ltd.

2 Project Organisations

Amal Abbas and Amos Haniff

Learning objectives

By the time you have completed this chapter, you should be able to:

☐ Understand how the project environment is influenced

☐ Recognize the main components of the corporate strategy model and how effective project management contributes to achieving strategic objectives

☐ Identifying critical project stakeholders and managing them within the context of project development.

☐ Understand the advantages and disadvantages of organising a project within a functional, project and matrix structure

☐ Discuss the roles of the Project Management Office (PMO).

☐ Understand key concepts of corporate culture and how cultures are formed.

2.1. Introduction

Today, project management practices play a crucial role in different industries and sectors. Project management is endorsed as an organizational strategic component that leads innovation, creates value and turns vision into reality. One way to understand projects is to view them as smaller, temporary organisations that are part of a larger, parent organisation. Typical of any organisation the project is influenced by a number of environmental factors, which includes the organisation that initiates the project, individuals participating within the project and individuals who have an interest in the project outcome. Before a project manager can begin to organise the work, the environment in which the project is operating must first be understood. The project manager must be aware of where the environmental factors originate. He or she must be able to identify the project stakeholders and assess their potential to affect the project outcome. Furthermore, the project manager must appreciate how the project will fit within the parent organisation and how the project will be organised within the existing organisational constraints.

2.2 The project environment

The key to good project management is being prepared; this includes being aware of the elements that could influence and constrain the project success. The project environment comprises of all the influences that affect the project throughout its life cycle. Most of these influences are outside the control of the project manager and in many cases beyond the control of the organisation commissioning the project. Conducting an analysis of the environment that the project is operating in will enable the project team to be ready for any eventualities and will determine the critical decisions that the project manager makes. However, doing this at the early stages of the life cycle would generate the knowledge and information to possibly influence the environment in a positive manner. It is accepted that there could be a number of factors that could influence the project, but Slack et al, (2006) identifies four environmental areas for consideration. These are as follows:

- **The geo-social environment:** This includes the geographical, climatic and cultural factors that may affect the project.

- **Econo-political environment:** This includes the economic, government and regulatory factors in which the project takes place.

- **The business environment:** The external environment in which the business commissioning the project operates. This could include industry behaviour, business competitors, suppliers and customers.

- **The internal environment:** The environment of the individual organisation or group commissioning the project. This includes structure, culture, recourses and corporate strategy

2.3 Project stakeholders

PMI (2013, p. 30), defines stakeholders as "the individual, group, or organization who may affect or be affected by, or perceive itself to be affected by a decision, activity, or outcome of a project, who may be actively involved in the project or have interests that may be positively or negatively affected by the performance of completion of the project".

Most projects, programmes and portfolios will have a variety of stakehold-ers with different, and sometimes competing, interests. These individuals and groups can have significant influence over the eventual success or failure of the work.

It would be very unlikely that all stakeholders groups would be in favour of the project. Some stakeholders may have a positive interest in the project and would normally seek to exert influence on the project to achieve a positive out-come. Other project stakeholders may have a negative interest in the project as its outcome would contradict their own personal objectives, beliefs or strategy. These individuals or groups would oppose the project and exert influence in a negative manner. In any respect, identifying and understanding the objectives of the various stakeholder groups should be one of the first priorities for the project manager.

Figure 2.1: Typical internal and external project stakeholders

As shown in Figure 2.1, project stakeholders may be either internal or external to the **project organisation**. The project organisation is the temporary organisa-tion established to manage the project. This differs from the **participating organi-sation**, which is the organisation who has commissioned the project.

2.3.1 Internal stakeholders

Internal stakeholders are those stakeholders within the project organisation who play an active role in the development and implementation of the project. Besides the project manager, typical internal stakeholders include:

- **The client:** This is the individual or group of individuals who have commissioned the project and commits and authorises expenditure on the project. The client may have commissioned the project for their own organisational use, or they may have commissioned the project for sale, rental or licenced to a third party organisation. It is the client who makes the final decisions on the project and can choose to change or stop the project at anytime.

- **The project sponsor:** Sometimes referred to as the **project champion** or **project owner**, this is the stakeholder responsible for identifying the business needs or opportunity for the project. According to the APM (2006), this role would be carried out by a senior executive, who ensures the project remains a viable proposition and benefits are realised. The project sponsor would also be responsible for resolving any issues outside the control of the project manager

- **The project team**: This is the individuals who plan, organise, implement and control the project throughout its life-cycle. Members of the project team will have differing expertise and skills that contribute to the success of the project.

- **Functional managers:** These are the managers who are responsible for assigning project personnel to the project from the various functional departments within the organisation. Functional managers are also a source of technical expertise and guidance for project difficulties.

- **Contractors:** These are the organisations external to the participating organisation, who offers services or expertise on the project. In some industries, such as construction, it will be the contactors who carry out the work on the project.

- **Project support:** No project can function without project support. This includes administrative, finance, IT, and maintenance. Some project support offices include the management of project documentation, such as updating schedules, budgets, risk registers and change requests.

◼ 2.3.2 External stakeholders

External stakeholders are the groups and individuals who may not actively participate in the project, but may influence the project outcome in either a negative or positive way. The project manger has no power over these stakeholder groups. External stakeholders include:

- **End users:** This is the group who will operate or use the project deliverable, once it is complete. They maybe part of the client organisation or external users of the end project.

- **Suppliers:** These are the external organisations or individuals who supply the materials and equipment for the project. Utility suppliers could also fall under this category. In some projects, suppliers may be considered internal stakeholders, as achieving the completion deadline within a project is often dependent on the reliability of suppliers.

- **Competitors:** This group of stakeholders will be affected by the project outcome. Conversely, client decisions regarding the project may be determined by the actions of the competitors.

- **Lobby groups:** These stakeholders may be positive or negative towards the project. They could include environmental groups who are opposed to major construction, energy or reclamation projects, or business leaders supporting the implementation of a major transportation or broadband infrastructure.

- **Communities:** This could include all the local, national and international communities affected by the project. For example a project to build a factory in a low employment area would expect to get local community support

- **Shareholders:** This is the group of stakeholders that own stocks and shares in the organisation and ultimately provide finance for the project. As a group they are highly influential and answerable to the board of directors.

- **Employees:** These stakeholders are the personnel who work in the client organisation. The project could either be of benefit to them or it may create increased workload, by project team members being relocated to the project.

- **Government agencies:** This includes all regulatory bodies who govern the project. For example, health and safety, licensing, employment and approvals.

2.4 Stakeholder management

Stakeholder management includes the procedures necessary to identify the individuals, groups and organizations that could affect or be affected by the project, to analyse stakeholder prospects and their influence on the project, and to develop proper approaches and procedures for efficiently involving stakeholders in the project. The stakeholder management plan aims to ensure that stakeholders are effectively involved in project decisions and implementation throughout the lifespan of the project, to gain support for the project and predict disagreement, conflict, or competing aims among the project's stakeholders. As shown in Figure 2.2 the stakeholder management process includes four stages:

- **Identify stakeholders** – identify by name and title the people, groups, and organisations that have significant influence on project direction and its success or who are significantly impacted by the project.

- **Plan stakeholder management** – identify the plans and techniques that will be used to attain the maximum support of stakeholders and minimize conflict.

- **Manage stakeholder engagement** – outlines the processes and steps that will be undertaken to communicate and working with the stakeholders to satisfy their needs.

- **Control stakeholder engagement** – describes the methods that will be used to monitor stakeholder engagement and alert the project team about.

The following section explain this process in more details.

Identify stakeholder

Input
- Project charter
- Procurement documents
- Enterprise environmental factors
- Organisational process assets

Tools and techniques
- Stakeholders analysis
- Expert judgment
- Meetings

Output
- Stakeholder register

Plan stakeholder management

Input
- Project management plan
- Stakeholder register
- Enterprise environmental factors
- Organisational process assets

Tools and techniques
- Expert judgment
- Meetings
- Analytical techniques

Output
- Stakeholder management plan
- Project documents update

Manage stakeholder engagement

Input
- Stakeholder management plan
- Communications stakeholder
- Change log
- Enterprise environmental factors

Tools and techniques
- Communication method
- Interpersonal skills
- Management skills

Output
- Issue log
- Change requests
- Project management plan updates
- Project documents updates
- Organisational process assets updates

Control stakeholder engagement

Input
- Project management plan
- Issue log
- Work performance data
- Project documents

Tools and techniques
- Information management systems
- Expert judgment
- Meetings

Output
- Work performance information
- Change requests
- Project management plan updates
- Project documents updates
- Organisational process assets updates

Figure 2.2: Project Stakeholders Management Overview

■   Identify stakeholders

Who are our stakeholders?

To develop an effective plan for managing stakeholders, there is a need to iden-tify clearly, and assess potential stakeholders in terms of defining their interests, involvement, interdependencies and impact.

Some questions that are relevant for deciding who should be considered a stakeholder for the project:

1   Will the person, group or organisation have direct or indirect effect on the project?

2   Will the person, group or organisation be affected directly or indirectly by the project?

3   Does the person, group or organisation have an impact on the project's resources (material, personnel, funding)?

4   Does the person, group or organisation have any special skills or capabilities the project will require?

5   At what point does the person, group or organisation have the greatest impact on the project?

Stakeholders analysis

Stakeholder analysis is a technique of systematically gathering and analysing quantitative and qualitative information to determine whose interests should be taken into account throughout the project. The analysis generally follows the next steps:

1   Identify all potential project stakeholders and relevant information.

2   Analyse the potential impact or support each stakeholder could generate and classify them according to that.

3   Assess how key stakeholders are likely to react or respond in different situations.

There are four major attributes that a project team need to consider when they conduct the stakeholder analysis: the stakeholders' position in the project, the level of influence (power) they hold, the level of interest they have, and the group/coalition to which they belong or can reasonably be associated with.

There are multiple classification models used for stakeholders analysis, e.g.:

■   Power/interest grid, grouping the stakeholders based on their level of power and interest regarding the project outcomes;

- Power/influence grid; grouping the stakeholders based on their level of power and interest regarding the project outcomes;

- Influence/impact grid grouping the stakeholders based on their level of power and interest regarding the project outcomes;

- Salience model; grouping the stakeholders based on their power, urgency and legitimacy regarding the project outcomes.

The power/interest matrix

One way to determine these key stakeholder groups is the power/interest matrix, as shown in Figure 2.3. Within the matrix, stakeholders are categorised according to their level of interest against the power they possess to exert their influence.

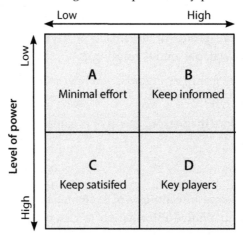

Figure 2.3: Stakeholder mapping: The power/interest matrix.

- **Group A: Low level of interest/low level of power**. Stakeholders within this group require little attention as it is unlikely that they will be able to impact on the project or wish to do so.

- **Group B: High level of interest/low level of power**. Stakeholders within this group have little power with which to exert on the project, but due to their high level of interest they should be kept informed of project progress.

- **Group C: Low level of interest/high level of power**. Stakeholders within this group could exert influence on the project but are unlikely to do so. However, due to the level of power they hold this group should be kept satisfied.

- **Group D: High level of interest/high level of power.** Stakeholders within this group are most likely to exert influence on the project and have the power to do so. This group of stakeholders are the key stakeholders and their expectations must remain the priority.

■   Plan stakeholder management

Plan stakeholder management is the process of developing appropriate management policies to effectively involve stakeholders throughout the lifespan of the project, based on the analysis of their needs, interests and potential impact on project success. The main benefit of this analysis is that it provides a clear plan to network with project stakeholders to sustenance the project's interests (PMI, 2013).

Based upon the data collected in the stakeholder analysis register and communication plan, the project manager will be in charge of involving stakeholders throughout the lifespan of the project. The level of engagement required for each stakeholder may vary over the course of the project.

■   Manage stakeholder engagement

Stakeholder engagement management is the process of communicating and working with stakeholders to meet their needs and expectations, and to address issues as they occur. The main aim of this process is to allow the project manager to increase support and minimize resistance from stakeholders.

To effectively manage stakeholder engagement, the project manager needs to utilise the communication plan and strategies identified in the previous stage to communicate project related information to key stakeholders in an active and promptly manner. Managing stakeholder engagement helps to increase the probability of project success by ensuring that stakeholders clearly understand the project goals, objectives, benefits, and risks. In addition to communicating information to stakeholders, the project team need to actively listen to feedback to make sure communications are being established and understood.

■   Monitor stakeholder engagement

Monitor stakeholder engagement is the process of monitoring overall project stakeholder relationships and altering policies and procedures for engaging stakeholders. Monitor Stakeholder Engagement involves collecting data, assessing the level of engagement in order to modify plans and procedures for engaging effectively with stakeholders.

2.5   Organizational breakdown structures (OBS)

■   Basic definitions

- **Organizing** is the process by which managers establish the structure of working relationships among employees to allow them to achieve organizational goals efficiently and effectively.

- **Organizational structure**, also known as **organizational breakdown structure,** is the formal system of task and reporting relationships that determines how employees use resources to achieve goals.

- **Organizational culture** is the shared set of beliefs, values, and norms that influence the way people and groups work together to achieve organizational goals.

- **Organizational design** is the process by which managers make specific organizing choices that result in the construction of a particular organizational structure.

The challenge facing all companies is to design a structure and culture that is able to:

- Motivates managers and employees to work hard and to develop supportive job behaviours and attitudes, and

- Coordinates the actions of employees, groups, functions and divisions to ensure they work together efficiently and effectively.

According to *contingency theory*, managers design organizational structures to fit the factors or circumstances that are affecting the company and causing them the greatest uncertainty. Thus, there is no one best way to design an organization.

Four factors are important determinants of the type of organizational structure or culture a manager selects: They are:

- The nature of the organizational environment,

- The type of strategy the organization pursues,

- The technology the organization uses, and

- The characteristics of the organization's human resources.

One of the biggest challenges for the participating organisation is creating a structure that facilitates teamwork, maximises efficiency and enables the project to achieve its explicit objectives. This is because projects contradict the normal culture and routines embedded within organisations, which typically evolve over time. Conversely, projects are temporary and non-routine; as such the established culture and norms of the participating organisation will not readily fit the project situation. Despite this, managers should seek to develop a project organisation structure that reflects the intersecting needs of the project, the needs of the team and the needs of individuals involved in the project (Burke, 2003). This is achieved by considering the following key elements:

- **The responsibility and authority:** Who has responsibility for each element of the work and who has authority over that element?

- **The communication and reporting relationship**. Who reports to whom? This includes the number of levels within the organisational hierarchy and the span of control of senior personal within the project.

- **The contractual arrangements.** Who are the contracting parties? And what is the nature of contact between parties? In most cases project team members will be in contact with the participating organisation. But this will not be the case with sub-contractors and some suppliers.

- **The functional departments participating within the project.** Which functional departments are contributing to the project? Projects often cut across organisational departments. These may be grouped in terms of function, product or geography.

Factors affecting the selection of the right structure

Table 2.1 outline the main factors that the project manager need to consider when selecting an organisational structure:

Table 2.1: Factors affecting the selection of the right structure

	Functional	Project	Matrix
Number of project	Few		Large
Cost of project	Small		Large
Level of uncertainty	Low level	High level	
Type of technology used	Project concentrate on technology mastered by one function	Several technologies with a need to employ full-time person	
Project complexity	Low level	High level	
Duration of project		Long project	Short project
Overhead cost			High

■   Functional organisational breakdown structures

The functional organisational structure, as shown in Figure 2.4, is perhaps the most widespread across industries. It is based on a clear hierarchy with senior executives at the top levels and operatives at the lower levels. Within the functional structure personnel within the organisations are grouped into functional departments or organisational units. Each organisational department specialises in a distinct discipline, is responsible for and has a high degree of autonomy over the management, performance and accounting of the functional area.

Under this arrangement projects are commissioned at the senior level and implemented within a particular functional unit. This is because the project would be of particular benefit to the participating functional unit. This being the case, within Figure 2.4, the project sponsor would be the Operations Director. However, different segments of the project may be delegated to other respective functional units with coordination remaining with the participating function. For example, a new project to implement a just-in-time process within the materials management area of the Operations Department may need to delegate procurement to the Finance Department and seek additional personnel through the Human Resource Department.

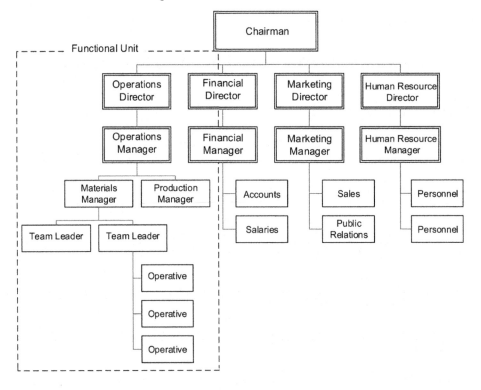

Figure 2.4: Functional organisational breakdown structure

Gray & Larson (2008) explains the advantages and disadvantages for using an existing functional organisational structure to organise projects. These are summarised as follows:

Advantages

1 **No change:** The existing routine operations and design of the participating organisation is maintained as projects are developed within the existing structure of the organisation.

2 **Flexibility:** The functional organisational structure enables maximum flexibility for staff as appropriate specialists can be temporarily assigned to work on the project, whilst remaining connected with their functional group.

3 **In-depth expertise:** The nature of functional organisational structures allows for development of in-depth knowledge and expertise. This expertise could be necessary at the critical stages of the project.

4 **Easy post-project transition:** Standard career paths within the functional organisational structure are maintained. This enables team members and specialist on projects to return to their normal duties once the project is complete or to seek advancement from contributing to the project.

Disadvantages

1 **Lack of focus:** Each functional unit tends to focus on its core routine operations. This often results in the project objectives becoming secondary to the obligations of the function and a silo effect between functions occurring.

2 **Poor integration:** Functional specialists tend be concerned only with their own particular segment of the project, rather than the project as a whole. This leads to a lack of integration across functions and between project personnel.

3 **Slow:** Functional organisations tend to be highly bureaucratic. It therefore generally takes longer to complete a project through this arrangement. Not only do projects need to be authorised through the normal channels of the hierarchy, but information and requests need to be communicated across functions and agreed within each department

4 **Lack of ownership:** The motivation of people assigned to projects could be weak. The project may be seen as burden to normal duties and not directly linked to career progression.

Exercise 1

Identify an organisation that is currently structured using the functional approach. How successful is it at managing projects? What prevents it from being successful?

■ Project organisational breakdown structure

Within some organisations all core business activities are performed as projects. This is typical of project-based industries such as construction, IT and advertising. As shown in Figure 2.5, temporary organisations, in the form of dedicated project teams, are created to work on the projects and fulfil the organisational objectives. Each project reports to the parent organisation, which provides assistance through its varied functional departments. The salient difference between this type of structure and a functional structure is that within a project-based organisation the main purpose of the functional unit is to support the project teams, rather than merely contributing to projects on an add-hoc basis.

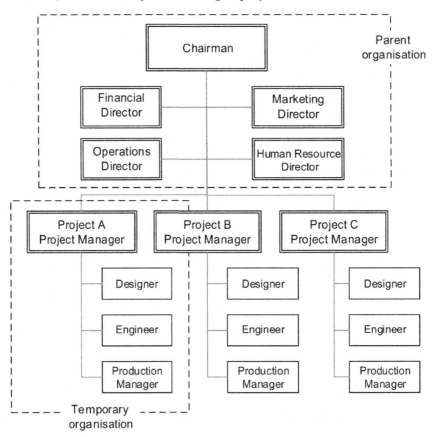

Figure 2.5: Project organisational breakdown structure

Despite being the accepted form of work organisation across project-based industries, both Gray & Larson (2008) and Shtub et al (1994) recognise that project organisational breakdown structures do have their weakness as well as strengths. These are summarised as follows:

Advantages

1 **Control:** As each project is responsible for its own management through a single project authority, the project manager can maintain strong control over the project and bypass the bureaucracy inherent in functional organisations.

2 **Fast:** Within project organisational structures most decisions are made within the project team. This enables rapid reaction time as the project manager does not need to refer to the organisational hierarchy or other functional units for project related decisions. Furthermore, as project team members tend to be working on the project full-time they devote their full attention to the project, rather than splitting their efforts with other duties.

3 **Cohesive:** Personnel within the project team are often loyal to the project. This results in a high level of motivation and cohesiveness across the project as team members share the common goal and responsibility for project success.

4 **Cross-functional integration:** The project organisational structure brings together specialists from different disciplines. With proper guidance from the project manager they become committed to optimising the project rather than their own respective area of expertise.

Disadvantages

1 **Duplication of resources:** As each project is created as a temporary organisation an insufficient use of resources due to the duplication of personnel and equipment across projects. This will inevitably increase operational costs and reduce economies of scale.

2 **Projectitis:** The nature of projects can result in project teams taking on an entity of their own and becoming so consumed within the project they begin to distance themselves from the parent organisation and other organisational projects. As motivation within the team is encouraged, the project team may prolong the project unnecessarily and may find it difficult to assimilate themselves back into functional units once the project is complete.

3 **Limited technical expertise:** The expertise of the project is limited to the experience and knowledge of its team members. This creates problems when higher expertise or other specialists are required. While outside expertise can be brought into the project, resource constraints and availability of specialist skills limit this possibility.

4 **Difficult post-project transition:** Assigning full-time personnel to a project creates the dilemma of what to do with team members once it is complete. If no other project work is available, transition back into their functional unit becomes difficult due to the prolonged absence whilst working on the project.

■ Matrix organisational breakdown structure

Developed as hybrid form of project organisation, the matrix organisational structure is probably the most contentious and publicised organisational structure of all. Certainly when it came to the forefront in the 1970s it received significant attention from both academics and project practitioners (Knight, 1976, Galbraith, 1971). Within the matrix arrangement, the project organisational structure is overlaid onto the functional organisational structure to create horizontal communication channels. Project teams are therefore created by employing specialist personnel within each functional unit, depending on the needs of the project. As shown in Figure 2.6, this results in two hierarchies being created within a single organisational structure. However, this also creates two lines of authority; vertical and horizontal, with project team members needing to report to both functional and project managers simultaneously.

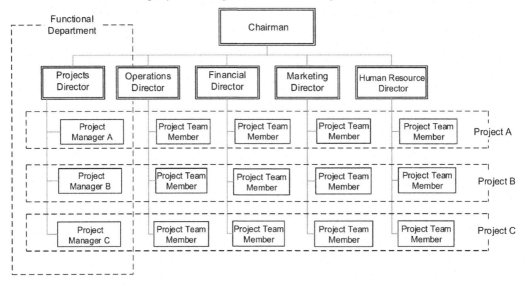

Figure 2.6: Matrix organisational breakdown structure

Organisations adopting the matrix structure manage projects in different ways to the functional and project organisational structure. In the first instance, rather than projects being controlled within a single functional unit, projects are directed within a dedicated project department, normally led by a formal Project Director. Members of the project team would remain within the functional unit, but would be allocated responsibility to a particular project. This optimises resource utilisation within the organisation by enabling those who are not working to full capacity within their functional unit to contribute to ongoing projects. Furthermore, it allows individuals to work on multiple projects whilst performing their normal functional duties.

However, this arrangement does lead to a situation of possible conflict between the project manager and the functional manager. In theory, the matrix structure should enable the project manager to select the specialist areas required for the project from each functional unit. But quite often this depends on the availability of staff as perceived by the functional manager. In principle, even though it is the project manager who is ultimately responsible for the success or failure of the project, all major project decisions, including resources must be negotiated between the project manager and the functional manager. Some of the possible areas of concern between the functional and project managers are summarised in Table 2.2.

Table 2.2: Areas of concerns between the project and functional managers.

Project Manager	Functional Manager
What is to be done?	How will each task be done?
When will the task be done?	Where will the task be done?
What is the importance of the task?	Who will do the task?
How much money is available to do the task?	How will project involvement impact on normal functional activities?
How well has the total project been done?	How well has the functional input been integrated into the project?

The success of negation between the project and functional manager is dependant on the type matrix system being used by the organisation. There are commonly three types of matrix structure that have an affect on the authority of the project manager, these are identified as follows:

1 **The weak matrix structure:** This type of structure varies little from the traditional functional organisational structure where each functional department retains responsibility for their own segment of the project. The only difference within this arrangement is r ole of the project manager, whose main responsibility it to coordinate the work and act as a communicator between functions. In the weak matrix structure, it is the functional managers who control the project, with the project manager having little authority over project decisions and resources.

2 **The strong matrix structure:** Conversely, within a strong matrix the project manager has ultimate authority and control over the project. Within this arrangement the role of the functional manager is to provide resources to the project as required by the project manager. This is beneficial when the project is of organisational importance, as it enables the project manager to select and have authority over the specialist skills required for project success with the full support of senior management.

3   **The balanced matrix structure:** This arrangement seeks to achieve a balance of power between the project and functional managers. Under a balanced matrix arrangement the project manager develops the overall plan for implementing the project, whilst the functional manager is responsible for assigning appropriate resources to the project. However, the difference between this arrangement and a strong matrix is that within a balanced matrix structure the resources remain under the authority of the functional manager. Thus, it essential under a balanced matrix that project manager and functional manager are able to understand the concerns identified in Table 2.1 and successfully negotiate for project success.

Regardless of the possible conflict between the project and functional units, the matrix structure does allow for efficient project management within organisations. However, it also has other important drawbacks in its use. Gray & Larson (2008) recognise the advantages and disadvantages of adopting the matrix organisational structure, which are summarised as follows:

Advantages

1   **Efficient:** As it is the functional manager who assigns resources to the project, allocation can be done in the most efficient manner to maximise resource utilization. The structure also allows for resources to be shared across multiple projects as needed, thus reducing resource duplication.

2   **Strong project focus:** Having a formal project management unit with project managers responsible for the coordinating and integrating functional contributions provides a stronger focus on projects within the organisation.

3   **Easy post-project transition:** As the project structure is overlaid over the functional structure, specialists who contribute to the project are able to return to their normal functional unit once the project is complete.

4   **Resource utilisation:** The nature of the matrix arrangement enables flexibility of resource utilisation and expertise within the firm, as under-utilised resources can be allocated across projects or project team members can return to assist functional needs.

Disadvantages

1   **Dysfunctional conflict:** Notwithstanding the importance of the project to the organisation, the functional manager needs to ensure the functional unit maintains performance and may be reluctant to release valuable resources to the project. Whereas the project manager requires specialist resources from the functional unit they remain, fundamentally, under the control of the functional manager. What can begin as a legitimate conflict may escalate to a

personal level, where both the project manager and the functional manager begin to make unprofessional judgements towards each other.

2 **Infighting:** Unlike the project organisation structure, the matrix structure often requires a sharing of resources and equipment across projects and functions. This could likewise lead to infighting as the varied project managers and functional managers would seek to ensure that their own project or unit takes priority.

3 **Stressful:** In considering the dysfunctional conflict and infighting between managers, it is without doubt that project participants would be exposed to stressful situations. This would be exacerbated by the need to satisfy two bosses from opposing directions. The difficulty arises when a project team member is forced to choose loyalty between the project and the function.

4 **Slow:** In theory the role of the project manager is to coordinate the project and accelerate the completion. However, due to the extensive negotiations, agreements and decision making required between the project and functional manger, in practice the process can frustrating and slow.

Exercise 2

Draw an organisational breakdown structure (OBS) of a typical small project. Who has responsibility over of each element? What is the reporting and authority structure?

■ The project management office

As more organisations begin to organise projects on a regular basis, there has been a need to support and manage projects centrally. This has resulted in the increasing practice of establishing a project management office (PMO). Within the organisational structure the PMO is created as a distinct functional unit that assists project managers in achieving project goals through the project expertise of formal project officers. A project officer may be the source of advice across the organisation or may be assigned responsibly to offer guidance on a particular project, as shown in Figure 2.7.

Created initially to reduce the risk of project failure, the PMO is seen as centre of excellence for project management within the organisation. The function of the project officer is not to act as a project manager or project sponsor for a project, rather to guide senior staff and project managers towards achieving the goals of the project. The PMO may contribute to project success in a number of ways, but the key responsibilities of the PMO are summarised as follows:

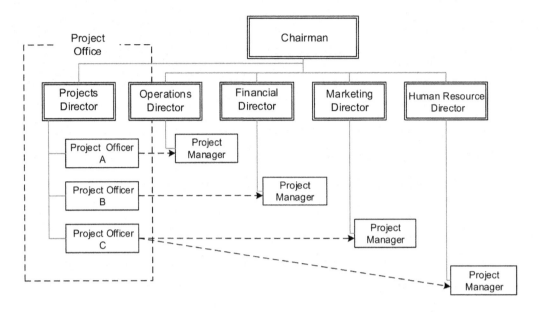

Figure 2.7: The project management office

■ **Provide guidance to project managers:** The key role of the PMO is to provide support to projects in terms of advice on aspects of the project or the provision of training and mentoring of project and functional personnel.

■ **Establish project management standards:** Is it important that projects within the organisation are managed and coordinated in a consistent manner. It is the responsibility of the PMO to design and create a uniform project management methodology to be used on all projects. This includes standardised forms for scope statements, risk plans, change requests and other project planning documentation. By standardising project processes, the PMO assures that projects are performed within the quality standards of the organisation.

■ **Provide administrative support:** Projects are highly complex and require a significant amount of project support. As few functional units have administrative support skilled in aspects of project management, the PMO could provide project support in terms preparation of schedules, budgets, resource planning and other project documentation.

■ **Provide a resource pool:** One of the fundamental objectives of the PMO is the provision of trained and skilled project personnel to work on organisational projects. This resource pool is developed internally through the development of project personnel within functional departments. As projects are initiated and completed the resource pool grows and subsequently the project management skills and lessons learned on projects are captured for use on future projects. Anyone in the organisations should be able to apply to the project resource pool. This allows for easier post-project transition as, in theory, those personnel who enjoy working on projects are able to remain in the pool and contribute to future projects, and those who do not can remain solely dedicated to their functional unit. The advantage of the arrangement is that the PMO essentially acts as an interface between the project manager and the functional manager and therefore minimises the conflict over scarce project resources.

2

Exercise 3

The concept of the PMO is relatively new and many organisations are committing investment in to the creation of them. What do you think are the negative consequences of a PMO would be on an organisations project?

2.6 Organisational culture

The second principal issue in organizational design is to create, develop, and maintain an organization's culture. **Organizational culture** is the shared set of beliefs, expectations, values, and norms that influence how members of an organization relate to one another and cooperate to achieve organizational goals.

- Organizational culture influences work attitudes and behaviors when employees *internalize* organizational values and norms, and then allow those values and norms to guide their decisions and actions.

- A company's culture is a result of its pivotal or guiding **values and norms.** **Values** are the shared standards which organizational members use to evaluate whether or not they have helped the company achieve its vision and goals. **Norms** are informal, yet powerful rules concerning how employees should behave in a company if they are to be accepted and help it to achieve its goals. Ideally, a company's norms help the company achieve its goals.

- Over time, members of a company learn from one another how to perceive and interpret various events that happen in the work setting and how to respond to them in ways that reflect the company's guiding values and norms.

■ Core cultural characteristics

There are six core characteristics that are valued collectively by members of an organization and make up the roots of an organization's culture.

1 **Sensitivity to others**. This is especially true when it comes to sensitivity to customers.

2 **Interest in new ideas.**

3 **Willingness to take risks.**

4 **The value placed on people.** How an organization values its people has a dramatic impact on the culture.

   ■ *Toxic organizational cultures*. Those in which people feel that they are not valued. Turnover is high in these organizations and profitability is problematic.

   ■ *Healthy organizational cultures*. Those in which people feel they are valued. In these organizations turnover is very low and profitability tends to be high.

5 **Openness of available communication options.** This characteristic relates to the ability of lower-level employees to easily access upper-level employees.

6 **Friendliness and congeniality.**

■ Strengths of organizational culture

Organizations differ with respect the degree to which the organizational cultures influence the people within them.

1 **Strong culture**. An organization in which there is widespread and intense agreement with respect to the core elements of the culture, making it possible for these factors to exert major influences on the way people behave. Strong cultures tend to exist in younger. organizations and may diffuse as companies get older and larger. Strong cultures have the following characteristics:

   ■ A clear philosophy exists about how business is to be conducted.

   ■ Considerable time is spent communicating values and beliefs.

   ■ Explicit statements are made to describe the organization's values.

   ■ A set of values and norms exist that are shared widely and rooted deeply.

   ■ New employees are screened carefully to ensure fit with the culture.

2 **Weak cultures**. An organization in which there is limited agreement with respect to the core elements of culture, giving these factors little influence on the way people behave.

■ The role of culture in organizations

Culture has three important roles in organizations.

- **Culture provides a sense of identity**. The more clearly an organization's shared perceptions and values are defined, the more strongly people can associate with their organization's mission and feel a vital part of it.

- **Culture generates commitment to the organization's mission.** In strong cultures people feel that they are part of the larger, well-defined whole and involved in the entire organization's work: issues that are bigger than any one individual's interests; culture reminds people of what their organization is all about.

- **Culture clarifies and reinforces standards of behavior.** Culture provides stability to behavior, both in respect to what an individual might do at different times, but also to what different individuals may do at the same time.

■ Forms of organizational culture

- **Hierarchy culture.** A form of organizational culture in which organizations have an internal focus and emphasize stability and control. Most effective leaders in this organization are good coordinators of projects and emphasize a smooth-running organization, often relying on formal rules and policies to do so.

- **Market culture.** A form of organizational culture in which organizations are concerned with stability and control, but are external in their orientation; core values emphasize competitiveness and productivity, focusing on bottom-line results.

- **Clan culture.** A form of organizational culture characterized by strong internal focus along with a high degree of flexibility and discretion; with goals that are highly shared by members of the organization and high levels of cohesiveness, such organizations feel more like extended families than economic entities. Most people prefer clan cultures to any of the other forms organizational culture.

- **Adhocracy culture**. Organizations that emphasize flexibility while also paying a great deal of attention to the external environment; characterized by the recognition that to survive and succeed an organization needs to be highly innovative and constantly assessing what the future requires.

■ How is organizational culture created?

Two key factors in the creation of organizational culture are the influence of the company founder(s) and the company's experience with the external environment.

- **Company founders**. These individuals often possess dynamic personalities, strong values, and clear visions of how their organization should operate. Their views become the accepted ones in the organization.

- **Experiences with the external environment.** Dramatic interactions with the external environment often cause an organizational culture to change.

■ Tools for transmitting culture

- **Symbols**. Material objects that connote meanings that extend beyond their intrinsic content. Material symbols are potent tools for sending messages about organizational culture.

- **Slogans**. Catchy phrases that companies use to call attention to their products or services. They also communicate important aspects of the organization's culture to both the public at large and its own employees.

- **Stories**. Organizations also transmit information about culture by virtue of the stories that are told in them, both formally and informally. These stories illustrate key aspects of an organization's culture and telling them can effectively introduce or reaffirm those values to employees.

- **Jargon**. The everyday language used in companies can help sustain its culture, especially the unique slang or jargon that is the company's own. The use of jargon helps people find their identities as members of a special group.

- **Ceremonies**. Celebrations of an organization's basic values and assumptions. These ceremonies convey meaning to people inside and outside the organization.

- **Statements of principle.** Explicitly written statements describing the principal beliefs that guide an organization. Such documents can help reinforce an organization's culture. This may include a Code of Ethics, which are explicit statements of the company's ethical values and expectations.

Summary

- The project environment consists of all the influences that affect a project. These include the geo-social, the econo-political, the business and the internal environmental areas.

2

- Project stakeholders are all the individuals or groups who have an active interest in the project, are affected by the project and can influence the project outcome, in some form or another. They may be internal or external to the project organisation. Each stakeholder group may have different and conflicting expectations of the project. As the project manager cannot satisfy all stakeholder expectations, compromises will need to be made.

- Stakeholder mapping is a tool which a project manager can use to understand individual stakeholder expectations. The map involves identifying each stakeholder and making an assessment in terms of unique facts about each stakeholder, their level of interest on the project, their level of influence on the project, and the relationship strategy to manage the stakeholder.

- Organisations tend to organise projects within the existing structure of the business. There are various methods in which the organisation can choose to organise itself, but the most common are functional, project and matrix.

- Within the functional structure people are grouped within functional departments, normally according to their specialism. Within this structure projects are commissioned at a senior level and implemented within a particular functional unit.

- Within project-based organisations, temporary organisations are created to fulfil organisational objectives. The purpose of the functional departments is solely to support the project teams in their fulfilment of the project goals.

- Matrix organisational structures are a hybrid of functional and project. By overlaying the project structure onto the functional and by drawing on project team members from each functional unit, projects can be managed within the organisation. Successful matrix arrangement requires negotiation between the project and functional manager. The strength of negotiation is dependant on the type of matrix adopted.

- The project management office has been created to reduce project failure within organisations. It is a separate functional unit designed to provide project support and guidance to project managers. This includes standardisation, resource planning and provision of a resource pool.

End of chapter questions

1 Discuss the four areas of the project environment and evaluate how they may influence the project outcomes.

2 Identify the typical internal and external stakeholders within a project and discuss how a project manager may attempt to understand their expectations of the project.

3 Evaluate the relative advantages and disadvantages of the functional, product and matrix organisational structures to managing projects. You should support your answer with diagrams.

4 Draw the distinction between a weak matrix, a balances and a strong matrix structure. Within this arrangement what actions should the project manager take to ensure the project is adequately resourced?

5 Evaluate the roles and responsibilities of the Project Management Office.

References

APM (2006) *APM Body of Knowledge* Bucks, Association of Project Management.

Burke, R. (2003) *Project Management: Planning and Control Techniques* West Sussex, England.

Galbraith, J. R. (1971) Matrix organizational design: How to combine functional and project forms. *Business Horizons,* **14,** 29-40.

Gray, C. F. & Larson, E. W. (2008) *Project Management: The Managerial Process,* New York, McGraw-Hill Irwin

Johnson, G. & Scholes, K. & Whittington, R. *(2008) Exploring Corporate Strategy; Texts and Cases.* Pearson Education Limited. Harlow.

Knight, K. (1976) Matrix organisation: A review. *Journal of Management Studies,* **17,** 111-130.

Packendorff, J. (1995) Inquiring into the temporary organization: New directions for project management research. *Scandinavian Journal of Management,* **11,** 319-333.

PMI (2013). *A Guide to the Project Management Body of Knowledge:* PMBOK guide. 5th ed. Pennsylvania Project Management Institute.

Pollack J. (2007) The changing paradigms of project management. *International Journal of Project Management,* 25(3):266–74.

Schwalbe, K. (2009) *Introduction to Project Management* Boston MA, Course Technology Cengage Learning.

Shtub, A., Bard, J. F. & Globerson, S. (1994) *Project Management: Engineering, Technology, and Implementation,* Englewood Cliffs, Prentice Hall

Slack, N., Chambers, S., Johnston, R. & Betts, A. (2006) *Operations and Process Management: Principles and practice for strategic management,* Harlow, UK, Pearson Education Limited.

Turner, R. J. & Muller, R. (2003) On the nature of the project as a temporary organization. *International Journal of Project Management,* **21,** 1-8.

van Donk, D. P., & Molloy, E. (2008). From organising as projects to projects as organisations. *International Journal of Project Management,* **26**(2), 129-137.

2

3 Project Financial Appraisal

Mohamed Sherif and Mohamed Salama

Learning objectives

By the time you have completed this chapter you should be able to:

☐ Understand the basic financial concepts in the context of project management

☐ Discuss project selection methods using discounted cash flow approach

☐ Apply relevant financial concepts to the project appraisal process

☐ Appreciate the impact of taxation on project financial appraisal

☐ Discuss the impact of inflation on project financial appraisal

3.1   Introduction

In general, project managers have to face the challenging task of selecting from within a number of investment options. This requires ample knowledge about the basic concepts of project financial appraisal and investment decisions. This chapter will present and discuss the most commonly used project financial appraisal tools and techniques that project managers need to know. Indeed, in big projects, specialized financial managers under the leadership of the project managers, take responsibility for two basic decisions: investment and the financial decision. Generally speaking, the investment decision is which real assets to invest in, while the financing decision is related to how these should be financed. To achieve the firm's goal or to maximize shareholders' wealth, the top managers, especially the financial managers, play crucial roles in making both decisions.

'Investment decision' = Purchase of real assets

'Financing decision'   = Sale of financial assets   (Brealey *et al.* 2011: 31)

The investment decisions are also referred to as 'capital budgeting' or 'capital expenditure' decisions because most firms prepare budgets for their future projects. The two primary goals of this chapter are to describe how to deal with rates of return and how to make an 'Accept' or 'Reject' decision on investment projects.

> *"To understand the use and application of most project evaluation methods, knowledge of basic engineering economics concepts such as equivalence, time value of money (TVM), cash-flow diagrams, and economic evaluation factors is required"*
>
> (Remer and Nieto 1995, p. 80).

Figure 3.1 show economic valuation 10-step for project appraisal proposed by Remer and Nieto (1995).

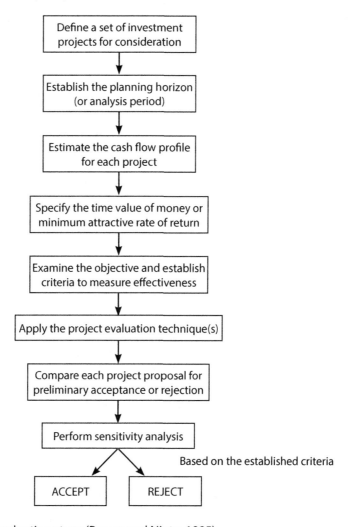

Figure 3.1: Economic evaluation steps (Remer and Nieto, 1995)

In the first section of Chapter 3, we assume that there are no taxes, no transaction costs, no disagreements, and no limits as to the number of buyers and sellers in the market. This is the so-called 'perfect market'. In Section 3.2, we start from the concept of the time value of money and the rate of return. Next, we explain a number of methods for project appraisal such as payback period, discount payback period, average rate of return, net present value, the internal rate of return and the modified internal rate of return. After studying this chapter, you should have an understanding of the techniques to use to arrive at the best investment decision when investment capital is rationed. This chapter will also help the reader understand the advantages and disadvantages of capital budgeting methods, as well as which to use in various situations.

3.2   Time value of money (TVM)

We start from the principle of the 'Time value of money'.

"£1 today is worth more than £1 tomorrow."

Future value and present value calculations rely on the concept of the time value of money. This section introduces the important concepts of future value, compound rate and present value. *Typical questions: if you gain 10% per year, how much will you earn over 5 years? If you earn 100% over 5 years, how much will you gain in each year?*

■   Compound interest versus simple interest

Before we calculate future value and present value, first of all, we should know the two basic types of interest: compound and simple interest. The first one occurs when the interest paid on the investment during the first period is added to the principal and in the following period interest is paid on the new principal. This is contrast with simple interest where the principal is constant throughout the period of investment. To explain the difference between simple and compound interest, we show an example as follows:

Example: Suppose an annual return rate of 10%, and the principal in a bank account is initially £50. After three years the balance on the account would be:

For simple interest: [£50 +(3×0.10×50)] = £50 + £5 + £5 + £5 = £65

For compound interest: [£50 ×(1.10)^3] = £50 + £5 + £5.50 + £6.05 = £66.55

The difference between simple and compound interest is the interest gained on interests. This difference increases over time with the interest rate and in the number of sub-periods with interest payments. Using the previous example, if you hold the same principal (£50) for longer, after 20 years, your bank account balance with compound interest will increase to £336.38 = [£50 ×(1.10)^{20}] while being only £150 = £50 +(20×0.10×50) with simple interest. Now, you notice the power of compound interest.

■ Future value calculation

Money can be invested to earn interest. Thus, the future value (*FV*) is the amount to which an investment will grow after earning interesting. The future value of a cash flow (*C$_t$*) is:

$$FV = PV(1+r)^n$$

Where *FV* is the future of the investment at the end of *n* years; *r* is the annual interest (or discount rate); *n* is number of years; and *PV* is the present value, or original amount invested at the start of the first year.

Example: You have £100 deposited in a bank account. Suppose banks are paying an interest rate of 5% per year on deposit. What will be the future value of £100 in 2 years?

$$FV = 100(1+0.05)^2=110.25$$

Your account will then gain interest of £10.25 and the value of your investment will grow to £110.25.

It is notice that future value can be increased by increasing the number of years (*n*), the interest rate (*r*) and the original investment (*PV*) (see Figure 3.1).

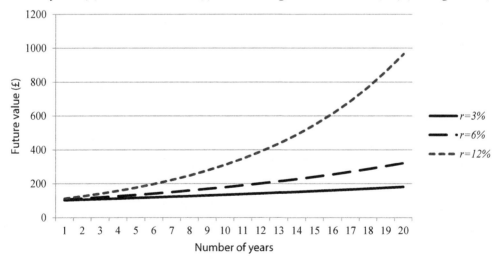

Figure 3.1: The future value of £100 initially deposited and compounded at 3, 6 and 12 percent

Example: Changing *r*, *n* and *PV*

You deposit £100 in the Royal Bank of Scotland (RBS) for 3 years. What is the *FV* at 3%? What is the FV if you change interest rate to 6%?

$$FV \text{ at } 3\% = 100(1+0.03)^3 = £109.27$$

$$FV \text{ at } 6\% = 100(1+0.06)^3 = £119.10$$

Continue the same example but change the time to 10 years. What is the *FV* now?

$$FV \text{ at } 6\% = 100(1+0.06)^{10} = £179.08$$

Continue the same example but change the contribution to £1,200. What is the *FV* now?

$$FV \text{ at } 6\% = 1,200(1+0.06)^{10} = £2,149.02$$

■ Present value and rate of return

Present value (*PV*) is the value today of a future cash flow. Thus, present value reflects the current value of a future payment or receipt.

$$PV = \frac{FV_n}{(1+r)^n}$$

Where *FV* is the future value of the future of the investment at the end of *n* years; *r* is the interest rate; *n* is number of years until payment is received; and *PV* is the present value of the future sum of money.

Example: What is the present value of receiving £6,500 three years from now if the equivalent investment return rate is 12%?

$$PV = \frac{FV_n}{(1+r)^n} = \frac{£6,500}{(1+0.12)^3} = £4,626,57$$

Thus, the present value of £6,500 earned three years from now is £4,626.57 if the discount rate is 12 percent.

■ Principle of value additivity or annuities

An annuity is a series of equal payments for a specified number of years. Where the payments occur at the end of each period, this is called an 'ordinary annuity'. A compound annuity invovles depositing or investing an equal sum of money at the end of each year for a certain number of years and allowing it to grow.[1]

Example: Future value annuity

What will be the *FV* of 5-year £500 annuity compounded at 3%.?

We can calculate the FV annuity and explain it by using a time line as follows:

---

1 Annuities due are ordinary annuities in which all payments (deposits) have been shifted forward by one time period. Each annuity payment therefore occurs at the beginning of the period instead of at its end.

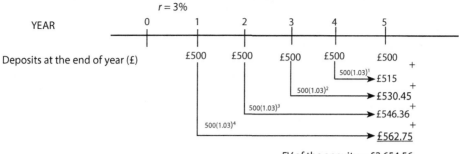

FV of the annuity = £2,654.56

Future value of an annuity using an equation:

$$FV_n = PMT\,[((1+r)^n - 1)\,/\,r]$$

Where FV_n is the future of an annuity at the end of the nth year; PMT is the annuity payment deposited or received at the end of each year; r is the annual interest rate (or discount rate); and n is the number of years.

Using the same example, What is the FV of 5-year £500 annuity compounded at 3%?

$$FV_n = PMT\,[((1+r)^n - 1)\,/\,\mathrm{r}] = £500\,[((1.03)^5 - 1)\,/\,0.03] = £2,654.56$$

In addition to the FV of an annuity, we need to know the present value of an annuity because pensions, insurance obligations, and interest hold on bonds are all annuities.

Example: Present value annuity

What will be the PV of 5-year £1,000 annuity with discount rate at 3%.

Again, we start to calculate PV annuity and to explain by using a time line:

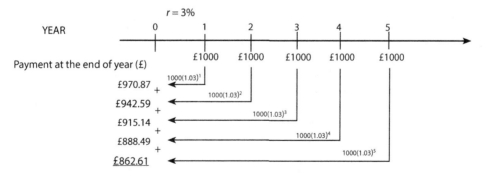

PV of the annuity = £4,579.70

Present value of an annuity using equation:

$$PV_n = PMT\,[\,(1-(1+r)^{-n})\,/\,r]$$

Thus, the *PV* of 5-year £1,000 annuity with discount rate at 3% is:

1,000 [(1-(1.03)$^{-5}$)/0.03] = £4,579.70

In practical, we can apply the concept of *PV* annuity for amortized loans. Loans paid off in equal installments over time are called amortized loans, e.g. home mortgages and auto loans. Reducing the balance of a loan via annuity payments is generally called amortizing. The payment period is fixed but different amounts of each payment are applied towards the principal and interest. With each payment, you owe less towards the principal. As a result, the amount that goes toward interest declines with every payment.

Example: Amortized loan

You want to finance for a new equipment with a purchase price of £12,000 at an interest rate of 8% over 5 years, what will your annual payment be?

Finding the payment: The payment amount can be found by solving for *PMT* using *PV* of annuity equation:

PV_n $= PMT [(1-(1 + r)^{-n}) / r]$

£12,000 $= PMT [(1-(1+0.08)^{-5}) / 0.08]$

PMT   = £3,005.48

Period	Annuity	Interest paid	Principal repaid	Balance
Year 0				£12,000.00
Year 1	£3,005.48	£960 (12,000x0.08)	£2,045.48	£9,954.52
Year 2	£3,005.48	£796.36 (9,954.52x0.08)	£2,209.12	£7,745.40
Year 3	£3,005.48	£619.63 (7,745.40x0.08)	£2,385.85	£5,359.55
Year 4	£3,005.48	£428.76 (5,359.55x0.08)	£2,576.71	£2,782.85
Year 5	£3,005.48	£222.63 (2,782.85x0.08)	£2,782.85	0

3.3   Further capital budgeting methods

In this section, you learn further about capital budgeting methods. Although net present value (NPV) is the well-known method, at least one other method, namely the internal rate of return (IRR), is commonly considered to compare the results. In the real world, there are a number of other methods and these sometime produce incorrect results; you should be wary of using them. Section 3.3 helps you to know which capital budgeting method CFOs usually rely on.

Typical questions: Should you invest in a new equipment in the hope of generating a profit next year?

There are two commonly used types of the payback period method. They are the conventional payback period method and the discounted payback period method. We recommend the discounted payback period method. However, the conventional or undiscounted payback period method is sometimes easier to explain to non-financial people who are unfamiliar with project evaluation techniques.

■ Payback period (PP)

3

The payback method is the most popular investment appraisal method. However, it suffers from such serious shortcomings that it should only really be regarded as a first screening method (Watson and Head 2007, p. 153). The payback period is the number of years that it is expected to take to recover the principal of an investment project. The decision rule for the payback period method is to accept a project if its payback period is equal to or less than a predetermined target value. This measure is simple and easy to apply and understand. It is calculated using cash flows, not accounting profits, and so should not be open to manipulation by managerial preferences for accounting policies.

Example: Project X requires £1,000 at the beginning of the project. We can see the future cash flows of Project X in Table 3.1. After three years, the project has generated a total cash inflow of £900. During the fourth year, the remaining £100 of the initial investment will be recovered. As the cash flow in this year is £200, and assuming that it occurs evenly during the year, it will take a further six months or 0.5 years. Thus, the payback period is 3.5 years.

Table 3.1: Table of cash flows and cumulative cash flows for Project X

Year	Cash flow (£)	Cumulative cash flow (£)
0	-1,000	-1,000
1	200	-800
2	400	-400
3	300	-100
4	200	100
5	300	400
6	200	600

Nevertheless, there are a number of drawbacks in using the payback method. First, it ignores any cash flows that are generated after the payback period. In addition, the payback period ignores the time value of money,

Thus, the payback method does seemingly not offer useful information when compared with other methods that we will show you in the later section.

■ Discount payback period (DPP)

The discount payback period is similar to the conventional payback period except that it uses discounted free cash flows instead of actual undiscounted cash flows. The discount payback period is therefore defined as the number of years required to recover the initial cash outlay[2] from the discounted free cash flows. Using the same example as with the payback period, the discount payback period is 5.73 years at discount rate of 15%. Table 3.2 shows the difference between traditional payback period and discount payback period methods. With undiscounted free cash flows, the payback period is only 3.5 years while the discounted free cash flows (at 15%), the discount payback period is 5.73 years.

Table 3.2: Table of discounted cash flows and cumulative cash flows for Project X

Year	Cash flow (£)	Discounted Cash flow (£)	Cumulative cash flow (£)
0	-1,000	-1000	-1,000
1	200	173.91	-826.09
2	400	302.46	-523.63
3	300	197.25	-326.38
4	200	114.35	-212.03
5	300	149.15	-62.88
6	200	86.47	23.59

■ Average accounting return (ARR)

The average accounting return (*ARR*) is the average project earning after taxes and depreciation, divided by the average book value of the investment during its life. Accounting profit is the difference between positive and negative cash flows. Depreciation describes the decline in value of a company's assets, such as buildings and equipment, over their useful lives. It is a method of capital recovery for accounting and book keeping purposes. Book value represents the initial cost of a project less any accumulated depreciation. Average book value is simply the sum of the annual book values divided by the number of years of the project's useful life. There are several methods for computing the depreciation of a project and thus, different book method results may occur depending on the depreciation method selected.

The accounting rate of return (original book method) may be known to readers by other names such as the return on capital employed (ROCE) or return on

---

2 The initial cash outlay is defined as the immediate cash outflow necessary to purchase the asset and put it in operating order.

investment (ROI). It provides a project's rate of return based on the ratio of average annual accounting profit to the original book value of the asset, or project. A variation of this method is the average book method, which obtains a ratio by dividing the average annual accounting profit by the average book value. A second variation of the original book method is the year-by-year book method, which examines the ratio of the yearly accounting profit to the yearly book value. Each of these methods needs a basis for comparison.

ARR formula (annual basis):

$$AAR = \frac{(Average\ net\ income)}{(Average\ investment)}$$

Decision rule: if *the rate determined ≥ Required Rate of Return,* **'Accept'** or otherwise, **'Reject'**

Example: Harvey Nichols and Company Limited is evaluating whether to construct a new store in Dubai. The initial investment is £1,000,000. We will assume that the store has an estimated life of 5 years and will need to be rebuilt at the end of that time. For simplicity's sake, the asset will be depreciated using straight line depreciation. The annual sales and expense figures are reported in Table 3.3.

Table 3.3: Harvey Nichols' project revenues and costs for average accounting return calculation

	Year 1	Year 2	Year 3	Year 4	Year 5
Revenue	£950,000	£900,000	£830,000	£750,000	£350,000
Expenses	£400,000	£350,000	£250,000	£200,000	£200,000
Before-tax cash flow	£550,000	£550,000	£580,000	£550,000	£150,000
Depreciation	£200,000	£200,000	£200,000	£200,000	£200,000
Profit before taxes	£350,000	£350,000	£380,000	£350,000	£-50,000
Taxes (tc = 30%)[a]	£105,000	£105,000	£114,000	£105,000	£-15,000
Net income	£245,000	£245,000	£194,000	£245,000	£-45,000

Note: [a] Corporate tax rate = t_c. The tax rebate in year 5 of -£15,000 occurs if the rest of the company is profitable. Here the loss in the project reduces the taxes of the entire firm.

Solution:

Average net income = $\frac{£245,000 + £245,000 + £194,000 + £245,000 + (-£45,000)}{5}$

= £50,000

Due to depreciation, the investment in the store becomes less valuable every year. Because depreciation is £200,000 per year, the project's value at the end of year 0 is £1,000,000, the value at the end of year 1 is £800,000, and so on. Thus:

Average investment = $\frac{£1,000,000 + £800,000 + £600,000 + £400,000 + £200,000 + £0}{6}$

$=$ £500,000

AAR = £50,000 / £500,000

=10%

If the company had required rate of return greater (less) than 10%, the project should be rejected (accepted).

There are several drawbacks with AAR method. First, AAR does not work with the right raw materials. It uses net income and book value of the investment, both come from the accounting figures. Profit figures are very poor substitutes for cash flow. The significant criticism of AAR is that it ignores the concept of time value of money.

■ Net Present Value (NPV)

Net Present Value (*NPV*) method is referred to as the net present worth criterion. In the most general terms, *NPV* examines the cash flows of a project over a given time period and resolves them to one equivalent present day cash flow. NPV is used by many people besides corporate finance teams.

> *"An investment proposal's net present value is derived by discounting the future net cash receipts at a rate which reflects the value of the alternative use of the funds, summing them over the life of the proposal and deducting the initial outlay"*

(Arnold 2013, p. 58).

NPV is calculated by using the present value of all free cash flows less the investment's cash outlay. It measures the net value of a project in today's pounds.

NPV formula:

$NPV = [(\sum FCF) / (1 + r)^n]$ - Initial Outlay

or

$$NPV = CF_0 + \frac{CF_1}{(1+r)^1} + \frac{CF_2}{(1+r)^3} + \frac{CF_3}{(1+r)^3} + \cdots + \frac{CF_n}{(1+r)^n}$$

Decision rule: if $NPV \geq 0$, **'Accept'** or if , **'Reject'**

Example: Project Y with an initial cash outlay of £8,000 with following free cash flows (FCF) for 5 years.

Year	0	1	2	3	4	5
FCF	£-8,000	£3000	£5000	£4500	£4000	£3500

The firm has a 15% required rate of return.

Solution:

$$NPV = [(\sum FCF) / (1 + r)^n] - \text{Initial Outlay}$$

$$= \left[\frac{£3,000}{(1+0.15)^1} + \frac{£5,000}{(1+0.15)^2} + \frac{£4,500}{(1+0.15)^3} + \frac{£4,000}{(1+0.15)^4} + \frac{£3,500}{(1+0.15)^5} \right] - £8,000$$

$$= £5,753.44$$

It can be seen that the *NPV* method is derived from the principle of the time value of money and the concept of PV.

Again, we start to calculate *NPV* of Project Y and to explain by using a time line as follows:

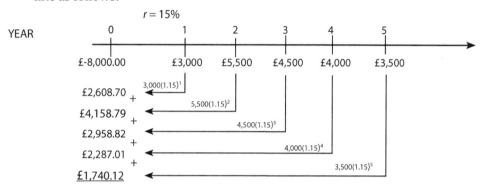

NPV of Project Y = £5,753.44

Project's positive NPV indicates that this project gives not only a return of 15% per annum but a large surplus above and beyond a 10% per annum return. This is an extremely attractive project (on a £8,000 investment the surplus generated beyond the opportunity cost of the shareholders is £5,753.44). Thus, if we accept this project, we would increase shareholder wealth by this amount.

Example: NPV analysis of two projects with equal lives

Year	Investment (£)	Income (£)	Operating and maintenance costs (£)	Salvage value (£)	Net cash flow (£)
Project A					
0	-1,000	0	0		-1,000
1		600	100		500
2		600	100		500
3		500	100		400
4		400	100	150	450
Project B					
0	-1,200	0	0		-1,200
1		800	150		650
2		800	150		650
3		700	150		550
4		500	150	200	550

Solution:

Projects A and B have been proposed to accomplished the same purpose. The require rate of return for both projects is 12%. The NPV of projects A and B can be expressed as follows:

$$\text{Project A } NPV = \left[\frac{£500}{(1+0.12)^1} + \frac{£500}{(1+0.12)^2} + \frac{£400}{(1+0.12)^3} + \frac{£450}{(1+0.12)^4} \right] - £1,000$$

$$= £415.72$$

$$\text{Project B } NPV = \left[\frac{£650}{(1+0.12)^1} + \frac{£650}{(1+0.12)^2} + \frac{£550}{(1+0.12)^3} + \frac{£550}{(1+0.12)^4} \right] - £1,200$$

$$= £639.55$$

Both projects are accepted because they produce positive NPV (greater than zero). However, Project B should be more favoured due to its greater value. An important issue to remember is that when using any of the equivalence methods, the same interest rate must be used for comparing both projects. Another important point to be aware of is that all projects must be compared over equal time periods. But, sometimes the projects to be compared have unequal lives. We will illustrate and solve this situation in a later section.

Berkvitch and Israel (2004) showed that simple *NPV* calculations can miss the real option value of a project. For instance, if the top managers (headquarters) can observe all possible projects at no cost, then following the *NPV* rule will lead headquarters to accept the project that maximizes shareholder value. But if headquarters cannot observe all proposed projects, then the divisional manager may manipulate the selection process by presenting projects such that managerial utility is maximised. McDonald and Siegel (1986), McDonald (1999) and Berkvitch and Israel (2004) suggested that when the firm cannot calculate the true *NPV*, it is best to use Initial Rate of Return (*IRR*) or the Profitability Index (PI) criterion instead of simple *NPV*.

Notes: The discount rate & cash flow calculation

Schall et al. (1978) surveyed and analysed capital budgeting methods of 424 US firms. Of those responding firms who indicated that a discount rate is applied for capital budgeting methods, 46% use a weighted average cost of capital (WACC), and only 8% use a risk-free rate plus a premium for their risk class. The most common method of predicting cash flow is to first predict net income and then adjust this with non-cash flow items such as depreciation. But only 7% indicated that they used net income directly, while 18% predict cash inflows and outflows directly. The remaining 13% use various different methods.

The profitability index (PI)

PI is the ratio of the present value of the free cash flows to the initial outlay. It yields the same accept or reject decision as NPV.

$$PI = \frac{PV \ of \ FCF}{Initial \ outlay} = \frac{\left[\frac{\sum FCF}{(1+r)^n}\right]}{Initial \ outlay}$$

Decision rule: if PI ≥ 1 , *'Accept'* or if PI < 1 , *'Reject'*

Example: BP Inc. is considering an exclusive project. Project X costs £50,000 and is expected to generate £15,000 in year 1, £18,000 in year 2, £20,000 in year 3 and £15000 in year 4. BP Inc.'s required rate of return for this project is 10%. What is the profitability index for Project X?

Solution:

$$PI = \frac{\left[\frac{£15,000}{(1+0.10)^1} + \frac{£18,000}{(1+0.10)^2} + \frac{£20,000}{(1+0.10)^3} + \frac{£15,000}{(1+0.10)^4}\right]}{£50,000}$$

$$= \frac{£13,636,36 + £14,876.03 + £15,026.30 + £10,245.20}{£50,000}$$

$$= 1.08$$

Project X's PI > 1, thus 'Accept'

Notably, when the present value of a project's free cash flows are greater than the initial outlay, the *NPV* will be a positive. *PI* will therefore be greater than 1. NPV and PI will always yield same decision.

Internal rate of return (IRR)

The internal rate of return method (*IRR*) is a measure of investment worth which calculates the interest rate for which the present worth of a project equals zero. The term 'internal' implies that the interest rate does not represent any 'external' or economic factors.

In general, *IRR* is the discount rate that equates the present value of a project's net future cash flows with the project's initial cash outlay (*IO*) and calculated as follows:

$$IO = \left[\left(\frac{FCF_1}{(1+IRR)^1}\right) + \left(\frac{FCF_2}{(1+IRR)^2}\right) + \cdots + \left(\frac{FCF_n}{(1+IRR)^n}\right)\right]$$

Decision rule: if *IRR* $\geq$*Required Rate of Return*, *'Accept'* or otherwise, *'Reject'*

If *NPV* is a positive (negative), *IRR* will be greater (less) than the required rate of return. However, if *NPV* equals to 0, *IRR* is the required rate of return.

Example: Tesco Co. is considering a new inventory system that will cost £4,500. The system is expected to generate positive cash flows over the next four years in the amounts of £1,500 in year one, £1,250 in year two, £1,100 in year three, and £1,000 in year four. Tesco's required rate of return is 10%.   What is the internal rate of return of this project?

Solution:

$$£4,500 = \left[\left(\frac{£1,500}{(1+IRR)^1}\right) + \left(\frac{£1,250}{(1+IRR)^2}\right) + \left(\frac{£1,100}{(1+IRR)^3}\right) + \left(\frac{£1,000}{(1+IRR)^4}\right)\right]$$

For IRR calculations without a financial calculator or computer software, the *'Trial and Error'* method is a common way to find it. We need the discount rate making NPV = 0. In this case, the present value of FCFs in the project should therefore be £4,500.

Let us try 5% of discount rate first:

$$\left[\left(\frac{£1,500}{(1+0.05)^1}\right) + \left(\frac{£1,250}{(1+0.05)^2}\right) + \left(\frac{£1,100}{(1+0.05)^3}\right) + \left(\frac{£1,000}{(1+0.05)^4}\right)\right] = £4,335.28$$

We might have too much discount rate. I will take a better guess now, and try a 3% interest rate:

$$\left[\left(\frac{£1,500}{(1+0.03)^1}\right) + \left(\frac{£1,250}{(1+0.03)^2}\right) + \left(\frac{£1,100}{(1+0.03)^3}\right) + \left(\frac{£1,000}{(1+0.03)^4}\right)\right] = £4,529.70$$

So close – maybe 3.30%?

$$\left[\left(\frac{£1,500}{(1+0.033)^1}\right) + \left(\frac{£1,250}{(1+0.033)^2}\right) + \left(\frac{£1,100}{(1+0.033)^3}\right) + \left(\frac{£1,000}{(1+0.033)^4}\right)\right] = £4,499.61$$

That is close enough. Thus, we would say that the Internal Rate of Return for is the Tesco's project is 3.30%. However, the *IRR* is lower than the required rate of return (10%). The project should be rejected.

The primary drawback of *IRR* relative to the *NPV* is the assumption of the re-investment rate made by the internal rate of return. Another problem with using *IRR* is that there can be more *IRRs* in the case of non-normal cash flows (-, +, -). When the cash flows of a project change sign more than once, there will be multiple IRRs. Non-normal cash flows are called unconventional cash flows[3].

Suppose the cash flows of a project are £-1600, +£10,000 and £-10,000 in years 0, 1 and 2 respectively. Because this project has a negative cash flow (cash out-flow), a positive cash flow (cash inflow) and another negative cash flow, it can be seen that the project's cash flows exhibit two changes of sign, or 'flip-flops'. This

---

3 Conventional cash flows occur when an outflow is followed by a series of cash inflows or a cash inflow is followed by a series of cash outflows.

pattern of cash flow might happen in some projects that have further investment during the project life period. It is easy to verify that this project has not only one but two IRRs (see Figure 3.3). Therefore, in the case of unconventional cash flows, NPV or other methods are preferred measures.

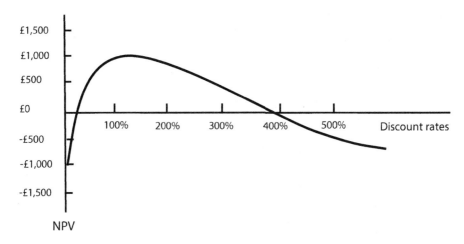

Figure 3.3: Multiple internal rates of returns

Example: Google plc has used the IRR method of project appraisal. The company has doubts about its usefulness after examining the project proposal.

Year	0	1	2
Cash flow	£-30,000	£150,000	£-130,000

Solution:

$$30 = \frac{150}{(1+i)^1} - \frac{130}{(1+i)^2}$$

$$30(1+i)^2 = \frac{150}{(1+i)^1}(1+i)^2 - \frac{130}{(1+i)^2}(1+i)^2$$

$$30(1+i)^2 = 150(1+i)^1 - 130$$

$$30(1+2i+i^2) = 150 + 150i - 130$$

$$30 + 60i + 30i^2 = 150 + 150i - 130$$

$$30i^2 - 90i + 10 = 0$$

$$\frac{30i^2}{30} - \frac{90i}{30} + \frac{10}{30} = 0$$

$$i^2 - 3i + 0.333 = 0$$

Solve *i* by following the formula thus:

$$i = \frac{-b \pm \sqrt{b^2 - 4ac}}{2a} \text{ thus, } i = \frac{-(-3) \pm \sqrt{(-3)^2 - 4(1)(0.333)}}{2(1)}$$

$(i - 2.884)\,(i - 0.155) = 0$

$i = 2.884 \text{ and } 0.155$

Due to unconventional cash flows of the project, we found multiple IRRs at 11.56% and 288.4%.

■ Modified internal rate of return (MIRR)

In the previous sections, with *NPV* it is assumed that cash inflows arising during the life of the project are re-invested at the required rate of return (discount rate) or cost of capital. In contrast, the *IRR* assumes that the cash flows can be re-invested at a rate equal to the *IRR* through the project's life. In practice, the intra-project cash inflows should be invested at the opportunity cost of capital. In the same vein, the company's normal discount rate is a suitable estimate of the re-investment rate.

The modified internal rate of return (MIRR) allows the decision maker to directly specify the appropriate re-investment rate. The MIRR is the rate of return which if used to compound the initial investment amount (the initial cash outlay), produces the same terminal value as the project's cash inflows. The future value of the project's cash flows at the end of the project's life, after they have been expressed in the terminal date's values, is achieved through compounding at the opportunity cost of funds.

Example: Project A costs £1,200 and is expected to generate £640 in year one, £860 in year two, but further investment (cash outflow) £300 in year three, and £500 in years four and five. The required rate of return for this project is 10%. What is the modified internal rate of return for Project A?

Solution: We do not need to use any formulas if we understand the concepts of *MIRR* and TVM (time value of money). There are three common steps for *MIRR* calculation.

1 Calculate the terminal value of the cash flows of the project by converting all positive cash flows to their future value at the end of project's life

2 Calculate the present value of the project by discounting all negative cash flows (cash outflows) backward to the beginning of the project's life

3 Now we have the terminal value (*FV*), present value (*PV*) and period of project's life. Thus, we can find the overall discount rate of the project – the modified internal rate of return (*MIRR*).

Again, it is easy to explain and show how to calculate *MIRR* by using a time line:

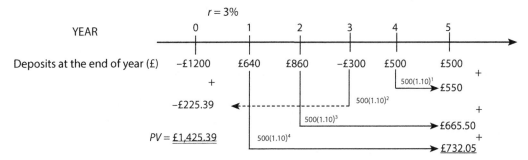

If you remember the concept of TVM, then $FV = PV(1+i)^n$. In this case, i is the modified internal rate of return (*MIRR*).

$$£2,447.55 = £1,425.39(1+MIRR)^5 \qquad MIRR = 11.42\%$$

Notably, the project cash inflows are now invested at the opportunity cost of capital. The *MIRR* method can also deal with the cases of unconventional cash flows (+, -, +) and solve the multiple *IRR* problem.

A survey study

Arnold and Hatzopoulos (2000) studied 300 UK companies in 1997 concerning project appraisal methods. They summarise the financial analysis techniques used for the appraisal of major investment and frequency of the use of combinations of appraisal methods in Tables 3.4 and 3.5.

Table3.4: Techniques employed for capital budgeting

	Small (%)	Medium (%)	Large (%)	Composite (%)
Payback Period (PP)	71	75	66	70
Average Rate of Return (ARR)	62	50	55	56
Initial Rate of Return (IRR)	76	83	84	81
Net Present Value (NPV)	62	79	97	80

Table 3.5: Frequency of the use of combinations of appraisal methods

	Small (%)	Medium (%)	Large (%)	Composite (%)
No method	3	-	-	1
Single method				
PP	3	-	-	1
ARR	-	-	-	-
IRR	6	-	-	2
NPV	-	4	8	4

Two methods				
PP + AAR	3	4	-	2
PP + IRR	3	4	3	3
PP + NPV	3	4	-	2
ARR + IRR	9	8	-	5
ARR + NPV	3	4	3	3
IRR + NPV	9	4	11	8
Three methods				
PP + ARR + IRR	12	4	-	5
PP + ARR + NPV	9	-	5	5
PP + IRR + NPV	12	33	24	22
ARR + IRR +NPV	-	4	13	6
Four methods				
PP + ARR + IRR + NPV	26	25	34	29

Note: The capital used ranges between £1.3bn and £24bn for the large firms, £207m and £400m for the medium-sized firms, and £40m and £60m for the small companies.

3.4   Capital rationing, taxation and inflation

In the previous sections, we agreed that if a project had a positive net present value (*NPV*), or required internal rate of return (*IRR*) or/and profitability (*PI*), then it both should be undertaken and could be undertaken. However, in the real business world, there are limits placed on the availability of project finance and a choice has to be made among a number of positive *NPV* projects. This is the capital rationing problem. Capital rationing occurs when funds are not available to finance all wealth-enhancing projects. Also, we ignored taxation and inflation rates that may distort cash flow projections and cost of capital calculations. The real business world it is not in line with these assumptions. The analysis is made more realistic in Section 3.4 by considering these assumptions.

■ Investment on unequal project lives

The unequal lives problem will occur when we have to compare over two mutually exclusive projects with different life spans. To compare unequal life projects, we, therefore, introduce the Equivalent Annual Annuity (*EAA*): an annuity cash flow that yields the same present value as the project's *NPV*. In the same vein, the *EAA* derived from the concept of present value of an annuity but we replace *PV* with *NPV* (see Section 2.2). As a result, the *PMT* will be *EAA*.

Therefore, *EAA* using equation:

$$EAA = NPV / [1 - (1 + r)^{-n}) / r]$$

Example:

If you need to accept only one project between Projects X and Y, with equal investment of £1,000, required rate of return at 15%, and following cash flows in years 1-3 (for Project X) and in years 1-6 (for Project Y).

Year	Project X's cash flow	Project Y's cash flow
0	£-1,000	£-1,000
1	£600	£400
2	£600	£400
3	£600	£500
4		£500
5		£400

Calculate the projects' *NPV*

X = £369.94 and Y = £463.79

Calculate the projects' *EAA*

EAA_X=£369.94/[1 – (1 + 0.15)$^{-3}$) / 0.15] and EAA_Y=£463.79/[1 – (1+0.15)$^{-5}$) / 0.15]

EAA_X = £162.03 and EAA_Y = £138.36

In this case, although Project Y (with 5-year project life) generate more *NPV* but we should accept Project X (with 3-year project life) due to larger *EAA*.

Incremental cash flow

Financial managers must consider what new cash flows in total the company will receive if it takes on a given project. Thus, incremental after-tax cash flows might play a significant role for capital budgeting. Because accounting profits do not reflect actual money in hand, free cash flow accurately reflects the timing of benefits and costs. After-tax free cash flows must be measured incrementally. Incremental cash flow is the additional cash flows (inflows or outflows) occurring in the project's life.

Taxation and investment appraisal

Taxation plays a crucial role in project performance. If managers are making decisions to maximise shareholders' wealth, they will place importance on the cash flows which are available for shareholders. They will therefore evaluate the after-tax cash flows of a project. Arnold (2013) suggested that there are two rules following capital budgeting in the real world with taxation:

> "Rule I: If acceptance of a project changes the tax liabilities of the firm then incremental tax effects need to be accommodated in the analysis."

> *"Rule II: Get the timing right. Incorporate the cash outflow of tax into analysis at the correct time. For example, it is often the case (for small firms) that tax is paid one year or more after the receipt of the related cash flows."*

However, tax rates can change at any time and any project presented using rates applicable at the time of evaluation may be soon out-of-date. This text book will not get too involved in the details of the taxation system. We would like to note that taxation should be taken in consideration for investment appraisal.

■ Inflation and capital budgeting

The inflation rates have fluctuated over the past 40 years. For instance, in the UK it has varied between 1% and 26%. It is important to adjust capital budgeting methods to deal with the inflation. However, future rates of inflation are difficult to predict. There are two types of inflations: specific inflation (changing in prices of individual goods and services) and general inflation (reducing the purchasing power of money). Inflation may cause two problems for capital budgeting. First, the estimation of future cash flows is incorrect. The company should estimate the degree to which future cash flows will be inflated. Second, the required rate of return will increase if the inflation rate rises. Therefore, inflation is positively associated with the discount rate used in project appraisal.

Summary

This chapter has provided insights into the key factors for a company when making financial decisions for investment. The analysis has been based on the goal of companies, which is to maximise their shareholders' wealth. To achieve this target requires an allowance for the time value of money (TVM) and the cost of capital as well as the analysis of relevant cash flows.

End of chapter questions

1 Given a project with an initial investment of £125,000 that provides annual cash inflow of £40,000 for the first two years and £30,000 per year three and £20,000 per year four through six. The required (discount) rate of return is 5%. What is the payback period and discounted payback period for this project?

2 Virgin Active Corp. is considering gym machines for the new branch at Stirling, Scotland that requires an initial investment of £150,000 installed, and has a useful life of 7 years. The expected annual after-tax cash flows are £25,000 for each of the 7 years and nothing thereafter.

a. Calculate the net present value of the machine if the required rate of return is 12%.

b. Calculate the IRR of this project.

c. Should Kingston accept the project (assume that it is independent and not subject to any capital rationing constraint)? Explain your answer.

3 Morrison Co. is considering a new inventory system that will cost £750,000. The system is expected to generate positive cash flows over the next four years in a total of £350,000 in year one, £325,000 in year two, £150,000 in year three, and £180,000 in year four. Morrison's required rate of return is 8%. What is the modified internal rate of return of this project?

     a) 10.87%   b) 11.57%   c) 13.68%   d) 15.13%

4 Project X has an internal rate of return (IRR) of 12%. Project Y has an IRR of 10%. Both projects have a required return of 8%. Which of these statements is most correct?

a. Both projects have a positive net present value (NPV).

b. Project X must have a higher NPV than project Y.

c. If the required return were less than 12 percent, Project B would have a higher IRR than Project X.

d. Project Y has a higher profitability index than Project X.

5 ASDA Co. is considering a new inventory system that will cost £450,000. The system is expected to generate positive cash flows over the next four years in the amounts of £250,000 in year one, £125,000 in year two, £110,000 in year three, and £80,000 in year four. ASDA's required rate of return is 10%. What is the payback period of this project?

a. 4.00 years

b. 3.02 years

c. 2.68 years

d. 2.42 years

6 What is the payback p eriod for a project with an initial investment of £180,000 that provides an annual cash inflow of £40,000 for the first three years and £25,000 per year for years four and five, and £50,000 per year for years six through eight?

a. 5.80 years

b. 5.20 years

c. 5.40 years

d. 5.59 years

7 The advantages of NPV are all of the following except:

    a. it can be used as a rough screening device to eliminate those projects whose returns do not materialize until later years

    b. it provides the amount by which positive NPV projects will increase the value of the firm

    c. it allows the comparison of benefits and costs in a logical manner through the use of time value of money principles

    d. it recognizes the timing of the benefits resulting from the project

8 Which of the following statements is most correct?

    a) If a project's internal rate of return (IRR) exceeds the required return, then the project's net present value (NPV) must be negative.

    b) If Project X has a higher IRR than Project Y, then Project X must also have a higher NPV.

    c) The IRR calculation implicitly assumes that all cash flows are reinvested at a rate of return equal to the IRR.

    d) A project with a NPV = 0 is not acceptable.

9 The disadvantage of the IRR method is that _____.

    a. the IRR deals with cash flows

    b. the IRR gives equal regard to all returns within a project's life

    c. the IRR will always give the same project accept/reject decision as the NPV

    d. the IRR requires long, detailed cash flow forecasts

10 A project requires an initial investment of £347,500. The project generates free cash flow of £600,000 at the end of year 3. What is the internal rate of return for the project?

    a. 72.66%   b. 42.08%   c. 28.44%   d. 19.97%

11 BP Corp. can purchase a new machine for £20,000 that will provide an annual net cash flow of £7,500 per year for five years. The machine will be sold for £800 after taxes at the end of year five. What is the net present value of the machine if the required rate of return is 15.5%?

    a. £5,563.78

    b. £5,235.59

    c. £4,532.98

    d. £4,457.18

Solutions

1 3.75 years for payback period method/ 4.53 years for discount payback period

Year	Payback Period		Discount Payback Period	
	Cash flow (£)	Cumulative cash flow (£)	Discounted Cash flow (£)	Cumulative cash flow (£)
0	-125,000	-125,000	-125,000	-125,000
1	40,000	-85,000	38,095.24	-86,904.76
2	40,000	-45,000	36,281.18	-50,623.58
3	30,000	-15,000	25,915.13	-24,708.45
4	20,000	5,000	16,454.05	-8,254.40
5	20,000	25,000	15,670.52	7,416.12
6	20,000	45,000	14,924.31	22,340.43

2 Virgin Active Corp.

a. NPV = (£-35,906.09)

b. IRR = 4.01%

c. No, the projects NPV is negative and the IRR is less than the required rate of return. Acceptance of this project would reduce shareholder value.

Keywords: NPV, IRR

3 Answer = b

Keywords: Modified Internal Rate of Return

4 Answer: a

Keywords: IRR, NPV, Required Return

5 Answer: c

Keywords: Payback Period

6 Answer: b

Keywords: Payback Period

7 Answer: a

Keywords: NPV

8 Answer: c

Keywords: IRR, NPV, Reinvestment Rate

9 Answer: d

Keywords: IRR

10 Answer: d

Keywords: IRR

11 Answer: b

Keywords: NPV

References and further reading

Arnold, G. (2013), *Corporate Financial Management*, 5th Edition, Pearson Education Limited: England.

Arnold, G.C. and Hatzopoulos P.D. (2000), The theory-practice gap in capital budgeting: evidence from the United Kingdom, *Journal of Business Finance & Accounting*, **27**, 603-626.

McDonald, R. and D. R. Siegel, D.R. (1986), The value of waiting to invest, *Quarterly Journal of Economics*, **101**, 707-727.

McDonald, R. (1999), *Real Options and Rule of Thumbs in Capital Budgeting, Project Flexibility: Agency, and competition: new developments in the theory and applications of real options*, Oxford University Press: New York.

Remer, D.S. and Nieto, A.P. (1995), A compendium and comparison of 25 project evaluation techniques, *International Journal of Production Economics*, **42**, 79-96.

Schall, L.D., Sundem, G.L. and Geijsbeek, W.R. (1978), Notes survey and analysis of capital budgeting methods, *Journal of Finance*, **33**, 281-287.

Sherif, M. (2014), *Corporate Financial Theory*, 2nd European Edition, McGraw-Hill Education: New York.

Watson, D. and Head, A. (2007), *Corporate Finance Principles & Practice*, 4th Edition, Pearson Education Limited: England.

4 Project Leadership

Isla Kapasi, Laura Galloway and Robert Graham

Learning objectives

By the time you have completed this chapter you should be able to:

☐ Identify modern leadership theories

☐ Understand and evaluate the difference between managers and leaders

☐ Appreciate the complexities of leadership in the context of project management

☐ Identify project management competencies

☐ Recognise the important aspects of project management success

4.1 Introduction

Leadership is a process where by a person influences others to accomplish objectives. Leadership occurs throughout organisations, including in projects. For project managers they must not only demonstrate efficiency in their use of the project management tools and techniques, but must also demonstrate leadership of the project and project team. As projects are discrete, unique and involve change, it is the role of the project manager to provide guidance, support and direction for the project stakeholders. It is the project manager who resolves the conflict of expectations among stakeholders at the start of the project. It is the project manager who develops a strategy for delivering the project and influences the stakeholders to support it. Most significantly it is the project manager who motivates individuals to work effectively together and strive for project success. This chapter reviews modern theories of leadership, the difference between managers and leaders, and sets out key project management competencies and some rules for project management success.

4.2   Leadership: Modern background theories

Leadership is about having people engage in and pursue activities to achieve some end or goal. Contemporary leadership theory points to leadership being based on flexibility to situation, context, followers and tasks. As per Situational Leadership (Hersey and Blanchard, 1977), the style of leadership should match to situation, and specifically to followers (how motivated and how skilled they are). Prior to that, Contingency Theory (Fiedler, 1967) posited that leadership style should be contingent on the wider context, and from a broad perspective, leadership can be defined as either task- or person-oriented. Situations are composed of Relations (between leaders and followers), Task, and Power (the extent to which reward and punishment can apply). From these bases, modern theories of leadership emerge, namely the continuum between the poles of Transactional and Transformational Leadership (Bass, 1985).

Transactional leadership is leading by reward and punishment; by offering incentives for effort, additional rewards for good work, and punishment, or at least the withdrawal of rewards, for lack of effort or output (Tracey and Hinkin, 1998). On the other hand, transformational leadership is about motivating people by engaging them in activities or tasks to the point where they are personally invested. Transformational leadership requires personalised leadership that engages followers on an individual level, matching the aims of the organisation with the aspirations and interests of followers. This is the basis of lots of modern styles of leadership, such as authentic leadership and charismatic leadership.

It is said that all commercial organisations operate leadership strategies somewhere on the transactional to transformational continuum (Avolio, 1999), depending on situation, follower context and level of knowledge required in the industry or for the task. For example, for high-skilled knowledge workers seeking a career in a technology or other professional sector, engagement with work, creativity and autonomy are all-important; personal development and career progression are the principle aims. On the other hand, routine or non-technical tasks that require low level skills might attract an employee motivated in a very different way, perhaps where reasonable pay and conditions are the motivator and long-term aspirations do not feature much. Thus, the most efficient form of leadership will lie on the point of the transformational–transactional continuum most appropriate for the organisational goals and the engagement levels and requirements of followers. In commercial organisations, payment of staff is a fundamental transaction – people are unlikely to return to work if they're not being paid. Other transactions are going on as well though, and indeed, the development opportunities and personalised treatment associated with transformational leadership might also be understood as transactional. So the two styles of leadership are not entirely distinct from each-other, and in commercial organisations, particularly in knowledge sectors, both are required to extract the best from people.

That concludes a short introduction to the theoretical backdrop of leadership. And a reasonable set of principles are underpinning these theories. But what can you do when you have no reward or punishment 'tools' available to you? Therein lies the dilemma and the challenge for the project manager.

4.3   Manager vs. leader

Although the terms tend to be used interchangeable, leadership differs from management in a number of ways. First, a 'manager ' is an official title given to an individual, which gives them authority over subordinates, sections, departments or processes. The main aim of the manager is to maximise the outputs with a particular function through administrative implementation. The manager's role involves organising, planning, directing and controlling resources. Management is about bringing order and consistency to a function (Kotter, 1996). Managers provide the stability within an organisation. They follow rules and implement business policy. Managers behave rationally and seek to ensure that processes are functioning efficiently and the status quo is maintained. Direct leadership may be a management responsibility but a manager is not necessarily always a leader. Thus managers are efficient.

Conversely, leadership is a behavioural characteristic. It involves having vision and developing a strategy to inspire, motivate and influence others in pursuit of organisational goals. Leaders set objectives. They embrace change, they work with risk and aim for effectiveness. Leaders tolerate chaos and a lack of structure as this part of the change process. Table 4.1 offers further insight into the difference between managers and leaders.

Table 4.1: The differences between managers and leaders

Managers	Leaders
Maintain control of subordinates by authority and ruling	Leaders influence individuals to follow
Focus on administration	Focus on relationships
Are concerned with the short term objectives	Are concerned with the long term goals
Deal with complexity	Deal with uncertainty
Follow policy	Establish principles
Find fact and solutions to problems	Identify opportunities and makes decisions
Are concerned with efficiency	Are concerned with effectiveness
Imitate other managers	Create own style

Project management is leadership intensive. Effective project managers are innovative, creative and entrepreneurial, whilst at the same time they enforce rules, provide stability and maintain order within the project team. This almost makes the project manager a hybrid between a leader and a manager. However, as with all leaders, the effective project manager recognises that the success of a project can only be achieved by a motivated team. It is for this reason that project management is often more about leadership than management.

Exercise 1

In general, organisations require both leaders and managers to perform. An organisation with too many managers will lack innovation, direction and vision. Conversely an organisation with too many leaders will be problematic, as there will be much debate and little productivity.

Consider the television programme *"The Apprentice"*. In the US version Donald Trump brings twelve determined leaders together to compete for a single six-figure salary position. Each week the contestants are split into two project teams, who compete with each other to achieve a specific objective. Even though the 12 contestants were selected for their business acumen, each week they have major conflicts, disasters and disorder.

What are the problems with a group of leaders working as a team?

4.4   Project management and leadership

Projects have become an integral component of modern organisations. Projects are now commonly used for organisational improvement, change and strategy implementation (Maylor, 2001; Winter *et al.*, 2006). As project knowledge and use have expanded, the focus on the traditional project control mechanisms (that have underpinned project management since the first edition of the *Project Management Body of Knowledge* in 1987), has been found to be limited. Correspondingly, a greater emphasis on effective leadership of project teams has emerged. In short, there has been a shift in emphasis in projects from managing project tasks to leading project teams; from viewing projects as task-oriented, to taking a more people-centred approach. This has had to happen as, like other forms of organisations, projects have been found to work best when leadership encourages engagement amongst those who comprise the team.

But how can project managers become leaders? How can projects be led when in most cases there is an absence of demonstrable authority or power, rewards or punishments? In project teams the designated leader is often unlikely to be a line manager, is likely to be managing crossfunctional, multi-stakeholder teams, and working in a 'matrix' organisational design (Cleland, 1995). Therefore he or she is unlikely to have limited 'formal' powers such as access to financial remuneration (or withdrawal), and has limited or no influence on other types of reward, such as promotion etc. So how do they lead?

Projects are most often based on a specific project aim. Projects are also time-bound; most often they are temporary. To deliver quality project outputs in that context project managers have to be able to do four main things:

1   Understand the project goal,

2   Personalise the mission,

3   Connect with the team/staff being led, and

4   Conduct the work to complete the project.

In the past, projects have been considered entirely task-focused. Therefore, the project team has been treated as a resource for task completion, just the same as any other resource. The leadership literature tells us this is not necessarily the best way to motivate people, and in fact, in knowledge sectors – or for knowledge-based projects – a person-centred approach is much more effective. Indeed, from the list of four things a project manager must do, there are clear person-based factors involved.

If we return to contemporary leadership theories, the issues of flexibility (to situation, context, team), communication, engagement and personalisation recur. Transformational leadership theory in particular lends itself to leadership by influence without the requirement of tangible rewards and punishments tools (Müller and Turner, 2007).

Transformational leadership

Transformational leadership has four component parts to it. These are divided into two groups; one focused on the leader; the other focused on the followers. These are:

The leader has:

- Idealised influence: where the leader motivates followers by his or her own conduct and behaviours and becomes something of a role model.

- Inspirational motivation: enthusiastic and engaging; inspires people to perform through his or her own conduct

The follower has:

- Intellectual stimulation: they are given challenging and interesting things to do and are afforded autonomy to develop their own solutions and ideas

- Individual consideration: followers are treated as individuals with their own talents, ambitions and are afforded opportunities to perform and to develop with their individual needs and aims in mind.

None of these elements requires line management or financial control. Instead, they all are based on engagement, respect, trust and most importantly, communication. It is these that have seen the best leaders through history and in commercial organisations; where a leader's vision and enthusiasm are clear, and are infectious; and where that leader appears (at least) to care about the development of followers in line with strategic goals of the organisation.

So how does this work then? What does a project manager have to do to become a real project leader? It is challenging – there is no easy way around it. In a limited time, with limited resources and often with a team selected by a third party from somewhere higher up in the organisation, the project leader still has to meet the four project management criteria listed above. Some ways in which each might be achieved optimally as a consequence of excellent leadership are presented below:

1 **Understand the project goal.** Have a clear understanding of the goals and start to plan how these might be achieved within the cost, time, quality framework.

2 **Personalise it.** Learn about the project and take the aims on personally, to the point where the project is envisioned. Invest and engage with it on a personal level – own it.

3 **Connect with the team.** Get to know the team: know everyone's name; know their professional backgrounds and experiences; know their professional aspirations – can these be enabled or assisted by experiences within the project; know something about them personally – such as their hobbies, talents, interests – these might be useful to the project; take time to take their opinions, requests, comments and criticisms – use their expertise and experience and trust them to have an opinion and allow them to voice it.

4 **Conduct the project.** Assign people to interesting tasks; delegate tasks, delegate responsibility, delegate authority; encourage ideas; encourage creativity and autonomy; operate a no-blame culture and take overall responsibility; join in, be seen to participate, be seen to have ideas and autonomy and be seen to be enthusiastic and engaged.

None of the principles of transformational or person-based leadership change the fact that the project management pillars remain concurrent priorities. Projects are bound by time, cost and quality. But where there are teams, there are leaders, and the differences between a failed project, a delivered project, and an excellent project are largely based on the effectiveness of the operation of the team; this in turn is entirely reliant on how well it has been led (Cleland, 1995). Really excellent leadership is hard to achieve and particularly so where you have few or none of the 'regular' tools at your disposal. Project managers cannot hire or fire; they cannot bonus, promote or demote. But they can still lead.

4.5   Project management competencies

The project management body of knowledge (PMBOK) has been developed by the Project Management Institute (PMI) and sets out eight important project management competencies which include: management of time, scope, cost, quality, contract, risk, communication and human resource (Barber and Warn, 2005). In addition, the study of competencies has further developed to include project management *leadership* (Müller and Turner, 2010). Cleland (1995) reports that in the case of project management it is competence rather than superior position within an organisations hierarchy that will be linked to leadership. Thus, all team members have the potential to be the leader of a project team (ibid.)

Müller and Turner (2010) identify in their recent study that there are 15 leadership competencies that can be combined to form three categories of leadership style: intellectual, managerial and emotional. Their findings indicate that a combination of emotional and intellectual intelligence are linked to the management of the most successful projects (ibid.). In addition, Geoghegan and Dulewicz (2008) identify the importance of managerial competencies. Furthermore, there are specific types of competency profiles which link to successful project management in different industrial sectors (Müller and Turner, 2010). This illustrates how important project management leadership competencies are. They are set out in Table 4.2.

Barber and Warn (2005) propose that to be a successful project manager, the leader needs to be able to incorporate both the maintenance behaviours of a project manager and the important leadership competencies. Research conducted by Geoghegan and Dulewicz (2008) confirms this with findings to show that managerial competencies (e.g. managing resources) are of principal importance to project success. Therefore, successful project managers need to be competent in managing time, quality and cost but also need to apply transformational leadership techniques such as clearly communicating a vision and having high emotional intelligence.

Table 4.2: Fifteen leadership competencies and three styles of leadership (Müller and Turner, 2010, p. 438)

Group	Competency	Goal-orientated	Involving	Engaging
Intellectual (IQ)	Critical analysis and judgement	High	Medium	Medium
	Vision and imagination	High	High	Medium
	Strategic perspective	High	Medium	Medium
Managerial (MQ)	Engaging communication	Medium	Medium	High
	Managing resources	High	Medium	Low
	Empowering	Low	Medium	High
	Developing	Medium	Medium	High
	Achieving	High	Medium	Medium
Emotional (EQ)	Self-awareness	Medium	High	High
	Emotional resilience	High	High	High
	Motivation	High	High	High
	Sensitivity	Medium	Medium	High
	Influence	Medium	High	High
	Intuitiveness	Medium	Medium	High
	Conscientiousness	High	High	High

Exercise 2

What competencies have you acquired or increased through your project management assessment so far?

4.6   Rules for project management success

Some project managers may be charismatic and have dynamic personalities, which enable them to negotiate and achieve the required activities and changes to deliver the project. Other project managers may be more subtle. They may quietly monitor project performance and support the team in achieving the project objectives by creating a productive and effective project environment. Research supports that different leadership styles are effective in different project types and industry sectors (Müller and Turner, 2007; Müller and Turner, 2010).

Whichever approach the project manager takes to lead a project, the following rules will assist as guide to leading the project.

1 **Keep everyone informed:** Do not keep information to yourself. People become frustrated when they do not have access to information or are not advised of project issues. The project team will feel alienated and become de-motivated if they are not adequately informed of project issues and clients will lose trust if they are advised of important project issues by someone other than the project manager.

2 **Show progress:** Due to the risk and investment required for a project, clients and stakeholders often become nervous and frustrated it they do not see physical progress on a project. This is despite all the work in planning and preparing for the project. It is therefore essential that the project manager shows progress at all times. This is either through communication, project documentation or regular project deliverables.

3 **Take ownership of the project:** The project is the project manager's baby. The project manager must nurture it and develop it until it is ready for handover. The more the project manager takes ownership of the project, the better he will be in motivating the project team to achieve project success.

4 **Support the project team:** No project will be successful without the efforts of the project team. The project manager must therefore motivate and lead the project team to achievement of the project goals. This involves ensuring that the needs of the project team are met, the project team respects and follows the project manager and the project manager gives credit and rewards to project team members for their efforts and achievement.

5 **Communicate:** As previously stated, communication is an essential skill of the project manager. The project manager must be able to communicate at all levels within the organisation. This not only involves directing, presenting and talking, but also involves listening and interpreting.

6 **Perception and control of forthcoming problems:** Try to avoid reactive behaviour and instead encourage proactivity by motivating teams to change and implement new or different work practices which actually prevent problems from occurring.

Above all it is critical that the project manager maintains control of the project and makes others aware that he or she is in control. However, it should be noted that the project manager does not need to know everything, but must have enough information and support to answer all the questions. Finally, Cleland (1995) identifies several key issues which are of importance to a project leader: the vision for the project, the resources that are required, the alignment of people and resources, gaining commitment of stakeholders, and the importance of communication to achieve that.

Conclusion

The greatest leaders throughout history, from Ghandi to Mandella, and through social life, from William Wilberforce to Woody from *Toy Story*, all have at the heart of their leadership strategy communication with and consideration of the people they lead. It is no different in the project management context. Even in commercial organisations, while financial and finance-related rewards (or withdrawal of them) are key elements, the real difference in terms of value is in the non-pecuniary forms of engagement and investment they get from the people who work there. Look at the leadership styles of the likes of John Rockefeller, Walt Disney, Richards Branson, Steve Jobs, Mark Zuckerberg, as just a few examples. And most of the commercial success stories emanating from Silicon Valley, construction, energy, through to the financial sector are heavy users of projects as organisational strategic and operational vehicle for development and change. Overall, transformational leadership is found to be the most valuable leadership style in projects which are successful (Prabhakar, 2005). Most importantly, individuals can develop project and leadership competencies associated with successful project management and thus, as Cleland (1995) says "every member of a team has an opportunity to be a leader" (p.86).

Project Leadership case study

John Smith is a project Leader in an internationally recognized, Scottish-based financial services company. The company is structured on product/divisional lines e.g. financial products, insurance, investments, mergers etc. but it also has a number of project teams which work across divisions and are relatively autonomous, with each project team reporting to a Project Leader. Project Leaders report to a Project Director who in turn reports directly to the main board of the company. It is essentially a 'project based' organisation and over the last five years or so project teams have been increasingly involved in change management initiatives in various parts of the firm.

Project leaders are selected firstly for their technical skills and secondly for their people skills. John was seen as an excellent financial products manager who was able to deliver on targets and he was highly regarded by senior managers. He was less well regarded by his peers though because he had a tendency to 'rub people up the wrong way' due to his task-focused approach. When John was made a project leader he was promised training in soft skills as most people were aware of his rather abrupt manner and many questioned his suitability for the role. John is the only member of the project team who does not have a university degree and many say this has caused him a measure of jealousy and is the source of his rude behaviour towards certain people.

Three months into the new role, things are not going well for John Smith or his team. John has not been given the training he was promised and he is leading on the basis of what he thinks is strong leadership. John cuts people off in team meetings and has become increasingly agitated when team members make comments or offer opinions and it has reached a point where people now say nothing in meetings as they are sure they will be browbeaten and undermined by John. Team members had originally had a grudging respect for John but that has now gone due to his constant criticism and micro-management and people want out of his team. Project milestones are being missed and the Project Director is becoming increasingly concerned at the poor performance of John's team. It was thought that John was a very good manager but he is proving to be a poor team leader. His team never know from day-to-day what kind of approach he'll adopt; one day he is autocratic and driving people, next day he seems distant and adopts a laissez-faire approach, and the next he is asking team members for their views and trying to involve them in decision making.

There are four people plus John in the project team and they are all from different work backgrounds. Joanne has worked for the company for ten years, is from IT and has worked in projects for the last four years. Joanne is highly regarded by everyone she has ever worked with but it has often been said that she thinks and acts like an engineer; she thinks everything in life is a system with inputs, processes and outcomes. Joanne likes clarity and direction and she feels this is now missing and that John is failing the team.

Jack is from an HR background and tries to see problems from different perspectives before making judgements. Jack is quiet and soft-spoken but is perfectly capable of fighting his corner and has strong views, but if he can achieve consensus on an issue he is happy. He avoids win-lose situations and tries at all times to ensure everyone has some input into decision-making. He is the person to whom most of the team look to calm things down when tempers begin to fray. Like Joanne, Jack is becoming increasingly frustrated at John's leadership style.

Lorenzo joined the firm recently having been recruited through the Advanced Graduate Recruitment Programme, and he has been marked out as future high-flyer. Lorenzo is supported by a mentor in the Senior Management Team and he was told by his mentor when he started, 'If you have any concerns or worries bring them to me and I'll get them sorted out'. He has been given an open-ended brief in the team and his role is to watch and learn as it is expected he will be running his own team in the not-too-distant future. While studying for his Postgraduate Master's degree Lorenzo studied project management and leadership and he is bemused at the disconnect between theory and practice; either the text books on leadership are works of fiction, or John Smith does not have a clue about leadership. Lorenzo studied approaches to leadership including autocratic, democratic and laissez-faire and he is familiar with the Managerial Grid developed by Blake and Mouton and from what he has seen, John Smith is all over the Grid. In common with others in the team, it is John's inconsistent leadership style that is causing Lorenzo difficulties. John allocates work to Lorenzo and just when he is getting comfortable with it he is asked to pick up another piece of work and feels as if he has to start all over again. Also, when Lorenzo asks for guidance John tells him 'You're a smart guy, work it out'. Lorenzo is a smart guy and he knows it is not in his best interests to start complaining about John to his mentor; going behind someone's back is bad form and it might make it look as if Lorenzo is incapable of sorting out problems when he knows he will have to be seen as a problem-solver, not a passer of problems.

Alice is from finance and she has been seconded to the team as maternity cover. Alice knows this is a short-term role but she wants into projects and she is determined that this opportunity is not going to pass her by. Alice has worked with the company since leaving university seven years ago and while she has been in finance for most of that time, she does not want to be stuck in it for the rest of her life. Alice's work has focused on Compliance and Regulations and she is now bored to tears by it and is looking for a change of career. Unlike the others, however, Alice is quite happy to go behind John's back and complain about him to other managers. She regards him as incompetent and possibly the worst manager she has ever worked with. Targets have been missed, the projects they have been given are over budget, and due to the nature of the organization, which operates a form of Just-in-time work flow, their failings are affecting other project teams further down the line.

Questions

It sounds as if John Smith is in need of advice and guidance before he loses his job.

1   What qualities and personal characteristics support a higher likelihood of success as a project manager? What qualities and personal characteristics would make it difficult? Compare these to John's behaviour.

2   Of the various elements of project manager competencies, which does John appear to exhibit? What evidence is there to support your contention?

3   What advice and guidance would you offer John regarding his leadership style that might help the project team get back on track? Develop an argument to defend your position.

4   To what extent does John's situation highlight the tensions between management and leadership? Cite examples from the short case study to support your answer.

End of chapter review questions

1 What are the key differences between transformational and transactional leadership?

2 What are the differences between a manager and a leader?

3 Why is project management leadership complex?

4 How can a project manager exhibit excellent leadership?

5 Why are project management competencies important?

6 What are the rules for project management success?

4

References

Avolio, B. J. (1999) *Full Leadership Development: Building the vital forces in organizations,* California: Sage

Barber, E. and Warn, J. (2005) Leadership in project management: from firefighter to firelighter. *Management Decision,* **43** (7/8), 1032-1039

Bass, B. M. (1985) *Leadership and Performance Beyond Expectations*: Free Press; Collier Macmillan

Cleland, D. I. (1995) Leadership and the project-management body of knowledge. *International Journal of Project Management,* **13** (2), 83-88

Fiedler, F. E. (1967) *A Theory of Leadership Effectiveness,* New York: McGraw-Hill

Geoghegan, L. and Dulewicz, V. (2008) Do project managers' leadership competencies contribute to project success? *Project Management Journal,* **39** (4), 58-67

Hersey, P. and Blanchard, K. H. (1977) *Management of Organizational Behavior: Leading Human Resources*: Prentice-Hall

Kotter, J. P. (1996) *Leading Change,* Boston, M.A.: Harvard Business School Press.

Maylor, H. (2001) Beyond the Gantt chart:: Project management moving on. *European Management Journal,* **19** (1), 92-100

Müller, R. and Turner, J. R. (2007) Matching the project manager's leadership style to project type. *International Journal of Project Management,* **25** (1), 21-32

Müller, R. and Turner, R. (2010) Leadership competency profiles of successful project managers. *International Journal of Project Management,* **28** (5), 437-448

PMI (1987) *Project Management Body of Knowledge* Upper Derby, IL: Project Management Institute

Prabhakar, G. P. (2005) Switch leadership in projects: an empirical study reflecting the importance of transformational leadership on project success across twenty-eight nations. *Project Management Journal,* **36** (4), 53-60

Tracey, J. B. and Hinkin, T. R. (1998) Transformational leadership or effective managerial practices? *Group & Organization Management,* **23** (3), 220-236

Winter, M., Smith, C., Morris, P. and Cicmil, S. (2006) Directions for future research in project management: The main findings of a UK government-funded research network. *International Journal of Project Management,* **24** (8), 638-649

5 Project Teams and Groups

Robert Graham

Learning objectives

By the time you have completed this chapter you should be able to:

☐ Recognise and understand the significance of teams in contemporary organisations

☐ Understand the process of creating the project team

☐ Understand the importance of virtual teams in contemporary organisations

☐ Gain an awareness of the stages of team development and group dynamics

☐ Understand the differences between a group and a team

☐ Consider some of the dysfunctional aspects of teams and barriers to their development

5.1   Introduction

There are many well-founded and apparently obvious reasons why organisations form teams. Teams have a strong intuitive appeal in that we assume a team must be more effective and efficient in achieving a task than a collection of individuals working alongside each other. It is claimed that people working in teams produce more, are happier and more confident, and share a commitment to the team and its objectives. It is also argued that teams harness the capabilities and capacities of each individual which in turn produces better decisions and allows for problem-solving and flexibility. It is further claimed that teams produce synergy, that a team is 2 + 2 = 5, where ideas flow from member to member and are turned into reality by people with a shared vision. As attractive as these arguments might appear, we cannot accept them at face value and must question and examine the role of teams in organisations, for if it were so simple each and every organisation could simply re-designate their various work groups as teams and all of their perceived benefits would flow to the organisation.

Some of the questions we will consider in this chapter include, what is a team and why do organisations form them? Is a team different from a group? Do teams come fully-formed or do they go through stages of development? What are the strengths and weaknesses of a team-based approach to work? What are the characteristics of an effective team?

Groups are by no means restricted to the workplace; they play a central role in our lives and Huczyniski and Buchanan (2015) point out that each of us is on average a member of five or six groups and they distinguish between primary and secondary groups. Primary groups are those such as family and close, life-long friends, that provide us with psychological and emotional support and to whom we have strong connections. Secondary groups are akin to associations or affiliations with like-minded people. For example, membership of a sport or hobby club such as country dancing or a member of a choir, and these are groups that people choose to join. Secondary groups also encompass work relationships, where labour is exchanged for payment and where the relationships between members might be termed transactional, but it is groups within a work context that we are concerned with here.

5.2   Team work in contemporary organisations

As organisations have become flatter and less hierarchical in recent years, they have placed an ever-increasing emphasis on the human resource (people) and explored ways of leveraging the knowledge and talents of employees by granting them greater autonomy and discretion over their work. Robbins (2012) cites research that demonstrates the extent to which teams have become the new norm in organisations. The same research highlighted the extent of this trend by pointing out that 66% of EU workers perform part of their work in teams and across Europe, team-working is most common in the UK where 81% of employees report working in teams, with the lowest levels found in Italy and Lithuania at 41 and 38% respectively. The predominance of teamworking is in manufacturing rather than service sectors, but in the USA 54% of the 600 leading companies use self-directed teams. In Europe, some form of teamworking exists in 36% of all workplaces. Australia witnessed a dramatic increase in the number of people working in teams, rising from 8% to 47% between 1988 and1991. According to Thompson and McHugh (2004), 72% of British workplaces have at least some core employees in formally designated teams, with 80% of workplaces with teams extending them to three-fifths of core employees and of these, 66% had trained some staff to be functionally flexible. Further, 21% had groups of non-managerial employees who met to solve specific problems such as quality or performance. These figures suggest strongly that teams are more than a passing fad and are here for the foreseeable future, so an understanding of them is critical to managerial and organisational success.

5.3 Project teams and virtual teams

You will be aware from other parts of your study of project management that a project team is a temporary organisation brought together for a specific purpose and it has many of the characteristics of a short-life team or cross-functional team. Many of these teams share common characteristics in that they are groups of people with complementary skills and knowledge brought together either to address a specific problem or deliver a project. A project team has a specific purpose, leadership of it will have been formally ascribed to a single person, everyone in it should be clear on their role and area of responsibility and they should be clear about who it is they report to. A project team can vary in size from three or four people based in the same building to one that is geographically diverse and with members based in different time zones.

A recent development in teams and groups has been the advent of virtual teams. According to Huczynski and Buchannan (2015; 337) a virtual team is one that "relies on technology-mediated communication, while crossing boundaries of geography, time, culture and organisation, to accomplish an interdependent task. A global virtual team is one that is nationally, geographically and culturally diverse and which communicates almost exclusively through electronic media". They also point out that a virtual team can be of the single-country or multi-country type and if it is the latter, it is termed a global virtual team. The question of whether a team might be identified as virtual or not is explored by Zigurs (2003) and she argues that rather than thinking of a team as either 'virtual' or not, it makes sense to consider them on a 'continuum of virtuality'. Zigurs identified four key features of virtual teams as geographic dispersion, temporal dispersion, cultural dispersion and, organisational dispersion, and she points out that virtual teams have a common goal and rely on technology yet they have to deal with dispersion on a variety of dimensions.

Many large multi-national, global organisations including Apple, Microsoft, Atkins Global, Rolls-Royce, EADS (Airbus consortium) and Boeing use virtual project teams. Atkins Global, a British multi-national, for example, has approximately 18,000 employees in 25 different countries with a number of virtual teams working on projects such as the Beatrice Offshore Wind Farm in the North Sea, with teams based in Epsom, London, Bristol, Glasgow, Birmingham, Rotherham, and Sharjah in the UAE. The tools used by team members to communicate include Skype for business calls and video chats, screen sharing, emails and online data transfer servers. They also utilise teleconferencing and have global network servers for data to be available to the entire company, and according to one of their project team leaders "it's as easy to talk to someone in Sharjah as it is in the UK". On the Hinkley Point C Nuclear Power Station project, Atkins had teams spread over the UK with other teams based in Bangalore, India, building models for use in project analysis which were then sent to project teams in the UK.

Several authors (Arnold and Randall, 2010; Ashleigh and Mansi, 2012) question whether, say, six people in six different geographical locations can be called a 'team' and it may be that our understanding of teams has been broadened to include virtual teams. Bergiel, Bergiel and Balsmeier (2008) explored the advantages and disadvantages of virtual teams or virtual teaming, and noted that one of the main advantages of virtual teams is that, in a global context, organisations that are capable of rapidly creating virtual teams of talented people can respond quickly to changing environmental circumstances and customer demands and thus gain competitive advantage.

Some of the advantages of virtual teams include:

- Significant reduction in travel time and costs
- Reduction in workplace disruption
- Access to a wider talent pool
- Increased quality of work and innovative ideas
- Engender creativity and originality
- Promotion of diversity and equality
- Millenials are comfortable with mobile technology
- May enable 'reverse learning' as Millenials transfer mobile technology knowledge to older workers

The disadvantages of virtual teams include:

- Time differences
- Cultural differences
- Interpersonal friction
- Technology breakdowns
- Language barriers even where there is a common language, e.g. English
- Unclear expectations of roles and behaviours

- Role identification

- The management of conflict and appeals

- Leadership impartiality – where does the team leader's primary loyalty lie?

- Greater task-orientation because team members have not previously met

- Lower satisfaction with group process compared to face-to-face teams

- Less exchange of social-emotional information between members

With one or two exceptions, the strengths and weaknesses of virtual teams are strikingly similar to 'traditional' teams. Both emphasise the importance of shared objectives, role and task clarification, information sharing and open communication, decisions arrived at by consensus, group learning, and a recognition of a common team identity. Equally, both recognise the ways in which team cohesion and effectiveness might be undermined by in-fighting, personality clashes, refusal to share information, failure to make an equal contribution to the task and the dangers of groupthink, amongst other things.

5.4   Creating the project team

An effective project team does not happen spontaneously. It requires a great deal of preparation and effort, from recruiting and selecting team members and to moving them to a state where the team is performing in an effective and efficient manner. The nature of projects is such that teams are temporary and it will be unlikely that a ready unified team will be waiting at the start of the project. It is quite possible that the team members have never worked together before and very often have not even met before the project starts. This creates a major challenge for the project manager. In a short space of time a set of diverse individuals need to be transformed into a high–performing, cohesive project team. Thus, one of the most important activities in project management is building the project team. Within most organisations this involves analysis, discussion and negotiation with functional or line managers in order to acquire suitable team members. Pinto (2007) presents a 4-step process for building the project team.

1   Identify the necessary skills sets

Projects are unique and therefore the requirements from the project team will differ with each project. The first stage of building the team is therefore to conduct a realistic assessment of specific types of skills the team members require in order to complement each other and perform their tasks as effective as possible. For example, in a typical construction project, the skills set would include architectural design, quantity surveying, structural, mechanical and electrical engineering, and building contacting. It might also require other specialist skills sets such as technical knowledge in solar panels, landscape design or even commercial kitchen appliances.

2   Identify people who match the skills:

The next stage after identifying the skill set required for the project is to find people who have the complementary skills to perform the project effectively. This may require hiring people both internal and external to the organisation. The difficulty arises when the specialist skills are required, as these tend to be rare and expensive. One option is to train current personnel to become proficient in the necessary skill set, although this takes time and training costs.

3   Negotiate for potential team members

The third stage in the team building process involves communicating with likely team candidates and negotiating for their employment. In the first instance, it is good practice to meet with potential team members to ensure their level of interest and commitment to the project. In considering the characteristics of an effective team, there would be little point in employing a team member who is not sufficiently motivated to achieve the project goals.

However, not all project team members have the sufficient authority to assign themselves to a project. In most cases the project manager needs to negotiate for suitable personnel through functional managers, as discussed in Chapter 2. Pinto (2007) warns that these negations can be complex and lengthy. Whereas most functional managers are in support of projects, they will be more concerned with the daily operations of the organisation and the vital contribution of key personnel. For this reason it will be necessary to negotiate on:

- *The length of time the project team member is required:* The main concern of the functional manager will be how long the team member will be unable to contribute to the functional department.

- *The actual person selected to join the project*: The project manager will provide a list of criteria, in terms skills, but it may be the functional manager who selects the particular team member according to the skill set.

- *Contingency plans:* In the event of special circumstances or an emergency, the functional manager may wish to retain the option of recalling the team member back to the functional department. In this scenario, the project manager must need clarification of what constitutes an emergency and how long the team member will be unavailable to work on the project.

4   Assemble the project team

The final stage involves assembly of the project team. This involves clarification of the roles and duties of each team member, expectations and establishing the standard operating procedures of the team.

5.5   Stages in team development

Labelling a group of people a 'team' will not necessarily lead to them acting as a team – they must evolve before they become effective and there are at least four stages, as described by Bruce Tuckman (1965). Tuckman and Mary Ann Jensen (1977) added a fifth stage, as shown in Figure 5.1

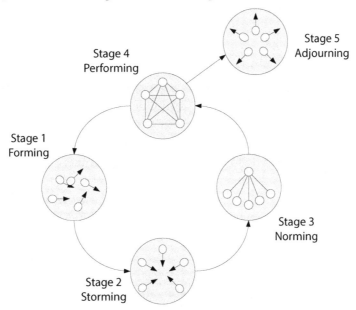

Figure 5.1: Stages of team development

Stage 1: Immature group - *Forming*

In a work context, when teams are formed there may be confusion and uncertainty over purpose and roles. It is often the case that people have been allocated to a particular team and initially members have to get acquainted, assessing the situation by testing ground rules, defining goals and making initial judgements about other people in the group. Communication is likely to be limited, superficial and impersonal.

At this stage the project manager needs to provide direction for all the team members. This involves clearly reiterating the project objectives and the aims of the project team. Responsibilities of each team member should be allocated, as should specific tasks and duties. The interdependencies between each activity should be clearly explained and team members must know which activities are dependant on each other. The project manager should also set out the rules of behaviour within the team and how the team will operate. This includes the project manager's own expectations as well as the expectations of each other. It is important that the team knows how decisions will be made and how much autonomy they have. Also, for motivation it is good practice to clarify from the beginning how feedback will be given on performance and any reward systems that will be implemented for good performance.

Stage 2: Fractional group - *Storming*

At this stage there may be disagreement over priorities and a struggle for leadership may emerge. There might be tension, open hostility and clique formation as team members begin to assess the nature of the task and the roles they have been allocated. There might also be frustration over the perceived lack of progress.

This is a frustrating stage for the project manager, as outlining the rules of behaviour and roles and responsibilities at the forming stage should, theoretically, eliminate any cause for conflict. However, unless the conflict is exposed and addressed it remains a hindrance to individual and team performance. The project manager needs to openly address any conflicts or disagreements. This may result in a reallocation of responsibilities or a different approach to tasks. It may also be necessary to revisit the agreements made by the team during the forming stage and either, ensure that the understanding is uniform across the team or change conditions within the agreement as necessary.

Stage 3: Sharing group - *Norming*

At this stage consensus begins to emerge, formal leadership is accepted as trust is established and communication is open. Roles should now be clarified and cooperation between team members as they focus on the team task.

The project manager at this stage would want to ensure that calm in the team continues. This is the beginning of unity and commitment amongst individual team members and effort should be channelled towards facilitating any issues and supporting individual capabilities. Despite being allocated roles, the team members may still not fully understand how their position within the team contributes to the project. It is therefore useful to reiterate the importance of the tasks in relation to the objectives of the team.

Stage 4: Effective team – *Performing*

As there is now agreement on roles, rules and the task, successful performance should follow. There is trust and an acceptance of individual weaknesses, people are flexible and supportive of each other.

At the performing stage the project manager can take a step back from managing the team and can focus on his own activities and responsibilities. Project tasks can be delegated with confidence, although team members would take on extra roles and responsibilities themselves, without the direction of the project manager. Although, there may be less need to instruct the team, members will still need guidance from the project manager for personal and interpersonal development.

Stage 5: Disbanding group: *Adjourning*

The group is at the disengagement stage and there is anxiety about separation and ending. Often the group has positive feeling towards the leader and view the past in a positive light as past conflicts and disagreements are forgotten about.

At this final stage, the key role of the project manager is to facilitate project closure. This can be a stressful time for the team. The nature of projects often means that team members will work together so closely, under intense pressure, that they develop close personal friendships and it is therefore difficult for team members to go their separate ways. It is for this reason that some authors refer to this stage as "mourning". Project managers need to be sensitive to the concerns of the project team and where possible smooth the transition from the project to back to their functional department or new project. There may be a requirement from the project manager to mentor team members or to provide some form of appraisal and feedback. But above all, it is essential that the performance of individual team members needs to be recognised.

The extent to which a team reaches the performing stage is dependent on a number of factors but it is by no means the case that team development is a naturally occurring phenomenon, moving from one stage to the next in a clear, linear fashion. Nor is it the case that these stages must occur in sequence for teams can move forward and then regress; indeed, they might pass through the same stage more than once and they can also become stationary for a period of time, languishing almost in limbo between stages and thus an understanding of group dynamics is essential for the team leader.

5.6   Team or group, what's in a name?

Within a work context the terms 'teams' and 'groups' are used interchangeably and the differences might seem unimportant but is essential to differentiate them. According to Kurt Lewin (1939) "…it is not the similarity or dissimilarity of individuals that constitute a group, but the interdependence of fate". Michael Hammer (1998) stated that "…a team is not just a group of people who work together or like each other or share opinions. A team is a group of people with a common objective." Shaw (1981) defines a group simply as "…two or more persons who interact with one another in such a manner that each person influences and is influenced by each other person". Torrington and Hall (1995) state that a team "…is more than the sum of the individual members. A team demands collaborative, not competitive effort, where each member takes responsibility for the performance of a team rather than just their own individual performance. The team come first, the individual comes second and everything the member does is geared to the fulfilment of the team's goals rather than their individual agenda."

Some of the key characteristics of a team are, then, unifying relationships, shared objectives, interdependence, a common purpose and a recognition of their particular group identity. A group can be a collection of individuals who lack a common identity and have no interdependence; they could work on their own and the job would still get done. A team will always be a group but not all groups are teams.

Within contemporary organisations we are likely to find some of the following types of teams: project teams, virtual teams, short-life working teams, problem-solving teams and self-managed work teams. The differences between them are relatively slight as they share a number of key characteristics including autonomy, are focused on a single objective, they are transient with a changing composition, membership is fluid and members are multi-skilled and flexible. According to Mullins (2013) effective teams are characterised by some of the following elements:

- Specific objectives

- Role differentiation and role clarity

- Rule clarity

- Open communication

- Conflict is open

- Decisions are made by consensus

- Shared aims and objectives

- A sense of commitment to the group

- Acceptance of group values

- Mutual trust and dependency

- Full participation by all members

- Low turnover, low absenteeism and few errors

The extent to which a team reaches the performing stage is dependent on a number of factors but it is by no means the case that team development is a naturally occurring phenomenon, moving from one stage to the next in a clear, linear fashion. Nor is it the case that these stages must occur in sequence for teams can move forward and then regress; indeed, they might pass through the same stage more than once and they can also become stationary for a period of time, languishing almost in limbo between stages and thus an understanding of group dynamics is essential.

5.6   Dynamics

Kurt Lewin coined the term 'group dynamics' and he examined groups from the perspective of their internal nature: how they form, their structures, processes and functioning and how they affect individual behavior. Lewin also explored how they affect other groups within an organization and ultimately, how they affect the organization itself. Cartwright and Zander (1968) define group dynamics as "a field of inquiry dedicated to advancing knowledge about the nature of groups, the laws of their development and their interrelations with individuals, other groups and larger institutions."

Luthan (1988) argued that managers need to understand the significant role that groups play in the dynamics of organisations and a review of the research literature on groups identified three key factors in determining group effectiveness:

1 *Task interdependence* (how closely group members work together)

2 *Outcome interdependence* (whether and how, group performance is rewarded)

3 *Potency* (the belief that the group can be effective)

Group dynamics is more than gaining insights into the forces among group members and understanding how groups should be organised and conducted; it is also a set of techniques such as role-playing, brainstorming and team-building. The purposes of team-building include analysis of the way work is performed, establish team goals and priorities, examine and understand its processes and examine the relationships among the people doing the work, and according to Beckhard, (2002) its ultimate purpose is to enhance individual and group performance. As we have seen, work is increasingly a group-based activity and thus it is important for managers to have an understanding of group dynamics; managers have a role in motivating group members and they must be aware of the need to adapt their leadership style to the team, the task and the situation. A knowledge of group development may help them to plan appropriate interventions and they need to understand the importance of informal groups. Team training plays a vital role in building competitive advantage and research cited by Ashleigh and Mansi (2012) shows that training improves the effectiveness of teams by highlighting weaknesses in team processes and decision making. The same authors cite a meta-analysis study carried out by Salas et al. (2008) on team training interventions for 2,500 teams which found that training improved decision making and task performance. These interventions can be useful when a team is failing to develop from one stage to another, e.g. from the storming to the norming stage. Group dynamics also distinguishes between formal and informal groups and an understanding of these differences is essential to our understanding of teams and groups.

Formal groups have the authority of the organization with officially prescribed goals. Relationships within them are formal as they have a hierarchical structure with a formally designated leader. Informal groups are formed by individuals and have no recognition within the organization but members share an identity which comes from membership of the group. They have no formal goals and relationships within them are informal and fluid and leadership varies according to the situation. Informal groups develop spontaneously, usually to meet the social needs of people; the need for affiliation, security, recognition and self-worth. What, then, might be some of the barriers to team development?

Exercise 1

Many of you will have, or have had, part-time jobs where you have been a member of a work team e.g. front-of-house team, sales team etc. and much of your university coursework will have been done in groups and thus you have first-hand knowledge of some of the strengths and weaknesses of a team-based approach to work.

5.8   Barriers to team development

Hackman (1998) highlights a number of reasons why teams fail to deliver on the promise. Hackman and his colleagues conducted a study of thirty-three different work groups of many kinds including athletic teams, prison guards, top management teams and airline crews with the intention of identifying what it was that made work groups effective. When analysing the results of their research they found that only four of the thirty-three groups could be considered effective. The rest of the groups had so many problems that the researchers turned their attention to analysing the reasons why they *did not* function effectively. Hackman stated that many of the claims made on behalf of teams in 'popular' management books cannot be dismissed, but he noted that even where there had been improvements in team performance and productivity, rarely could they be attributed solely to the creation of the team itself. Once teams have been formed in organisations, their work is typically compared with other 'conventional' units but, said Hackman, this may be an invalid comparison for rarely is a work group established without other changes being introduced; for example, changes in technology, management style, new leadership, reward systems and so on. Was it the team that triggered the improvements or was it one of the other factors? In addition to these factors, Hackman and his colleagues questioned the extent to which improvements are sustained over an extended period of time – what they termed the 'staying power' of performance improvements – and noted that short-term gains might also be the outcome of the notorious 'Hawthorne effect'. Hackman and his colleagues posed the question of whether or not teams lead to improved organisational performance and concluded that it is a question that has no general answer. What the researchers were able to identify, however, were the main mistakes made when putting people into work teams:

Mistake 1: Using a team for work that is better done by individuals

There are some tasks that only a team can perform, such as a band or a choir, but some are inimical to teams, with creative work as an example.

Mistake 2: Calling the performing unit a team but really manage members as individuals

To gain the benefits of team work, a team must actually be built; real teams are interdependent and with a shared purpose. Teams can vary in size and do not have to meet face-to-face but they must agree on boundaries, task definition and the group process, i.e. the decision-making process.

Mistake 3: Fall off the authority balance beam

The exercise of managerial authority often triggers anxiety amongst team members. What team members look for is clear direction with an appropriate level of authority delegated to them. How the task is to be achieved should, however, rest with the team.

Mistake 4: Dismantle existing organisational structures so that teams will be fully 'empowered' to accomplish the work

An enabling structure has three components:

1 A well-designed team task.

2 A well composed group of mixed backgrounds and who are not too similar to each other but neither are they completely mismatched.

3 The basic norms of conduct are clear and explicit, the small number of dos and don'ts that allow team members to pursue their objectives without having to continually discuss what behaviours are, and are not, acceptable.

Mistake 5: Specify challenging team objectives but skimp on organizational supports

Even if the team's direction is clear and it has an enabling structure, it will fail if it is not given sufficient resources. Team functioning requires four key supports including:

1 A reward system that recognises and reinforces excellent team performance.

2 A system that provides teams with training and technical consultation that may be needed to supplement members' knowledge and expertise.

3 An accurate management information system that provides the team with accurate data.

4 The day-to-day, routine aspects such as suitable working space, staff, equipment and the tools needed to get the job done.

Mistake 6: Assume that members already have all the skills they need to work well as a team

Managers often assume that once the team has been formed their work is done. Effective teams need on-going support, coaching and mentoring for individuals in sharpening their team skills. There are three crucial pints in the team's life when it needs such support:

1 At the beginning when the team is starting its work.

2 The mid-point, when half the work has been done but recognition that half of still has to be completed.

3 The end when the work has been completed.

5.9   Dysfunctional aspects of teams

From this overview of Hackman's work, it should be evident that simply labelling a collection of people a 'team' is almost guaranteed to lead to failure and there are several reasons why teams fail to develop and perform effectively, As we saw from Hackman's research, some of these barriers are institutional or systemic while others are influenced by individual differences. Organisations are made up of teams, groups and functional departments and it is inevitable that conflict within and between teams will emerge. These dysfunctional aspects assume various forms and here we will outline several elements which undermine team effectiveness.

■ Group conformity

Work groups develop norms – unwritten and often unspoken assumptions about how group members behave towards each other, how the work will be done, the roles members adopt, the pace of work and what the group will do to ensure its continuity and survival. These shared or 'superordinate' goals create the basis for group conformity, a crucial feature of a team, but might a point be reached at which one or more members go along with a group decision against their 'better judgement'?

Research from as early as the 1930s (Sherif, 1936; the Hawthorne Studies 1924-32) demonstrated how group norms emerge and how a group can influence a person's perception of other members and the total group situation. Sherif (1936) demonstrated that in a situation characterised by doubt and uncertainty and where there is limited first-hand information, an individual member's views will shift to conform with other members, even where the others had incomplete information. Several subsequent studies on group conformity and roles (Asch, 1956; Zimbardo, 1973; Milgram, 1974) confirmed the extent to which members of a group will conform either to the will of the majority or to an authority figure.

■ Groupthink: Irving Janis (1972)

Janis was a social psychologist who studied political decision-making and examined how close-knit groups of apparently clever people consistently make bad decisions and he concluded that groups are prone to irrational decision-making. On the question of why this should be the case, Janis noted that the critical situational factors underpinning groupthink are the ideological homogeneity of the group and the stress of the situation. In these situations maintaining team cohesion is the key priority for the team and determines future actions and Janis noted the following symptoms or signs of groupthink:

- **Illusion of invulnerability:** group members become convinced they have a sense of power that prevents them from making mistakes. This in turn leads them to downplay warning signs and emboldens them take risky decisions.

- **Collective rationalisation:** group members tend to ignore evidence that contradicts the consensus they have arrived at and information that does contradict their assessment of the situation is ignored or explained away.

- **Belief in the morality of the group:** group members are convinced that their actions are moral and ethical and that people outside the group are 'unethical' or acting in their own self-interest.

- **Direct pressure on dissenters:** group members conform to the will of the majority because they want to retain membership of the group.

- **Self-censorship:** another form of conformity; group members are aware of the consequences of publicly disagreeing so they do not articulate their doubts or fears to other group members.

- **Illusion of unanimity:** an outcome of self-censorship; silence is viewed as tacit acceptance of the group's actions and thus decisions are made by default.

Janis set out a number of measures a group can adopt to guard against group-think and these include:

- **Appoint a devil's advocate:** have people challenge the prevailing view by arguing against untested assumptions.

- **Encourage everyone to be a critical evaluator:** foster an open climate where people feel free to express their views and opinions and add to the quality of decision-making.

- **Do not have the leader state a preference up front:** avoid the leader coming out and stating a view at the start of any discussion.

- **Divide into subgroups:** break the group into smaller groups to explore the same issue and then funnel their views back to the main group.

- **Discuss what is happening with others outside the group:** in a work context, get people from outside the immediate work-group involved in discussions as they might have insights into how the work of one group may affect others in the organisation.

■ Social loafing

According to Huczynski and Buchanan, social loafing can be defined as the 'tendency for individuals to exert less effort when working as part of a group than when working alone'. (p.396) Social loafing is an example of negative synergy and teams, as we have seen, are prone to infighting, personality clashes, and rivalries and unless these are managed the team will operate sub-optimally and the total group output may be equal to or less than that of the weakest team member. Social loafing is where a team member contributes less effort than other team members but expects to share equally in the rewards. Social loafing differs from free-riding in that with the latter, the individual contributes little or nothing to the task but gains from membership of the group. Many students will have first-hand experience of this tendency while involved in a team project at university, where a fellow student is awarded the same mark as the other team members while having contributed nothing to the team task.

Conclusion

The evidence suggests that teams are now one of the most commonly used forms of work design in contemporary organisations and this holds true across different industries, sectors and geographical locations. Teams act as a linking mechanism, connecting organisational and individual objectives and they provide people with the opportunity to develop their skills and abilities in an environment where their contribution is valued by other team members. Effective teams do not become effective by chance, however. The role of the team leader in building a positive working environment, one in which everyone is committed to team goals, where people are clear on their roles and responsibilities, where team learning is encouraged and ideas are shared, takes a particular set of skills and abilities that few team leaders have. A leading authority in the area of organisational change and innovation, Bernard Burnes (2015), estimates that the failure rate for innovations in team-working in areas such as Total Quality Management (TQM) and Business Process-Re-engineering is 75% to 80%.

We have identified a number of barriers to team development and some of the interventions that the team leader might adopt to allow the team to function and perform. The team leader must also be aware of the nature of group dynamics as it gives them insights into both the functioning of the group and what they can do to promote team cohesion and allow each member the opportunity to maximise their contribution to the group. The group cannot be viewed as a mere collection of individuals. A team must be built into a single entity where there is collective responsibility for its performance and the team leader must avoid falling into the authority trap; they cannot direct every task and role and for the team to function there must be mutual trust and accountability.

Short illustrative case study: Phil Jones' dilemma

Phil Jones is a project leader at Engineering Co and leader of a team operating in six different geographical locations across two time zones. Phil is a mechanical engineer. His technical skills have been recognised by Engineering Co and he has made steady progress with the company since leaving university.

Phil has been the Senior Project Team Leader for six months on a blue chip project, an integrated rail and metro system in the Gulf region of the Middle East. The project went out to global tender and Engineering Co won the contract for supplying rails, switching gear, electrical supply and the metro stations, and it secured the contract largely on its ability to deliver high quality projects on time, on budget and fit for purpose. Engineering Co did not submit the lowest tender for the project but the client was convinced of its technical and managerial capabilities, which have given it a clear competitive advantage. The company enjoys a strong industry reputation, and for engineering and management graduates, it is an 'employer of choice' as it is widely regarded as having one of the best graduate development programmes in Britain. Engineering Co is essentially a project-based organisation but its structure is nominally a combination of functional and divisional units. There is a clear division between planning and execution in Engineering Co and while strategy is 'owned' by the senior management team, the majority of the work is delivered through project teams.

Phil Jones is only thirty years of age but he is seen as having senior management potential and has been given leadership of one of the key project teams. Phil is based in Surrey, close to London. He travels frequently throughout the UK to meet project team members and is on-site in the Gulf every six to eight weeks but crucially, he is the only one in the team who has met the other members face-to-face. The project is still at the planning stage of the work and has gone reasonably well up to now, but Phil believes that performing 'reasonably well' means it is operating sub-optimally and that is not good enough; Phil wants it to be an exceptional team and he is determined to drive it towards that objective. The project team members were all internal applicants and Phil was given the final say on who would be recruited to the team. There was a significant number of internal applicants and the selection process was exhaustive, with each member being selected across a range of competencies. Phil was certain that he had the right people with the rights skills in the right jobs at the right time, but six months into the project, he senses undercurrents of tension amongst team members. In several instances team members have agreed with each other and it seems to Phil that they are doing this to avoid any overt conflict. Phil is not going out of his way to generate conflict but he believes that a certain level of it would be good for the team as it might bring some of the undercurrents into the open where they could be acknowledged and addressed and which might allow the team to develop into a more effective and efficient unit.

Phil is angry at the way it is going for he feels he is losing focus on the project as his time is increasingly being taken up with 'people issues', an area where he is the first to admit his strengths do not lie. Some of the issues Phil has had to deal with include team members stating that they are still not 100% sure of their role in the team and consequently work has been duplicated and that has cost the project time and money. Phil was pretty sure everything would somehow have fallen into place as at first people appeared to be committed to the project and the team. He thought he had made the immediate project goals clear and he assumed everyone knew what it was they had to do, as he thought he had given the team clear boundaries. Phil has also found that there are cultural issues around authority and responsibility, and when it comes to decision-making, several team members look to him to make the calls. This irritates Phil as he has told people repeatedly that they are empowered to make decisions and they must stop referring every problem back up the line, but several team members countered that they are unsure of *what* they can make decisions on and that Phil is inconsistent, telling people to be pro-active and then over-ruling them later.

Phil is a problem-solver and he decided that the best course of action was to get some books on teams and groups to gain insights into what teams are, how they function and to gain a better understanding of some of the dysfunctional aspects of teams. Initially, Phil approached these issues as an engineer; the team is a system and if the problems are analysed dispassionately the analysis will generate solutions which should be accepted by everyone as they are the outcome of a rational decision-making process. Phil takes comfort in certainty and he wishes at times that people would just act rationally and accept his decisions as they are based on what is best for the project. Grudgingly, Phil has come to the view that he is a mini HR Manager first and a Project Team-Leader second, and the project team is in danger of losing focus and momentum. Phil read Bruce Tuckman's stages of group development with interest and he is now convinced that the team is stuck at the storming stage and he is unsure of what has to be done to get it to the performing stage. He is desperate for the team to succeed, not only for his own career. Phil wants all of the team members to be able to look back on their time on the project team as a positive experience and he wants people to be proud to have on their CV that they were part of the Gulf Metro Project Team.

Questions

1   To what extent would you agree with Phil Jones' diagnosis of the situation?

2   What interventions do you think are needed to get the team back on track and reach the performing stage as defined by Tuckman?

3   Could it be argued that some of the problems within the project team are problems of the team leader's own making?

4   To what extent could it be argued that a project team leadership role is a combination of project specialist and HR manager?

End of chapter questions

1 Discuss the process a project manager would need to go through to build an effective team.

2 Evaluate the stages of team development and explain how a project manager may facilitate each stage.

3 Discuss the difficulties in managing a virtual project team

4 What are the barriers to team development and how would a project manager overcome them?

Bibliography

Arnold, J. and Randall, R. *et al.* (2010) *Work Psychology: Understanding Human Behaviour in the Workplace* Fifth Edition Harlow: Pearson

Ashleigh, M and Mansi, A. (2012) *The Psychology of People in Organisations.* Harlow: Pearson

Bergiel, Bergiel and Balsmeier (2008) Nature of virtual teams: a summary of their advantages and disadvantages', *Management Research News* **31** (2) 99-110

Bushe and Chu (2011) 'Fluid teams: solutions to the problems of unstable team membership' *Organizational Dynamics* **40** (3) 181-8

Cartwright and Zander

Coutu, D. (2009) Why teams don't work, *Harvard Business Review* **87**(5)

Hackman, J. R. (1998) 'Why Teams Don't Work' *Leader to Leader* **7**, 24-31

Huczynski, A. and Buchanan, D. (2013) *Organizational Behaviour.* 8th Ed. Harlow: Pearson

Huffman & Killian (2012) The flight of the Phoenix: interpersonal aspects of project management, *Journal of Management Education* **36**(4), 568-600

Janis, J. L. (1972) *Victims of Groupthink.* Boston: Houghton Miffin

Jarvenapa and Leidner (1999) Communication and trust in global virtual teams, *Organizational Science* **10**(6), 791-815

Lewin, K. (1939:1997) Experiments in social space, *Reflections* **1**(1), 7-13.

Mullins, L. (2010) *Management and Organizational Behaviour*, 9th Ed., Harlow: Pearson

Noon, M., Blyton, P. and Morrell, K. (2013) *The Realities of Work: Experiencing Work and Employment in Contemporary Society* 4th Edition Basingstoke: Palgrave

Pinto, J. K. (2007) *Project Management: Achieving Competitive Advantage*, New Jersey: Pearson

Sherif, M. (1936) *The Psychology of Group Norms*. New York: Harper and Row

Shaw, M. E. (1981) *Group Dynamics: The Psychology of Small Group Behaviour*, 3rd Ed. New York: McGraw-Hill

Shin, Y. (2005) Conflict resolution in virtual teams, *Organizational Dynamics* **34**(4), 331-45

Tuckman, B. and Jensen, M.A. (1997) Stages of small group development revisited, *Group and Organizational Studies* **2**(4), 419-27

Zander, Mockaitis and Butler (2012) Leading global teams, *Journal of World Business* **47**(2), 592-603

Zigurs (2002) Leadership in virtual teams: oxymoron or opportunity?, *Organizational Dynamics* **31**(4), 339-51

5

6 Project Scope Management

Reza Mohammadi and Amos Haniff

Learning objectives

By the time you have completed this chapter you should be able to:

☐ Define the project scope

☐ Understand the importance of defining the project scope

☐ Prepare a detailed scope statement

☐ Outline the contents of a project charter

☐ Break down a project into deliverable, sub deliverables and work packages

☐ Create a product break down structure

☐ Create a responsibility assignment matrix

☐ Develop a project communication plan

6.1 Introduction

Project scope management involves describing the product, service or result of the project, and identifying the activities that need to be achieved in order to deliver the expected final outcome. Far too often an initial project brief is given to a project manager with little guidance as to what the project includes or the extent of the work required to deliver the business objectives. This should be of little surprise. After all, the primary concern of the client is to recoup the benefits from commissioning a project or exploiting an opportunity through a project.

The process of defining the project, in terms of deliverables, objectives, requirements and detail, becomes the responsibility of the project manager.

This chapter guides the processes of developing and defining the project scope. This involves assessing the project objectives, identifying main deliverables and subdividing these into structures that enable the project manager to generate responsibilities, cost estimates, control points, work packages and a basis for detail planning.

6.2   Defining the project scope

The project scope is everything about the project. This includes the final deliverable of the project and all the work that must be done in order to achieve the deliverable. Defining the project scope involves identifying *what is* and *what is not* included in the project. This provides the point of reference against which the project is authorised, measured and controlled.

Project scope is defined to be "the sum of products and services to be provided as a project" (PMI, 2013). The scope of project must be written down in the Scope Document. The level of details should be sufficient to define to all stakeholders just exactly what the project is about. The scope is different from the objectives. Objectives set out the actual deliverables of the project in some details. The scope, on the other hand, defines just what aspects of the project are the responsibility of the project team and are covered by the budget and the timescale.

A very common example of poor scope is maintenance. Often a project ends with successful delivery of the stated objectives but no-one has thought about maintenance. There is no budget or resources to cover maintenance because they were all used up in delivering the objectives. Consequently, it is vital before the project starts to specify the scope exactly, to eradicate or resolve any unreasonable expectation as to what aspects of the project the team are expected to deliver.

The best way to specify the scope is to specify: What **IS** included in the scope, followed by what is **NOT** included in the scope. This would eliminate a possible scope issue arising from unreasonable expectations in discussion with stakeholders.

It is the project manager's responsibility to define the project scope, normally conducted under the guidance of the project sponsor and following consultation with the key stakeholders as described in Chapter 2. It is accepted that all stakeholders may not be in full agreement of the project objectives, but a clear definition of the scope will establish a common understanding of the agreed project outcome. It is critical that the boundaries of the project are defined at the early stages of the project, as there is a tendency to add deliverables to the project during the planning and execution stage. The project scope therefore becomes the baseline against which the work content required to create the project deliverables are planned and measured. Without a clear definition of the project scope, it would be impossible to estimate durations, calculate costs, and determine resources and establish when the project is officially complete. Finally, the scope document should be written in such a way as to best communicate the intension of the project to all of the stakeholders.

■ The project charter

Sometimes referred to as a *project initiation document* (PID) (OGC, 2005), the project charter is the document that formally authorises the project. Drawing on the defined project scope, the project charter is created, issued and sanctioned by senior management.

As the main purpose of the charter is to formally recognise the existence of a new project within the organisation, it is normally a short document that only outlines the broad objectives of the project. It also identifies the main stakeholders and authorises the project manager to officially acquire the resources required to achieve the project objectives. Once authorised the project becomes part of the ongoing work within the organisation. Identity codes are created, budgets are allocated, resources are assigned and performance measures are established.

As the project charter is a high level document, its primary concern is to document the business needs and justify the investment for the project. It should demonstrate an understanding of the customer requirements and show how the end deliverable of the project intends to satisfy those requirements. Typical contents of the project charter would therefore include:

- The project title
- The project's mission and brief
- The project focus
- The critical success factors (CFSs)
- The project risks
- Project authorisation
- The assigned project manager
- The project team management structure
- The project approach
- The project quality plan

- A communication plan
- Customer needs and expectations
- Identification of stakeholder needs and expectations
- A summary of the business case
- Justification for commitment to the project
- Financial information, including return on investment and a summary of the budget
- Identification of the key milestones
- Project constraints

In some organisations a project is not formally initiated until after the completion of a formal feasibility study. The feasibility study is the initial justification needed to determine if a project is 'do-able'. Feasibility studies are normally carried out for larger or riskier projects, or projects that are ill-defined. The feasibility of a project is measured against a detailed statement of the project scope. It is useful to add a key statement from the stakeholder analysis and key performance objectives.

The scope statement

The scope statement is the **detailed** description of the project deliverables and the work required to accomplish those deliverables. It reflects the project team's efforts at documenting and seeking approval of all important project parameters prior to proceeding to the planning phase (Pinto, 2013). Significantly, it determines the baseline on which the project team will plan the project and on which the project manager will make project related decisions, and defines the criteria on which completed projects are accepted. In some organisations the scope statement also becomes a contractual document used to specify the work content to be delivered by an external organisation. For example, if the project involves a market research survey, the major deliverables could be design, data collection, data analysis and providing recommendations by 21 March 2017, for a cost not to exceed £ 200,000.

One of the responsibilities of the Project Management Office (PMO) is to produce a scope statement template as shown in Figure 6.1. This ensures that all projects commissioned by the organisation provide the relevant information in sufficient detail, and ensures standardisation across all documentation.

Project Scope Statement					
1. Business Objectives					
Project name:					
Prepared by		Date		Revision	
Project Manager		Project sponsor			
2. Business Objectives					
Business Objectives	Describe the business need/opportunity/objectives				
Product Description	Describe how the project satisfies the business need/opportunity/objectives				
3. Project Description					
3.1 Project Objectives					
3.2 Project Scope					
Includes					
Does not include					
3.3 Project Requirements					
3.4 Project Constraints					
3.5 Project Milestones				**Target date**	
Project start					
Project Completion					
3.6 Project Assumptions					
3.7 Critical Success factors					
3.8 Schedule of supporting documentation					
4. Scope Statement Approval					
Signed	Date		Approved		Date

Figure 6.1: Sample template of a scope statement

Although the level of detailed required will vary according to each project, typical elements of the scope statement include following:

- **Project objectives**: These are what the project aims to achieve. They consist of the benefits the organisation expects as a result of investing in the project and any particular targets the project means to accomplish. Therefore, a project may have varied objectives that need be realised, and these include business, technical, cost, schedule and quality.

  Objectives must be described in measurable terms. To be measurable each objective will have an attribute attached it, that success can evaluated against. For example, a project to implement a new computerised library management system could have as its objectives that it will provide higher levels of service to patrons; recoup printing and copying costs within six months; reduce waste by 60%; be implemented within 12 months at a cost not exceeding £250000.

- **Project scope description**: This is the section that fully describes the product, service or result the project is expected to accomplish by the project. This includes the use of the outcome, the end user, colours, size or any other relevant characteristics.

- **Project requirements**: This section describes the requirements of the project deliverables in terms of standards they are expected to achieve. These could be specified quality standards, technical standards or minimum performance requirements, e.g. the required output of particular piece of machinery, delivered by a project, could have a minimum capacity of 200 units per hour.

- **Project deliverables**: These are the expected outputs throughout the project lifecycle. This comprises of the final project outcome, any part outcomes delivered as phases and any supporting deliverables. This may include a list of specifications, technical manuals, prototypes or sections of the project.

- **Project boundary**: Any deliverable not explicitly included within the scope statement is implicitly excluded from the project. However, when the project forms part of a larger programme it may be necessary to document the items not included in the scope.

- **Project constraints**: As discussed in Chapter 1, all projects have constraints that should be defined from the outset. These include the limits in terms of time, cost, resources or equipment.

- **Project milestones**: These are the specific dates imposed on the project for meeting certain stages in the project. More often milestones can be addressed as a project constraint.

- **Project assumptions**: As the scope statement is produced at the early stages of the project, a number of decisions may not yet have been made. The project

6

team therefore needs to make assumptions of any uncertainties and document them accordingly.

- **Critical success factors**: These are those essential elements of the project that must be achieved for the project to be considered successful. This could be measured in terms of deliverables, levels of quality or objectives. The CSFs define the acceptance criteria for the project.

■ Scope creep

Many projects suffer from **scope creep**, which is a tendency for the project scope to expand over time – usually by changing requirements, specifications, and priorities. This can be reduced by carefully writing your scope statement. Scope creep can have a positive or negative effect on the project, but in most cases scope creep means added cost and possible project delays. Changes in requirements, specifications, and priorities frequently result in cost overruns and delays. For example, on software development projects, scope creep is manifested in bloated products in which added functionality undermines ease of use. If the project scope needs to change, it is critical to have a sound change control process in place that records the change and keeps a log of all product changes. The log identifies the change, impact and those responsible for accepting or discarding a proposed change. All the project management institutes recommend the dedication of significant quantities of effort to scope management at the outset and throughout the project. One of the reasons may be seen in this real world example.

Example: The Sinclair C5

Initially conceived in the mid-1970 as a four-seater electrically powered vehicle for under £1000, the concept of the Sinclair C5 grabbed a lot of attention because it came from such a renowned inventor – Sir Clive Sinclair, famous for one of the first calculators and personal computers. It was highly popular idea and had no shortage of backers, including Hoover, which kitted out part of its factory for its manufacture. The result at the end of the process was rather different as shown

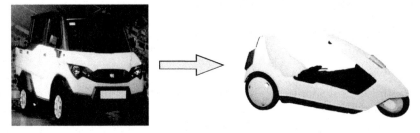

Figure 6.2: Scope creep of Sinclair C5. Source: (Cited by Harvey, M 2010). Reproduced courtesy of Austin Area Electric Automobile Association and Mark Polglaze, with permission from Mike Chancey.

Exercise 1

You are in charge of organizing a dinner-dance concert for a local charity. You have reserved a hall that will seat 30 couples and have hired a jazz combo.

Develop a scope statement for this project that contains examples of all the elements. Assume that the event will occur in 4 weeks and provide your best guess estimate of the dates for objectives.

6.3   The work breakdown structure (WBS)

Once the scope and deliverables have been established, the project manager will need to define all the major deliverables and sub deliverables of the scope. The responsibility for accomplishing each deliverable also needs to be allocated to the relevant team member. The project management tool used to identify the project deliverables is a hierarchical process called the work breakdown structure (WBS).

The WBS helps the project manager to:

- Facilitates evaluation of cost, time, and technical performance of the organization on a project.

- Provides management with information appropriate to each organizational level.

- Develop of the organization breakdown structure (OBS). which assigns project responsibilities to organizational units and individuals

- Manage, plan, schedule and budget.

- Define communication channels, and

- Coordinate the various project elements

Developed by the US Department of Defence (DOD/NASA, 1962), the WBS has become the critical pre-planning process used to identify all the activities and work elements incorporated within the project scope. Using a hierarchical structure, the WBS presents a framework showing how the total project scope is grouped into the project deliverables and manageable work packages. Breaking down the project in this manner provides the project manager with an invaluable structure of what will be required to deliver the final project outcome. According to Obradovitch & Stephanou (1990) use of the WBS serves six main purposes:

1 **Reiterates the project objectives**: Drawing on the scope of the project, a WBS identifies the main deliverables and activities required to accomplish the

project objectives. All the work elements identified within the WBS must be completed as part of the project.

2 **Offers a logical structure**: As we learnt in Chapter 2, the OBS provides a logical hierarchy for the organisation. Similarly, the WBS provides a logical structure for the project by identifying the main project deliverables, the various sub-deliverables and the logical flow between activities.

3 **Establishes a method of control**: The WBS is the first stage in establishing a comprehensive method of control; this is done by assigning the lowest level work elements identified within the WBS a control account and individual performance expectations.

4 **Monitor project status**: Each element identified within the WBS can be assigned to a responsible team member and monitored in terms of achieving the project objectives. The WBS can also be used to determine the stage of each activity and the dependency on other activities.

5 **Improve communication**: The WBS provides a picture of how each element of the work fits together to form the project. As a result team members are aware of how their component contributes to the project, who is responsible for dependant activities and how their element affects the project downstream. This increases communication within the project and enhances motivation among team members.

6 **Demonstrates a control structure**: Identified work elements and the general structure of the WBS provide logic on how the project will be controlled and the most appropriate control methods to use during the project life-cycle.

■ Developing the WBS

Figure 6.3 defines the various levels of the WBS hierarchy. At the highest level will be the final project outcome – this is the starting point for developing the WBS. The next level below will be the all the major project deliverables. This will be followed by the sub deliverables required to accomplish the major deliverables. These are further subdivided into smaller elements, which are divided even further until a level is reached where a detailed set of activities that can be managed and controlled.

This breakdown groups work packages by type of work within a deliverable and allows assignment of responsibility to an organizational unit. This extra step facilitates a system for monitoring project progress. The WBS in Figure 6.4 has been broken down to four levels of a hierarchy using appropriate WBS coding. These could be broken down further, but as a rule six levels is the maximum.

Within the **Virtual Learning Environment** (VLE) project, Level 1 represents the final project deliverable, which is a completed VLE system. This level could be defined by the project title. The next stage is defining the main requirements for the VLE. These are the main deliverables, which could be defined in phases, sections or major parts of the project. Within this example, the main deliverables of Level 2 are represented by main tasks to be completed as part of the VLE. Level 3 are the sub-deliverables identifying what needs to complete each main deliverable. This could involve breaking down each deliverable into its component parts. The final level of each major deliverable is the detail work packages. This is the point at which the control measures are made. Once you have generated your WBS, you will begin to see the way that the three project dimensions – Time, Cost and Quality interact with and influence each other.

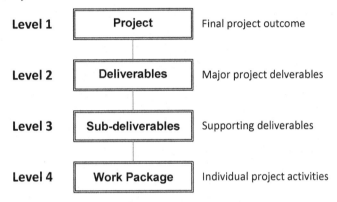

Figure 6.3: Hierarchical structure of the WBS

■ Work packages

Focusing on the micro deliverables of the WBS, ensures that the deliverables at the upper levels are realized. The lowest level of the WBS is the work package. This is the point from which:

■ The activities are defined

■ The schedule is formed

■ Cost estimates are made

■ Resources are assigned.

Work packages are parcels of work that are individually planned, resourced and have a cost associated to them. Normally work packages are short-duration tasks, lasting around 2-3 weeks, but on major projects this could be longer. The salient criterion of a work package is that it represents a control point within the project.

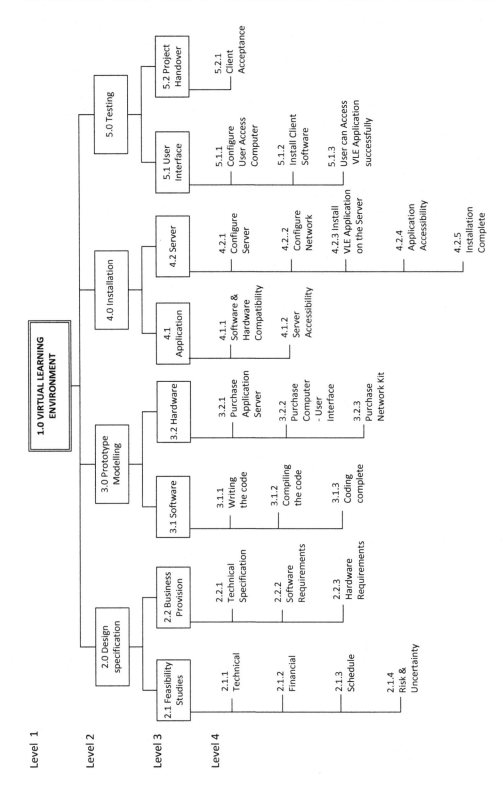

Figure 6.4: Work breakdown structure for Virtual Learning Environment (VLE)

Responsibly for ensuring that the work package is delivered on time, to budget and to the technical specification is allocated to a dedicated **work package manager** (WPM). Typically, a WPM would have responsibility for a number of work packages throughout the project life cycle. However, each work package should be as independent as possible from others within the project. Furthermore, no work package is included in more than one sub-deliverable of the WBS. A work package is the lowest level of the WBS. It is output-oriented in that it:

- Defines work (what).
- Identifies time to complete a work package (how long).
- Identifies a time-phased budget to complete a work package (cost).
- Identifies resources needed to complete a work package (how much).
- Identifies a person responsible for units of work (who).
- Identifies monitoring points (milestones) for measuring progress and success (how well).

As a rule of thumb, a task shown not be shown as a separate activity if its duration is less that 5 percent of the total project duration, but remember that, irrespective of project total duration, there will always be short duration activities that are so important that they must be included in your WBS and project plan – such as getting planning permission or authorisation to proceed.

Let us consider the work-package '2.2.2 Software Requirements' in Figure 6.5. This will include all the Software programming language/Coding and application required to ensure the compatibility between software and hardware are planned as part of VLE project design specification. Work packages have their own scope, objectives and deliverables, which will be documented in a **work package statement**, by the responsible WPM. For 'WP 2.2.2' the scope could include the exact programming language to be chosen for coding etc. Finally there must be a cost and a schedule associated to the work package.

It is the responsibility of the WPM to ensure that work package starts on time and is monitored to ensure that completion of the works is according to the project schedule. It is most likely that other work packages would be dependent on its timely completion. However, once all the work packages within sub-deliverables 2.2.1, 2.2.2 and 2.2.3 are complete, the Business Provision (2.2) will be complete. In fact when all the work packages are complete, the project is complete. It would therefore appear that a project is basically a series of work packages that are grouped together to form sub-deliverables, deliverables and objectives. For this reason, the work package becomes the basic unit for planning, scheduling, costing and controlling the project. Consequently, the Project Manager must ensure that mechanisms are in place to review progress on packages at regular intervals.

6

1.0	**Virtual Learning Environment Project**	**Resources**
2.0	**Design Specification**	
2.1	**Feasibility Studies**	
2.1.1	Technical	AGM
2.1.2	Financial	AGM
2.1.3	Schedule	AGM
2.1.4	Risk and Uncertainties	AGM
2.2	**Business Provision**	
2.2.1	Technical Specification	WPM
2.2.2	Software Requirements	WPM
2.2.3	Hardware Requirements	WPM
3.0	**Prototype Modelling**	
3.1	**Software**	
3.1.1	Writing The code	COL
3.1.2	Compiling The Code	COL
3.1.3	Coding Complete	COL
3.2	**Hardware**	
3.2.1	Purchase Application Server	REM
3.2.2	Purchase Computer - User Interface	REM
3.3.3	Purchase Network Kit	REM
4.0	**Installation**	
4.1	**Application**	
4.1.1	Software and Hardware Compatibility	AHR
4.1.2	Server Accessibility	AHR
4.2	**Server**	
4.2.1	Configure Server	AHR
4.2.2	Configure Network	AGM
4.2.3	Install VLE Application On The Server	WPM
4.2.4	Application Accessibility	REM
4.2.5	Installation Complete	REM
5.0	**Testing**	
5.1	**User Interface**	
5.1.1	Configure - User Access Computer	COL
5.1.2	Install Client Software	AGM
5.2.3	User Can Access VLE Application Successfully	WPM
5.2	**Project Handover**	
5.2.1	Client Acceptance	REM

Figure 6.5: Work breakdown structure in tabular format

Exercise 2

Consider planning a class party to celebrate passing your examinations.

1 Identify the main deliverables.

2 Identify the sub-deliverables.

3 Identify the work packages.

■ Cost breakdown structure

The WBS was actually developed as a method of cost control to manage budgets on major defence projects (Morris, 1997). However, this use of the WBS is now often referred to as **cost breakdown structure** (CBS). The CBS represents a hierarchical breakdown of the total project budget into the budgets for the deliverable, sub deliverables and work packages, although it is does not allow for the set-up and running costs of the project. Despite this, the CBS is the first attempt at estimating the budget costs of a project. The accuracy of the estimate will increase progressively as the level of detail of within each package increases.

The expenditure of each work package is made up of three elements:

■ The cost of resources required to deliver the work package

■ The cost of materials required to deliver the work package

■ The cost of equipment use required to deliver the work package – this includes the hire or purchase of special equipment specifically for the work package.

Costs are estimated using a process of 'roll-up'. Rather than the dividing the project from the top down, as within the WBS, the cost of each work package is accumulated and rolled up to the ascending sub deliverable at the next level. Each sub deliverable is rolled-up to the next level, thus providing an estimated budget for each main deliverable, as shown in Figure 6.6.

A **cost account** (CA) is created for each work package within the CBS. This is a control point created where the performance of the work package is monitored and controlled. Analysing the data from each individual control account enables the project manager to identify which work packages deviate from the budget, and the reason for the deviation. However, on larger projects where the number of work packages could run into thousands, the CA is created at the next level above the work packages, in order to reduce the complexity of analysis.

6

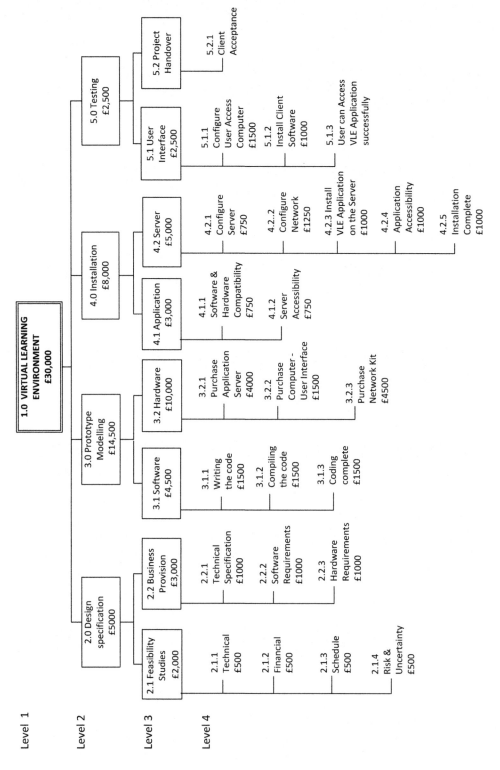

Figure 6.6: Cost Breakdown structure showing "roll-up"

6.4   Responsibility assignment matrix

As we have now established, projects are complex arrangements with a significant number of activities, tasks and responsibilities. These all need to be controlled and directed by the project manager. The responsibility assignment matrix (RAM) also called a linear responsibility chart, summarizes the tasks to be accomplished and who is responsible for what on the project

The RAM is a control chart that lists all the activities identified from the WBS and allocates responsibility of the tasks to the available resources. It effectively integrates the responsible personnel identified within the OBS, with the scope of work identified within the WBS, as illustrated in Figure 6.7.

Project Responsibility Matrix (RAM)											
Project Details											
Project name:											
Prepared by			Date			Revision					
Project Manager			Project sponsor								
Resource Allocation											
WBS	Activity Title		Project Manager	Assistant PM	WP Manager						
	Key X Executes the task R Responsible A Authorisation S Support C Confirmation of completion										

Figure 6.7: Sample responsibly assignment matrix

At a basic level the RAM identifies the project personnel responsible for delivering each element of the project scope. This is useful for identifying the responsible work package managers and those project team members responsible for managing the deliverables and sub deliverables. However, a more complex RAM will also identify:

■ The person/team/organisation responsible for executing the work element.

■ The person responsible for authorising the work element. This would either be the project manager or other senior project team members.

■ The person accountable for delivering the work element. This is the person who reports on its progress. Normally, the work package manager.

■ Any supporting personnel or assistants required to manage the work activity.

■ The person responsible for signing of the work element and formally confirming completion of the work package.

Not only do RAM's formalise the project responsibilities, they also provide a means for the project team to review the work load and agree on who is doing what within the project. This becomes invaluable further on in the project life cycle, where the project personnel can clarify the responsible bodies of dependant activities and those personal contributing to the current activities.

Exercise 3

You have been asked to manage a graduation ball for 100 guests. This will be held at a local hotel and will include catering, entertainment, photography, speeches and dancing. Each guest will pay £25 and the total cost of the project should not exceed the income generated. Develop a work breakdown structure for this project and try to identify all of the major components and provide four levels of detail.

6.5 Project communication planning

The final stage of the project definition phase involves communicating the project documents to the project team members and determining the information and communication needs of the project stakeholders. It is surprising, but 90% of the project manager's duties involve project communication, yet it is rare that a project manager dedicates sufficient effort to developing a project communication plan (Schwalbe, 2009). This is very short-sighted of project managers. Unless the responsible stakeholders have the necessary project information they will be unable to fulfil their project obligations, make project-related decisions confidently or contribute to the project effectively. It is the responsibility of the project manager to ensure that all stakeholders have the necessary project information.

Table 6.1: Shale oil research project communication plan

Type of information	Target audience	Frequency of communication	Method of communication	Provider
Milestone report	Senior management and project manager	Bi-monthly	E-mail and hardcopy	Project office
Project status report & agendas	Staff and customer	Weekly	E-mail and hardcopy	Project manager
Team status report	Project manager and project office	Weekly	E-mail	Team recorder
Issues report	Staff and customer	Weekly	E-mail	Team recorder
Escalation reports	Staff and customer	As required	Meeting and hardcopy	Project manager
Outsourcing performance	Staff and customer	Bi-monthly	Meeting	Project manager
Accepted change requests	Project office, senior management, project manager, staff and customer	As required	E-mail and hardcopy	Design department
Oversight gate decisions	Senior management and project manager	As required	Meeting and hardcopy	Oversight group and/or Project office

The project communication plan is a quality planning document that provides the communication guidelines for the project. All project team members must adhere to the communication plan and there must be a process for recording that the information required has been communicated and the date of the communication. Whereas communications may vary depending on the project, a typical communication management plan should include:

- What information needs to be collected and when?
- Who will receive the information?
- What methods will be used to gather and store information?
- What are the limits, if any, on who has access to certain kinds of information?
- When will the information be communicated?
- How will it be communicated?
- Stakeholder communication requirements.
- Information to be communicated. This should include the format, content and level of detail required.
- The person responsible for communicating the information.

- The project stakeholder who will receive the information.
- The method of sending the information (e-mail, post, internal memorandum).
- Frequency of the communication.
- Escalation procedures for resolving issues.
- Revision/edition of the communication management plan.
- Glossary of common project terminology, including acronyms.

■ Document management systems

The advancement of communication technology has enabled project information to be managed and communicated over the internet using an online document management system. This does have a number of advantages:

- Allows documents to be uploaded and accessed from any location by authorised personnel.
- Allows the project manager to track communications and ensure that the relevant stakeholders are receiving the relevant project information.
- Creates a file management system using the project WBS coding.
- Automatically tracks iterations of project documentation and advises all team members when new documents are uploaded.
- Provides fast retrieval of documentation using the software search engine.
- Automatically logs and confirms receipt of project information.

Document management systems also have the added advantage of:

- Saving time through instant correspondence.
- Saving cost by eliminating printing, photocopying and postage.
- As the projects involve an immense amount of documentation, moving to a paperless system makes a small contribution to the environment.

Major organisations tend to create their own document management system hosted on the company intranet. However there are a number of secure generic packages available online that allow for web-based project communication. Furthermore, project management packages, such as Microsoft Project have a facility to share Gantt charts and project plans online. In considering the benefits of this form of communication and the ever increasing technological advancement, it is likely that all project documentation will soon be managed this way.

The importance of establishing up-front a plan for communicating is important project information cannot be overstated. Many of the problems that plague a project can be traced back to insufficient time devoted to establishing a well-grounded internal communication plan.

Exercise 4

Develop a communication plan for an airport security project. The project entails installing the hardware and software system that (1) scans a passenger's eyes, (2) fingerprints the passenger, and (3) transmits the information to a central location for evaluation

Summary

The **project scope** is a description of the final outcome the project expects to achieve and the work content required to achieve the final outcome. It is concerned with *what is* and *what is not* involved in the project.

The **project charter** is the document that formally authorises the project and allows the project manager to acquire project resources. It is primarily concerned with the business needs and justification for investment in the project. It therefore only requires a statement of the broad project scope and objectives.

The detailed scope is presented in the **scope statement**. This document provides the baseline against which the project is planned and progress is measured. At a minimum it defines the project objectives, deliverables, project boundary, constraints, milestones and critical success factors.

Project authorisation is often dependant on a satisfactory **feasibility study**. This is detailed study that evaluates the project scope on technical, operational, financial and schedule feasibility. The feasibility study should also identify possible solutions as well as identify risks.

The **work breakdown structure** (WBS) divides and groups the total scope of the project into the major project deliverables. These are further subdivided to the descending levels until the work package level is reached where the activity can be controlled in terms of progress, cost and resources. All elements within the WBS must have a logical code assigned, for referencing and easy identification. Variations of the WBS include the **cost breakdown structure**.

The **responsibility assignment matrix** (RAM) successfully integrates the work content of the WBS with the allocated resources within OBS to provide a control chart assigning the responsibility of activities.

The **project communication plan** is a quality planning document that provides the communication guidelines for the project. This includes the lists of stakeholders receiving and sending the communication, details of the communication and frequency of the communication.

6

Case study: The wedding planner

Photo: Eric Chan, Wikimedia Commons

The past 100 years have seen the wedding industry evolve from hiring a local village dressmaker to becoming a multi-billion dollar industry involving bridal wear, tailors, wedding venues, caterers, magazines, retailers, fashion designers, jewellers, florists, hair dressers, beauty therapists, printers, photographers, web designers and wedding planners. Frequently used for society and high profile weddings, it is the responsibility of the wedding planner to organise and manage the wedding on behalf of the wedding party. This includes:

- ☐ Advising the wedding party on themes, venues and process
- ☐ Coordinating all the suppliers who are providing services to the wedding
- ☐ Scheduling the event
- ☐ Managing the budget
- ☐ Organising guests
- ☐ Arranging travel accommodation
- ☐ Facilitating communication between parties
- ☐ Allocating responsibility of task
- ☐ Managing all risks and emergencies

It is essential that before the wedding preparations begin, the wedding planner must clearly understand the expectations of the bride and groom. This is done through the initial consultation period where the scope of the project is developed. The wedding planner will need to establish the particular theme, preferred venues, suppliers, dates, and the budgets, number of guests and any special arrangements. The planner must also establish the scope of their responsibilities. Are they organising only the ceremony and reception, or does the extent off the project extend to arranging the honeymoon, dealing with the media and organising the bachelor party and bridal shower?

The work breakdown structure will serve a number of purposes. In the first instance it will define all the activities within the total scope of the project; secondly, it will verify budget and budget allocation on each activity; most importantly for the wedding planner, it will enable development of the project responsibility matrix, identifying the suppliers responsible for executing the work and the method of ensuring the work is complete. As shown in Figure 4.11, level 2 of the WBS define the main deliverables as identified during the client consultation exercise. Some these deliverables will be managed and executed by a specialist company, such as a photographer or security firm. In these cases the wedding planner has only one point of control for the main deliverable. Whereas, major deliverables such as '5.0 Reception' would be broken down to work package level, with control points created at levels 4 and 5. These items will need greater control and coordination, and it is the wedding planner's responsibility to ensure activities occur according to the schedule of day. Therefore, tools such as responsibly charts and check-list are invaluable to the wedding planner, as through these everyone knows what they are supposed to do and when they are supposed to do it.

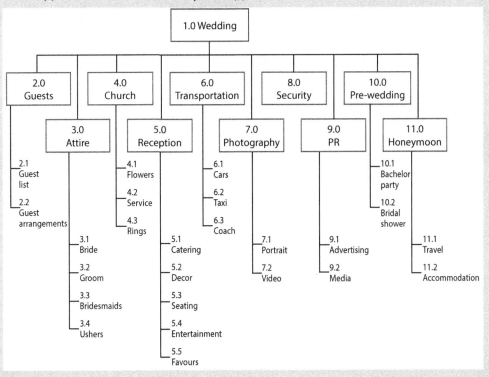

Figure 6.8: WBS for society wedding

Although the focus of the event is on the actual wedding day, the wedding planner needs to maintain control before and after the wedding. Before, the wedding all stakeholders involved in the wedding need to be coordinated. Whether they are suppliers, support or the bridal party, they must be advised as to their roles and responsibilities from the wedding planner. During the wedding all attendants, waiters, waitresses, photographers and drivers must be in the right place at the right time and all must know exactly what they are supposed to do and when. All guests must be assisted in being where they should be and at the right time. This includes advising of the day schedule, seating arrangements and guidance for toasts. After the wedding, it is the responsibility of wedding planner to ensure that all suppliers and assistants are paid.

Case study questions

1   What work packages would be included in the major deliverable 5.0 Reception?

2   What methods of communication would be suitable for managing an event such as a society wedding?

End of chapter review questions

1   What are the main elements of a typical scope statement?

2   What questions does a project objective answer and what would be an example of a good project objective?

3   What kinds of information are included in a work package?

4   When would it be appropriate to create a responsibility matrix rather than a full-blown WBS?

5   How does a communication plan benefit management of projects?

References

APM (2006) *APM Body of Knowledge* Bucks, Association of Project Management.

DOD/NASA (1962) *DOD/NASA PERT/ Cost Guide*, Washington, DC, US Government Printing Office.

Morris, P. W. G. (1997) *The Management of Projects*, London, Thomas Telford.

Obradovitch, M. M. & Stephanou, S. E. (1990) *Project Management: Risk and Productivity*. Oregon, Daniel Spencer.

OGC (2005) Managing Successful Projects with PRINCE2, Norwich, The Stationary Office.

Pinto, J. K. (2013) *Project Management: Achieving Competitive Advantage*, New Jersey, Pearson Education Inc.

PMI (2013) *A Guide to the Project Management Body of Knowledge: PMBOK guide*, Fifth Edidition. Pennsylvania Project Management Institute Inc.

Schwalbe, K. (2009) *Introduction to Project Management* Boston MA, Course Technology Cengage Learning.

6

7 Project Risk Management

Mohamed Salama and Amos Haniff

Learning objectives

By the time you have completed this chapter you should be able to:

☐ Understand the importance of risk management in projects

☐ Explain and implement a risk management process

☐ Describe the role of contingency planning on a project

☐ Design and complete a risk information sheet

☐ Create and control a risk register.

☐ Discuss Agile methodology in the context of risk management.

Introduction

Regardless of variations in time or place and size or type of project, risk will always exit. Intuitively, almost all rational human beings get involved in risk management activities on a daily basis, one way or another. Since the time one wakes up in the morning there are so many risks that face all one of us. Waking up late may result in missing the bus or a train or even a flight. Driving to work involves a number of possibilities that can have negative consequences. It is not a pleasant experience when the car does not start due to a flat battery or cannot run due to a flat tyre. Every driver is aware that road accidents are likely to happen and some accidents can unfortunately be fatal. Yet people do not stop using their cars in commuting both for business and leisure. Similarly, all projects are prone to risk and some risks can have very serious consequences, but this does not stop project managers from delivering their projects. It is imperative that project managers should be aware of how to manage project risks effectively.

■ Conditions of certainty, risk and uncertainty

Whenever there is an event that is known will happen sometimes, somehow, but that will certainly not happen at any specific known time with a predetermined level of severity, it is said that there is a *condition of risk*. If the event is certainly going to happen, i.e. there is no probability involved, and the consequences are known then this becomes a *condition of certainty*. When neither the event nor its probability is known, it is a *condition of uncertainty*.

For example, prior to 1992, Egypt had never experienced any earthquakes. Hence, the code for building never considered earthquakes as a risk. It was regarded by project risk analysis as an uncertainty unlike the case in other countries like Japan where construction experts are familiar with earthquakes and the code for buildings, particularly foundations, is designed to take this risk into account. In 1992, Egypt was hit by a strong earthquake that had serious impact on buildings and people. Many buildings either cracked or completely collapsed with subsequent casualties in people either injured or died. Since that date, risk analysts in Egypt regard earthquake as a risk event and the code for buildings has changed to account for, the now, possible event of earthquake.

All project managers know that projects can face many unpleasant events, such as bad weather during winter time in Canada, when it is quite difficult to do any road works due to the very heavy and almost continual snow. However, there are days during winter where the weather is milder; at least no storms. So for a project manager who is requested to undertake some urgent roadwork that cannot wait until the spring/summer time, there is a risk that the weather forecast might not be accurate. Hence, there will be implications on both the cost and the progress of the project, as work will stop during severe weather conditions. Project managers know that forecasts can be inaccurate sometimes, so the event is known but what is the probability of this event happening and how this will impact the project? This is what needs to be determined through a detailed risk analysis process.

Conditions of certainty on the other hand are different. In golf, the probability of getting the ball in the hole depends on a number of variables, but if the ball is right on top of the hole, there is no probability involved. Even some wind may blow it down the hole! If someone is shooting at a distance, there is a probability that it will be a miss, but if the gun is very close to the target, almost touching the target body, then there is no probability of missing. In this case, the probability of hitting is said to be 100% and the consequences are determined for sure.

To summarize this section it might be useful to use the well know jargon 'known-known', 'known-unknown' and 'unknown-unknown' to refer to the conditions of certainty, risk and uncertainty respectively.

7.1 Project risk management

A risk can be defined as "the combination of the probability of an event and its consequences" (ISO, 2002). For something to be considered a 'risk' there must be a number of determining factors: First of all there needs to be an 'event' or specific occurrence of the risk. Second, there needs to be a possibility of the risk occurring. Third, if the risk does occur, it would have either a negative or positive outcome. In terms of projects, a risk is commonly viewed as having an adverse impact on the project.

Project risk management is the proactive approach of dealing with the inherent conditions of risk within projects. It is concerned with developing a systematic process to manage all the possible risks on a project, before and after they occur. This involves identifying, analyzing and responding to any risks throughout the project life cycle and seeking to control the level of impact, should a risk occur.

Project risk management should be an iterative process that continues throughout the project lifecycle. This is because project risks can occur at any time in the project and some risks will not be apparent until its later stages.

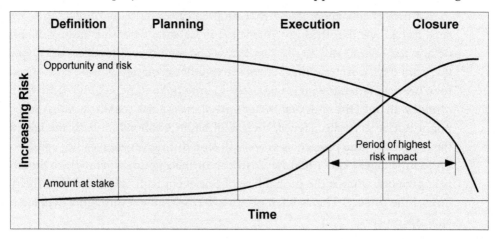

Figure 7.1: Risk versus the amount at stake

As demonstrated in Figure 7.1, the level of risk is greatest at the early phases of the project. This is because during the definition and early planning stages there is a greater degree of ambiguity regarding the future and the greatest degree of unknowns regarding project details. As the project progresses the level of ambiguity is reduced as decisions are made, designs are implemented and the remaining unknowns become known, until a zero point is reached (Burke, 2003). Conversely, the amount at stake, in terms of investment, is minimal at the start, as only a few resources have been committed to the project. As the project progresses, the level of resources and financial capital increases dramatically, with the highest point at project closure. The highest exposure to risk for the organisation therefore occurs during the final phases of the project life cycle. This is when the conditions of risk are still relatively high and the amount at stake is rising rapidly.

7.2   The risk management system

Effective risk management requires sufficient knowledge about the project scope, the project objectives, the project environment and the performing organisation. It is therefore best performed either by the project team, or by a dedicated risk management team directed by the project manager. The objective of the risk management process is to seek answers to the following questions and develop a suitable strategy for dealing with the risks identified:

- What are the risks and where do they come from?
- What is likely to happen should the risk occur?
- What is the probability of the risk occurring?
- What are the consequences of the risk occurring?
- What are the signs that the risk is going to occur?

The risk management plan generally consists of the output of the six sequential stages shown in Figure 7.2.

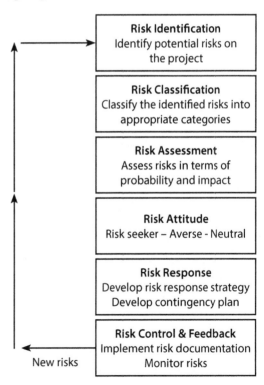

Figure 7.2: The risk management system

7

7.3   Risk identification

The first stage of the risk management process involves generating a list all the possible risk events that could have an adverse affect on the project. The most efficient method to risk identification is to conduct a brainstorming session as described in the risk clinic (see Section 7.8). However, complimentary methods include:

- **Lessons learned:** Historical documentation on similar projects will identify the majority of highly probable risks.

- **Delphi technique**: This involves reaching a consensus by asking a panel of carefully selected experts specific questions regarding possible risks to the project.

- **Interviewing:** Experienced project managers, stakeholders and experts are a great source of knowledge for identifying risks.

- **SWOT:** A common business practice of examining risks through the strengths, weaknesses, opportunities and threats within the project.

- **Risk breakdown structure:** Typically derived from the work breakdown structure (WBS) whereby each activity can be analysed in attempt to answer the question: "what may go wrong?" Rolling up an integrated risk scenario can be developed. This technique can be embraced by any of the above mentioned methods.

A risk event should be defined in two parts. The first part should identify the source of the risk, for example "unstable supply network". The second part should identify the consequence of the risk, for example, "failing to meet the project schedule". Hence the team may identify the risk as *"instability of the local supply network results in the delayed supplier delivery and failure to meet the project schedule"*. This provides a clear definition of the risk and identification of the root cause of the problem. Without identification of the risk source, an effective risk response cannot be developed.

7.4   Risk classification

Complementary to risk identification is the creation of categories for the classification of risks. This acts as a checklist where risks can be identified. It is sometimes a good practice to develop specific risk categories even prior to or concurrently with the risk identification process. This can be done by drawing on similar projects and tailoring the categories to suit the current project.

■   Risk categories

Risk event can be divided into different categories. Strategic risk is different from project risk in both context and management approach. Financial risk is dynamic in nature whereas risk of theft, fire and other accidents is typically static. Market risk can be seen as mostly external risk compared to operational risk that is more likely to be internal. In this section, the main different categories of risk will be discussed briefly.

Strategic risk

The traditional view recognizes projects as stand-alone vehicles whose purpose is to deliver the organizational strategic objectives following fixed time, cost and quality targets. Contemporary project management theory regards projects as adding value through the realized benefits to the organization. This is a step beyond just the strategic alignment between the project objectives reflected in the key deliverables of the project and the organizational strategic objectives. If there is a change in strategy during the execution of the project, then this will reflect on the project deliverables and might need the project manager to re-plan some of the forthcoming activities. This cannot be dealt with in an ad-hoc manner if and when it happens, hence, it should be part of the risk analysis during the planning phase of the project.

Needless to mention, some of the strategic changes are initiated by external influences due to legal, political, environmental and socioeconomic factors. For example, the change in building regulations in Dubai following the green building initiative imposed significant changes on the design and execution of building projects. The same happened in Saudi Arabia following the introduction of imposed thermal insulation to all external walls within new and to some extent existing buildings. The political turbulence in the MENA zone following the Arab Spring that started in 2011 and that in 2016 still has some countries like Syria and Lybia in turmoil, has undoubtedly affected projects that were either running or were planned to run in this part of the world. In some developing countries, there will be significant shortage in the supply of unskilled labourers in the construction industry during harvest season, particularly in rural areas where most labourers belong to families who are primarily farmers. This is a typical example of the socioeconomic environment of these areas and its impact on local construction projects.

On the other hand, some strategic changes are purely internal due to stakeholder influence, technological or financial reasons. The emergence of a new technology as part of the R&D in any organization will impact the existing product development projects, leading to the evolution of an entirely new family of products and the demise of the old ones, in some cases. A typical example was the smart phone. Major players such as Motorola who could not anticipate this change and cope with it, could not survive in this sector. What about Nokia?

Project risk

Project risk is mainly related to the individual project rather than the bigger picture of the organization or the industry as a whole. Project risks can be operational risks such as absenteeism, quality issues, time creep, cost overrun, budget errors, default of suppliers or drop in supply of resources due to socioeconomic factors as mentioned above. Project managers can utilize analytical tools such as SWOT analysis to identify the strengths, weaknesses, opportunities and threats, to perform an internal analysis of the organization and identify subsequent risks. Typically project risks are easier to identify and manage compared to other categories of risk, due to the more confined context. In the following sections of this chapter there will be more emphasis on this type of risk yet the other categories will be addressed in context. It is worth mentioning that other categories such as financial risk and static risk can be predominantly categorised as project risk.

Financial risk

The main difference is that the financial risk can also be considered at the organizational level, in some cases, and therefore can be a driver for strategic changes. However, the level of financial planning and the details of the analysis will vary significantly, whether at the project or strategic level. Furthermore, the financial risk can be due to external drivers beyond the control of the project manager.

During the last decade, the financial crisis led to the global economic crisis, whereby many countries are still trying to emerge from the economic slowdown. This had significant impact on many ongoing projects as well as planned projects worldwide, in various sectors. In projects, the lack of resources due to shortage of funding or cost creep due to price changes is amongst the common financial risks typically considered during the risk analysis as part of the planning phase. It is worth noting that the financial risks and the economic risks can be highly correlated in most cases, in sectors such as construction, oil and gas, tourism, etc. The variation in demand would have impact on both the revenues and the cash flow due to the drop in the price levels; both can have serious implications on the finances of organizations and subsequently the projects delivering the strategic objectives of those organizations.

The drop in oil prices from over $100 per barrel to the $40 level in 2016 was claimed to be a result of the economic slowdown of key global players such as China. Subsequently the oil and gas industry worldwide witnessed major layoffs and many of the intended projects were put on hold. The impact of this drop in revenues has not been limited to the oil and gas projects, but extended to hit other service sectors that catered for the oil and gas sector, such training and development service providers amongst other suppliers and service providers. Hence the impact can be claimed to have extended throughout the supply chain whereby various types of projects form the vehicle of delivery.

In Dubai the financial crisis had serious implications on the real estate sector, which is one the pillars of the economy alongside construction sector in general. Starting in 2008, the sheer drop in demand caused many of the ongoing projects to stop, while many other projects were cancelled. The drop in prices due to the change in demand resulted in the review of credit conditions and many of the credit buyers defaulted, thus fuelling the slowdown further. This was part of what is known the domino effect of the financial crisis. Some of those projects were only resumed in 2014 ,with many serious contractual problems due to price changes. One of the mega projects that was affected was the Dubai Metro. The ambitious plans of having an extended coverage to reach out to many key areas in Dubai was reviewed and the project was limited to two lines that cover two main axes only in the Emirate, mainly due to lack of funding.

Market risk

Perhaps this is the most influential type of risk yet the most challenging to manage. Project managers need to realize that the successful project is a means to an end, which is competitive advantage for the organization. The survival of the organization in the market is the prime aim of any business. This cannot be achieved unless there is continual review of the market and the market changes, well in advance, in order to maintain a proactive approach in managing any foreseen changes effectively. Typically, markets tend to reflect an array of factors that include but are not limited to the economical, political, technological, legal, social and environmental factors, with different time lags between cause and effect. Competition conditions within any market can change due to any of those factors. Furthermore, the need for the project can even become obsolete, which will require a review of its feasibility if still in the planning phase. Things can be worse if such changes occur during the execution phase. When Airbus managed to sell A380 to Emirates Airlines and Singapore Airlines, this was not good news to competitors such as Boeing. It is a characteristic of that market that whoever manages to get their product to market first, will block the market for around 25 years.

Project managers should be aware of the characteristics of their markets and the subsequent risks. In addition, the risk analysis should encompass all the above mentioned PESTEL factors since the latter can be drivers for risk factors. The utilization of other analytical tools such as Porter's Five forces can help elucidate other market risks relevant to the industry and its subsequent impact on the project under study. In general, other market risks can fall into one of the following broad categories:

■ **Technical risks:** A common risk in all projects is the dependency on technology. Technical failure has an impact on the performance and reliability of the project. It also has an impact on the quality of the project. Risks within this category include project requirements, interfaces and levels of complexity.

■ **External risks:** These are the risks that are normally out with the direct control of the project manager. They include meeting regulation and legislative conditions, government and political intervention, changes in market conditions and exposure to subcontractor and supplier forces.

■ **Organisational risks:** It stands to reason that the project could be vulnerable to internal issues within the performing organisation. Priorities may change, funding may not be available and dependant projects may not be complete on time.

■ **Project management risks:** These are the risks that are the ultimate responsibility of the project manager and include exposure to poor quality plans, schedules and estimates.

■ **Health and safety risks:** It is the responsibility of the project manager to ensure that all personnel working on the project do so in safe environment. In many countries health and safety is covered by government legislation and failure to act accordingly can result in prosecution.

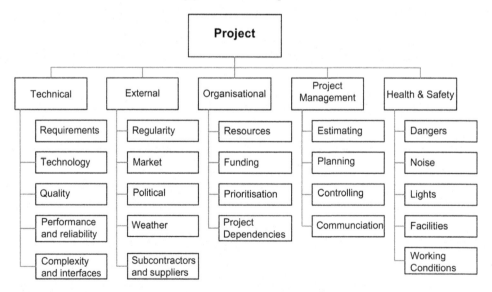

Figure 7.3: Risk breakdown structure

Risk categories can also be presented in highest high level of a risk breakdown structure (RBS). Using the same principles as a WBS, the RBS ensures a comprehensive process of systematically identifying risk to a consistent level of detail and contributes to the effectiveness and quality of risk identification (PMI, 2004).

7.5   Risk assessment

Not all risks identified within the risk identification process require the same level of attention. Some risks may be trivial and pose little threat to the project, whist others would have severe consequences if they occurred. The project manager therefore needs to determine which risks require constant monitoring and which can be ignored. The next stage in the risk management process involves prioritising each risk according to the severity of the threat to project success. The significance of a risk is assessed on two dimensions:

■ Probability of occurrence

■ Impact of the event

Probability refers to the likelihood that a specific risk will occur. For a risk to be of concern there must be a probability that the risk will take place. For example, an alien spaceship abducting the entire project team during the final phases of the project may have an impact on achieving project success, but the likelihood of this happening is extreme. Conversely, the probability of rain affecting construction on a building site in Seattle during the winter months is relatively high. In many cases probability can be assessed using expert judgement or historical information. Available data, such as climate and national statics, are also invaluable.

Impact refers to the consequence of the risk occurring on project success. This should be assessed against each of the project objectives:

■ **Cost:** The increased cost of the project as a consequence of the risk. This could be the cost of rectifying the problem or minimising the exposure to the client.

■ **Schedule:** The delay in project deliverables as a consequence of the risk. These could minor deliverables that delay dependant activities or a significant delay to the project deadline.

■ **Quality:** The effect on the quality of the project outcome as a consequence of the risk. This could range from a minor deviation from the specification to the end outcome being unfit for purpose.

■ **Scope:** The effect on the scope of the project as a consequence of the risk. This could range from a minor decrease in the work being included to the project deliverables not being attained and the project being abandoned.

Gray and Larson (2008) recognise that te assessment of impact can be problematic. This is because adverse risks affect project objectives differently. For example, late delivery of a component may only have a minor impact on the schedule, but could have a significant impact on cost if the project deadline is missed. The impact on the project would be dependant on the priority of each objective. If the schedule is more important than cost, then the impact is only minor. On the other hand, if the project is cost driven, the impact would be severe.

■ Risk probability / impact matrix

The typical approach to prioritising potential risk is the **risk probability and impact matrix**. This tool demonstrates evaluation of all the risks within a project on a single chart. Using the data collated to assess the probability of a risk occurring and the impact of the risk on the project objectives, each event is categorised on a scale of either 'low', 'medium' or 'high' depending on the assessment across both dimensions.

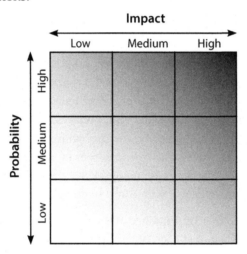

Figure 7.4: Risk probability / impact matrix

- **Low impact / low probability:** Risks at the lowest left hand corner of the matrix are of the lowest priority and can be ignored. They are unlikely to occur and even if they did, the project objectives would not be affected.

- **Low impact / medium probability:** These risks are of low priority, but should be noted by the project team. They have a reasonable chance of occurring, but would have little consequence on the project objectives if they do.

- **Medium impact / low probability:** These risks are also of low priority, but should be monitored and recorded. Although, there is little likelihood of the risk occurring, they would have an affect on the project objectives.

- **Low impact / high probability:** Risks within this zone are of medium priority. These are the minor risks that frequently occur within the project. They are manageable, but a nuisance and effort should be made to reduce the likelihood of occurrence.

- **Medium impact / medium probability:** Risks within this zone of are of medium priority. These are risks that could occur and would have a reasonable affect on the project objectives if they did occur. Effort should be made to reduce the likelihood and consequence of the risk transpiring.

- **High impact / low probability:** These risks are of medium priority. They are unlikely to occur, but if they did they would have severe consequences on the on the project. Effort should be made to reduce the risk consequence.

- **Medium impact / high probability:** Risks within this zone of are of high priority. These are risks are likely to occur and would have an affect on the project objectives if they did. Effort should be made to reduce the likelihood and consequence of the risk transpiring.

- **High impact / medium probability:** Risks within this zone of are of high priority. These are risks have a reasonable chance of occurring and would have a severe affect on the project objectives if they did. Effort should be made to reduce the likelihood and consequence of the risk transpiring.

- **High impact / high probability:** Risks at the top right hand corner of the matrix of are the critical risks and of the highest priority. They are likely to occur and will have severe impact on the project if they do. They should be monitored at all times and where possible eliminated.

Sometimes it may be more beneficial to apply a numeric value to each risk by weighting the potential severity of each risk event. Probability can be assessed by ranking the likelihood of occurrence on a scale of 1 to 10, whereas, impact can be assessed by ranking the consequences of the risk occurrence on a scale of 1 to 10. Risk severity is therefore calculated by the equation:

$$\text{Risk severity} = \text{Probability} \times \text{Impact}$$

Alternatively, a severity scale of between 0 and 1 could be applied to the risk probability and impact matrix, as shown in Figure 7.5. By assessing the likelihood and consequences of each risk, a value representing the potential risk severity can be applied. The closer the overall risk is to 1, the greater the severity of the risk occurring. Risks within the matrix can be further classified by the use of a colour coding system where low, medium and high risks could be represented by green, amber and red zones, for example.

	Impact					
Probability	1.00	0.20	0.40	0.60	0.80	1.00
	0.80	0.16	0.32	0.48	0.64	0.80
	0.60	0.12	0.24	0.36	0.48	0.60
	0.40	0.08	0.16	0.24	0.32	0.40
	0.20	0.04	0.08	0.12	0.16	0.20
		0.20	0.40	0.60	0.80	1.00

Figure: 7.5: Severity scale risk probability / impact matrix

Providing a detailed classification of risks using a numerical method does have added benefits.

- In the first instance it allows the organisation to define an appropriate level of acceptance for all risks. Depending on the type of project, an acceptance level may be for all risks that fall below a value of 0.60. Any risk above this number may be deemed to be too critical to the project and should either be avoided or eliminated. This is sensible practice for projects that have high health and safety concerns, such as rescue or medical projects.
- Second, it allows for sub groupings of risks by providing a detailed colour coding dependant on the risk value.
- Third, the method allows for a development of a more appropriate risk response for individual risks and groups of risks within a particular numeric scale.

7.6 Risk attitude

Different project managers will demonstrate different attitudes towards the same risk event. In general, there are three main types of risk attitude; risk averse, risk seekers and neutral. The former typically attempts to avoid risk as possible and opts to less risky event thus decisions are sometimes regarded as pessimistic. On the opposite end of the spectrum comes the risk seeker where the motto is "the higher the risk the higher the returns". This justifies decisions that are sometimes seen as quite optimistic. A risk neutral manager would seek a balanced decision based on a detailed analysis.

7.7   Risk response

Once risks are assessed in terms of probability and impact, the next stage in the risk management process is to develop an appropriate response strategy. A starting point is to understand that the less information and knowledge available about any event, the more the perceived risk. So it is always advisable to seek adequate information about the risk event under investigation before embarking on selecting a response strategy. In general, there are five possible responses to a risk that could have a negative impact on the project objectives:

1   **Risk mitigation: Also known as risk reduction.** Mitigation of a risk begins as soon as the assessment process is concluded. This is because taking early action towards a potential risk is more effective than repairing the consequences of a risk if it occurred. Risk mitigation involves reducing, or trying to eliminate the potential severity of a risk on the project. This is done by:

    ■ Reducing the likelihood that a particular risk will occur, and/or

    ■ Reducing the impact of the risk on the project objectives

    In many cases risks can be reduced through risk awareness and taking precautions should the risk occur. For example, to reduce the **likelihood** of car accidents, the car should have regular maintenance, particularly for the tyres and the brakes; the drivers should have adequate training and should abide by good practice and speed limits. On the other hand, the built-in safety measures within the vehicle such as airbags and seat belts should reduce the **impact** if and when an accident happens. Other mitigation strategies involve building a prototype of the product to identify any potential problems, or testing the product at various stages of development to eliminate risks. For example, system-based projects would be tested on an isolated computer, before being installed on a network. In addition, training and development of staff should reduce the probability of errors and serious mistakes that can impact the quality of the project deliverables.

2   **Risk avoidance.** Risk avoidance does not mean discarding the entire work package but rather involves taking a different course of action from the original plan in order to steer clear of the potential high impact / high probability risk occurring. This is typically a sensible decision when the anticipated outcome of the high probability event is intolerable. For example, selecting local suppliers rather than international suppliers in order to avoid the risk of prolonged delivery times. Another example is opting for an indoor event rather than an outdoor venue when there is high probability of rain and gusty winds that can ruin the event. However, it should be recognised that selecting

a different course of action, often results in a new set of risks that need to be identified and managed.

3 **Risk transfer:** Risk transfer is common practice. In this strategy a third party take on board the responsibility and consequences of the risk in return for a premium. The typical example is insurance. For example, almost all projects are subject to fire and theft. Both can be managed through appropriate insurance whereby an insurance firm would pay the costs of project expenses as a result of a risk occurring. The level of payment and extent of coverage would be dependent on the level of premium paid to the insurance firm.

4 **Risk sharing:** Sharing of risks has become a common business practice. This is because increased global competition has resulted in a greater amount being at stake should something go wrong. A number of organisations are opting for partnering arrangements and joint ventures in order to reduce their own exposure to risk. The benefit that each party wishes to get from a project is dependant on the amount of risk they wish to take. For example, organisations that have a 60% stake in a project would normally retain 60% of the risk. Another example is the case in fixed price contracts, where the contactor accepts the risks in return for a fixed sum which is usually higher than the standard contract price. However, if the contractor defaults then the client will have to bear the risk. Hence, it is a form of risk sharing.

5 **Risk acceptance:** Also known as **risk retention.** There is always a great deal of risks that needs to be retained in any project. These include the small risks that can be managed, such as minor delays of certain activities or small cost overrun on some work packages. In general, any risk response will be associated with a cost. If this additional cost is not justified due to the comparatively low impact, then risk retention might be a rational decision.

Conversely, some risks are so large that cannot be transferred, mitigated or avoided. For example, severe weather, such as earthquakes or gale-force winds cannot be controlled or managed, but a contingency plan could be put in place for such events occurring.

■ Contingency planning

A contingency is an alternative plan that is put into action should certain risks occur. The purpose of a contingency plan is to mitigate the impact of the risk on project success. It should attempt to ensure that project objectives remain consistent, although most contingencies will impact on the cost, time or quality of the project. Despite this, the absence of a contingency plan can result in a risk occurrence becoming an emergency. The project will inevitably be delayed whilst management establishes an appropriate course of action and implements the strategy, which is often formed in a state of panic resulting in poor decisions being made.

A contingency plan should be developed early enough in the project for the plan to be communicated and all team members to be aware of the responsibilities and actions required for smooth implementation. It needs to clearly identify any alternative equipment, resources or process required for successful execution of the plan. It also needs to take into consideration the lead time required to acquire the alternative equipment, resources and processes. There also needs to be a **contingency fund** to cover the cost of implementing the contingency plan and any other risk strategies. The size of the fund will vary dependant on the level of risk within the project, but 7-10% of the overall project budget is normal.

The contingency plan should be executed under certain predefined conditions and there should be sufficient warning given in order to implement it in good time. Contingency plans must identify a trigger point that causes the plan to be activated, such as missed milestones, non delivery of materials or testing failure.

7.8   Projects in action – the risk clinic

7

Project Risks

1. Missing report deadline because I have to attend a Risk Clinic
2. Lack of Sleep through having to work all night to complete report

Solution: Sleep through Risk Clinic!

Unfortunately not all project team members appreciate the importance of risk management. Yet, identifying and assessing risks is best done as a team exercise, where experiences, knowledge and expertise can be shared. Holding a risk clinic is a simple approach to creating a risk management environment. It also has the added advantage of bringing all the team members together to focuses on project issues and generally generates some innovative solutions to risk problems.

The clinic should be held in appropriate comfortable environment where the team are allowed to be creative without any distractions. A facilitator is required to manage the proceedings. This is best done by someone from outside the project team, but if this is not possible the project manager would be the best option. The risk clinic has three main stages.

Equipment required:

Post-it notes, marker pens, clip-chart paper or white-board.

Stage 1: Risk identification and Classification

Drawing on the WBS and project scope, all members of the project team suggest as many risks as possible within a short space of time.

The objective is to create a significant pile of risks from various categories and sources. Therefore brainstorming rules apply

Brainstorming rules:

- Write down ALL suggested risks on the post-it, no matter if they are unlikely, repeated or absurd.
- All risks should be placed in a pile at the centre of table
- Do not debate or discuss suggestions.
- Do not dismiss any other team members suggestion
- Fix a target number of risks to be identified (minimum 70) or fix a time limit of when the identification stage will be end.

Stage 2: Risk assessment

This stage involves analysing the identified risks and prioritising them accordingly.

- Using the clip-chart paper or white board, draw a 3x3 risk matrix with a scale of 1-10.
- Taking one identified risk at a time, place the post-it note in the appropriate zone of the matrix. The team needs to assess each risk on:
  - ☐ Probability: what is the likelihood of the risk occurring?
  - ☐ Impact: what are the consequences of the risk occurring?
- A consensus needs to be agreed as to where each risk should be placed. Therefore there will be discussion and rearranging of the risks.
- Discard all repeated risks
- Within each zone arrange each risk to give a severity value based on the scale. This is calculated by:

$$\text{Risk Severity} = \text{Probability} \times \text{Impact.}$$

- Record the score on the post-it note.

Stage 3: Risk attitude and response

The final stage of clinic involves generating an initial response for each risk. Again as a team, each risk should be discussed to reach a consensus as to the best approach. These should be recorded and used to develop the risk information sheets and the risk register.

- **Mitigate risk:** How will the likelihood be reduced? How will the impact be reduced?

- **Avoid risk:** How will the risk be evaded? Will this course of action create other risks?

- **Transfer risk**: Who will the risk be transferred to? What will the cost of transfer be?

- **Share risk:** Who will we partner with? What will be the conditions of contract?

- **Accept:** If we accept the risk, who will we advise? What is the plan if this occurs?

While the risk clinic will not identify all risks on the project, it is an excellent starting point for generating the risk register and understanding the possible risk events that could occur on a project.

7

7.9   Risk control

The final stage of the risk management process involves developing and implementing appropriate processes and procedures for control of identified risks. The outcome of the risk assessment process should be a **risk information sheet** (RIS) for each identified risk, as shown in Figure 7.6. Sometimes referred to as a **risk assessment form**, the RIS documents the important risk criteria required for control of risks. This must include:

- A description of the risk, clearly identifying the source

- The risk owner or assigned project team responsible for monitoring the risk, reporting on the risk status and implementing the risk response strategy and contingency plan.

- A time frame determining when the risk is likely to occur and when the mitigation strategy needs to be executed.

- A detailed description of the contingency plan and the trigger point to warn of the risk occurring.

Project risk information sheet					
Code		Revision		Date Identified	
Risk title					
Probability			Risk owner		
Impact			Source		
Severity			Time frame		
Risk description					
Mitigation strategy					
Contingency plan and trigger					
Risk status					
Submitted			**Date**		

Figure 7.6: Sample risk information sheet

More often the risk information sheets will be controlled within a risk database and updated accordingly. Each risk within the database is summarised and presented in a **risk register**, as shown in Figure 7.7. This becomes a key component of the project management plan and is used for reporting, meetings and evaluation of the project. The risk register logs all risks identified within the risk management process. It is a dynamic document that needs to be updated regularly as the status of risks change and new risks are identified. It should code and categorise each risk within the project for quick reference, and should contain sufficient information for the project manager and project team to discuss and monitor the risk situation.

Project risk register						
Project name:						
Prepared by			**Date**		**Revision**	
Project manager			**Project sponsor**			
Project risks						
Risk code	**Risk event**	**Probability**	**Impact**	**Value**	**Response**	**Risk owner**
Signed		**Date**		**Approved**		**Date**

Figure 7.7: Sample risk register

As previously stated, the risk management process is reiterative. It does not end until completion of the project. Identified risks need to be continually monitored for any change in status. However, as the process of risk management often leads to new risks being occurring, it is essential that risk is an item on the agenda at all project team meetings, that risk reporting is done a regular basis and that the risk database and risk register are updated and current at all times. It is critical that risks are visible and that are there are no nasty shocks during the project.

7.10 Agile project management (APM)

Traditionally, the project management methodology (PMM) builds on the thorough analysis (planning), monitoring (control) and review of the project at set phases known as the project life cycle. The initiation phase, followed by the planning phase, depend on a well defined scope, based on a clearly defined set of deliverables whereby the characteristics of the sought product, whether it be a new building, a new software, an event or any new product/service development (NPD / NSD), are clearly stated and agreed upon by the client and the project team. Such approach is sometime referred to as the waterfall model as shown in Figure 7.8 which presents the project stages for developing a new system.

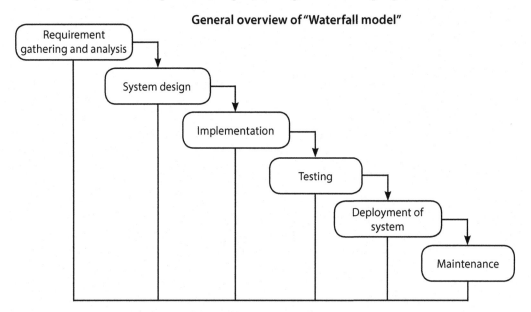

Figure 7.8: The waterfall model

The waterfall model is claimed to have some advantages including:

- Simple and easy to understand;
- Process is rigid whereby each phase has a defined set of deliverables;
- Phases do not overlap and
- Project plans can be replicated for future use.

On the other hand, the disadvantages of the Waterfall model are as follows:

- Inflexible to change;
- Working product is developed late in the project life cycle;
- High level of risk;

- Not suitable for projects with changing requirements and
- Poor model for long and ongoing projects.

Such disadvantages could not cope with the requirements of the current dynamic business environment and the emergence of new sectors and applications such as IT/ software development; change management across various sectors and New Product Development (NPD) projects, etc. These are in continual need of the project management set of tools and techniques as a vehicle to deliver the strategic objectives.

It was therefore imperative that new methodologies such as Agile project management (APM) would emerge to address such disadvantages. The traditional methodology is based on a predictive approach. For example, in traditional software development life cycle (SDLC) models, teams work with a detailed plan and have a full list of characteristics and tasks that must be completed in the next few months or the entire life cycle of the product. Predictive methods entirely depend on a well defined scope and thorough planning at the beginning of the cycle. Any future changes will be dealt with through the pre-set change control management system. (Stoica et al., 2013).

The Agile model uses an adaptive approach that eliminates detailed planning and only considers the tasks related to the product/service characteristics to be developed. The *Agile Manifesto of Software Development* outlines the four core values of Agile methodology:

1 Individuals and interactions over processes and tools;

2 Working software over comprehensive documentation;

3 Customer collaboration over contract negotiation and

4 Responding to change over following a plan.

In contrast to traditional methodology, Agile methodology develops projects in an iterative cyclic way. Modulation of work is referred to as 'iterations' or 'sprints'. For every sprint, it is expected to deliver a usable product increment to the customer. The ability to inspect and evaluate the deliverable at the end of each sprint provides significant advantages in terms of risk reduction as well as control over costs and time to market. Moreover, the interactive participation of the client and flexibility to changes in requirements promotes customer satisfaction (Abrahamsson, 2005).

In one of the most popular agile methodologies, Scrum (after rugby), the self organising team (SOT) adapts to dynamic changes in the product requirements. The product is frequently tested, minimizing the risk of major faults in the future. Interaction with the clients is the strong point of Agile methodology and open communication and minimal documentation are typical characteristics of the Agile development environment. Scrum teams are cross-functional, with all of the skills as a team necessary to create a product Increment (Schwaber and Sutherland, 2014., p5.). Self organising teams exhibit team autonomy and adaptability. Takeuchi and Nonaka (1986) describe self-organizing teams as exhibiting autonomy, self-transcendence, and cross-fertilization. Team autonomy means that project leaders establish the tasks the team must perform. During iterations, the team is free to decide how to work, primarily seeking to enhance team productivity. Scrum does not impose specific software development techniques, but rather provides an instrumental risk management approach for various phases, in order to reduce the anticipated ramification due to project complexity and unpredictability. (Stoica et al., 2013).

In the case of software development projects, agile software development methodologies include: Adaptive Software Development (ASD), Feature Driven Development (FDD), Crystal Clear, Dynamic Software Development Method (DSDM), Rapid Application Development (RAD), SCRUM, Extreme Programming (XP) and Rational Unify Process (RUP) (Cockburn, 2004; Stapleton, 2003; Palmer & Felsing, 2002; Schwaber & Beedle, 2001; Beck, 2000; Beck, 2004).

To conclude this section, a comparison between traditional project management methodology (PMM) and Agile project management methodology (APM) as applied to software development projects and encompassing the above mentioned points, is shown in Figure 7.9. It is worth noting that the detailed discussion of Agile, and Lean, methodologies is out with the scope of this text book. However, it was resolved that a brief reference to the emerging methodologies in the context of project risk management was essential due to the momentum currently witnessed, particularly in software development and new product development projects. The in-text citations provided in this section, the details of which can be found in full within the reference list at the end of this chapter, can provide those interested to read more about this topic with an up-to-date and quite comprehensive list of valuable sources.

	Traditional development	Agile development
Fundamental hypothesis	Systems are fully specifiable, predictable and are developed through extended and detailed planning	High quality adaptive software is developed by small teams that use the principle of continuous improvement of design and testing based on fast feed-back and change
Management style	Command and control	Leadership and collaboration
Knowledge management	Explicit	Tacit
Communication	Formal	Informal
Development model	Life cycle model (waterfall, spiral or modified models)	*Evolutionary-delivery* model
Organizational structure	Mechanic (bureaucratic, high formalization), targeting large organization	Organic (flexible and participative, encourages social cooperation), targeting small and medium organizations
Quality control	Difficult planning and strict control. Difficult and late testing	Permanent control or requirements, design and solutions. Permanent testing
User requirements	Detailed and defined before coding/implementation	Interactive input
Cost of restart	High	Low
Development direction	Fixed	Easily changeable
Testing	After coding is completed	Every iteration
Client involvement	Low	High
Additional abilities required from developers	Nothing in particular	Interpersonal abilities and basic knowledge of the business
Appropriate scale of the project	Large scale	Low and medium scale
Developers	Oriented on plan, with adequate abilities, access to external knowledge	Agile, with advanced knowledge, co-located and cooperative
Clients	With access to knowledge, cooperative, representative and empowered	Dedicated, knowledgeable, cooperative, representative and empowered
Requirements	Very stable, known in advance	Emergent, with rapid changes
Architecture	Design for current and predictable requirements	Design for current requirements
Remodeling	Expensive	Not expensive
Size	Large teams and projects	Small teams and projects
Primary objectives	High safety	Quick value

Figure 7.9: Traditional versus Agile development. *Source*: (Nerur, et al., 2005)

Summary

- The concept of 'known-known', 'known-unknown' and 'unknown-unknown' to refer to the conditions of certainty, risk and uncertainty respectively.

- The risk management process is a 6-stage iterative approach for minimising the consequences of unforeseen events on the project. These stages are risk identification, risk classification, risk assessment, risk attitude, risk response and risk control.

- Risk identification and classification involve identifying all the possible risks on project. When identifying risks it is important that the source of the risk is also identified. In general risks fall into one of the following categories: technical, external, internal, project management and health & safety.

- Risk assessment involves analysing each risk in terms of the probability of the risk occurring and the impact on the project objectives if the risk does occur. The severity of the risk is a result of the probability × impact.

- Risk response is based on risk attitude and involves developing an appropriate strategy for managing the risks. The five possible options for responding to a risk are: mitigate, transfer, avoid, share and accept. For some risks there needs to be a contingency plan in order to avoid any unnecessary surprises.

- Risk control involves generating and controlling the appropriate risk management documentation. These include a risk information sheet for each risk and a risk register for monitoring and controlling all the risks. Risks must be monitored on a regular basis to report on the status and identify if new risks have occurred.

- A contemporary methodology such as Agile project management (APM) is compared to project management methodology (PMM) in managing risk with emphasis on special types of project such as software development projects.

End of chapter review questions

1 Evaluate the stages of the risk management process

2 Discuss the importance of having an efficient risk control process.

3 You are part of a team to climb Mount Everest. Prepare a risk management plan for this project, explaining the importance of each stage.

4 Drawing on a project you are familiar with, explain the difference between the various risk response strategies.

References

Abrahamsson. (2005). Information Technology for European Advancement (ITEA) Innovation Report, *Speeding up embedded software development*.

Beck, K., (2004) *Extreme Programming Explained: Embrace Change*, 2nd ed., Addison-Wesley.

Burke, R. (2003) *Project Management: Planning and Control Techniques*, West Sussex: John Wiley & Sons.

Cockburn, A & Highsmith, J. (2001) Agile software development: The people factor. *Computer*, **34**(11), 131–133.

Cockburn, (2004) *Crystal Clear: A Human Powered Methodology for Small Teams*, Addison-Wesley.

Gray, C. F. & Larson, E. W. (2008) *Project Management: The Managerial Process*, New York, McGraw-Hill Irwin

Hoda, R., Noble, J. & Marshall, S. (2010.). Organizing Self-Organizing Teams. Proceedings of the IEEE/ACM International Conference on Software Engineering (ICSE2010), Cape Town, South Africa, May

ISO (2002) ISO/IEC Guide 73:2002. International Standardisation for Organization.

Lalsing, V., Kishnah, S. and Pudaruth, S. (2012). People factors in Agile software development and project management. *International Journal of Software Engineering & Applications*. **3** (1),117-137.

Nerur, S. Mahapatra, R. & Mangalaraj, G. (2005) Challenges of migrating to agile methodologies, Communications of the ACM (May) 72– 78

Peterson, K. (2009) A comparison of issues and advantages in Agile and incremental development between state of the art and an industrial case. *Journal of System and Software* **82**(9), 1479–1490

PMI (2004) *A Guide to the Project Management Body of Knowledge*: PMBOK guide, Pennsylvania Project Management Institute Inc.

Schwaber, K., Beedle, M. (2001) *Agile Software Development with Scrum*, Prentice Hall, Upper Saddle River.

Schwaber, K. and Sutherland, J. (2014). The Scrum Guide: The Definitive Guide to Scrum: The Rules of the Game. ScrumInc. http://www.scrumguides.org/docs/scrumguide/v1/scrum-guide-us.pdf. Last accessed 16th July 2016

Spark, N. T. (2006) *A History of Murphy's Law*, Nick Spark.

Stoica, M., Mircea, M., Ghilic-Micu, B. (2013). Software Development: Agile vs. Traditional. *Informatica Economică*. **17** (4), 64-74.

Takeuchi, H. & Nonaka, I. (1986)The new new product development game. *Harvard Business Review*, **64**(1)

7

8 Cost Estimating and Budgeting

Mohamed Salama

Learning objectives

By the time you have completed this chapter you should be able to:

☐ Discuss the concept of cost estimating

☐ Understand the various stages of cost estimating

☐ Compare and contrast the micro and macro approaches to cost estimating

☐ Discuss the various cost items and different methods used in cost estimating.

☐ Discuss the factors that affect the accuracy of cost estimates.

☐ Compare and contrast different bidding strategies.

☐ Construct a time-phased project budget

☐ Draw a project s-curve to illustrate project cash-flows

☐ Appreciate the importance of cost provisions and contingencies.

Introduction

Project schedules cannot be finalised until the resources have been allocated to different activities and work packages. A resource can be any entity required to accomplish the scheduled activity. This includes all the funds, people, equipment and materials required to achieve the project deliverables. This is sometimes known as the four Ms, referring to Money, Man, Machinery and Materials. All resources have costs associated to them which determine if the project is viable in the first instance. It is the project manager's responsibility to monitor the estimate of the project costs and ensure the availability of resources required for completion of the project. This chapter begins by discussing the different approaches to cost estimating, investigating the main cost items and the key factors that should be considered during the cost estimating process amid the resource constraints imposed on a project. The chapter then discusses the accuracy of cost estimates and concludes by demonstrating how to create a time-phased budget, which is used to monitor and control project expenditure.

8.1   Types of project costs

Besides the cost of resources, the total project expenditure also includes other cost drivers such as overhead expenses and facilities. It is essential that all cost drivers are identified at the early stages of the project lifecycle as this ensures that budgets are based on accurate information and include all the costs associated with the project. Within any project, cost drivers fall into two categories:

- Direct dosts

- Indirect dosts

■   Direct costs

These are costs that are clearly specific to a project or individual work package and include:

- **Labour:** These are the human resources working on the project and often represent its biggest cost. They include the project team, external consultants and all personnel identified on the OBS. Labour costs are calculated either by set fixed fee or by an hourly rate.

- **Equipment:** People working on a project normally require some form of equipment in order to perform their task. This could range from a computer to specialist machinery. Equipment costs are calculated by the daily/weekly hire of the equipment or when necessary, the purchase of equipment

- **Material:** Most projects require materials in order to be realised. These are the inputs of the project that are transformed into a project deliverable through the project being executed. For example, brick for construction projects, film for advertising projects or paper for printing projects. Material costs are calculated on the quantity of the material required.

- **Facilities:** Some projects are performed remotely from the participating organisation and require independent facilities such as office accommodation, utilities and other consumables.

8

■   Indirect costs

These are costs that cannot be clearly specified to a particular project and are incurred by multiple projects within the organisation. Indirect costs include:

- ■ **Overheads:** Many projects are performed within the participating organisations facilities. Overhead costs include rent, rates, utilities and other consumables.

- ■ **Salaries**: Projects draw on the support of administrative staff, senior management and even janitorial personal.

- ■ **Equipment and machinery**: Essential equipment such as photocopiers, computers, telephones and facsimiles all have associated costs that cannot be directly apportioned to a project. This also includes software and licenses required by the organisation to perform the project.

8.2   Project cost estimating

Realising the project scope within the allocated costs is one of the key project management objectives. Quite often the success of a project is measured on the ability to deliver a project within the cost constraint, as evidenced by a recent survey conducted by the Standish Group (2004). This report found that an astonishing 83% of IT projects failed to be delivered within the allocated budget.

■   Cost estimating versus price forecasting

The definition for the term 'estimating', as stated in the *Concise Oxford Dictionary* refers to "a contractor's statement of a sum of money for which specified work will be undertaken" whereas the same source defines the term 'forecasting' as "a foresight or conjectural estimate of something scheduled to happen in the future".

Academic studies in the field of construction project management, for example Ashworth (1991) and Ferry & Brandon (1994), made no distinction between the two terms. Also, the Chartered Institute of Building (CIOB and the RICS codes of practice used the term 'cost estimating' when they were referring to 'price forecasting'.

In some sectors, such as construction projects' cost planning and control, the following terms are commonly used: cost estimating, price forecasting and prediction. *Forecasting* is exclusively reserved for a future (uncertain) event whereas an *estimate* may also be applied to existing observable (measurable) situation. It might be argued that forecasting is an objective assessment while prediction is a subjective assessment of uncertain future events. A correctly formulated forecast should contain statements that are explicitly: a) quantitative, b) qualitative, c) related to time, and d) probabilistic in acknowledging the uncertainty of the future event (Ashworth & Skitmore, 1983). It was resolved that the term 'cost estimating' will be used in this context. It is important, though, to clarify the domain from the outset. The term 'cost' in this chapter refers to the cost for the client, which is the asking price by the provider, also referred to as the 'tender price'.

8.3   Cost planning and cost estimating

In general, cost management, which involves cost planning and cost control, is a process that extends throughout the various stages of the project from inception to decommissioning (Ashworth, 1999). The output of the cost planning cycle, that is the cost estimate, will obviously affect the cost control cycle. The more accurate the cost estimates, the less the variation and consequently the more limited need for remedial actions. Cost estimating is also seen as the process of approximating the expenditure of resources, materials, equipment, overheads and other expenses required to complete the project.

The accuracy and reliability of project cost estimates are critical as:

- They determine the viability of a project in terms of return on investment. If the estimate is deemed to be high, the organisation may not pursue it.

- They determine the level of funds allocated to the project. It is the project estimates that dictate the budget. If the budget is exceeded, it will be the responsibility of the project manager to either negotiate additional project funding or seek a reduction in the quality or scope of the project.

- They determine the cash flow and funds made available for the project throughout the project life-cycle.

- They provide a mechanism for measuring progress of the project by drawing comparison between the project estimates and actual costs.

Typically a good cost plan should "reduce project risk" and "ensure that the tender figure is as close as possible to the first estimate, or that any likely difference between the two is anticipated and within an acceptable range" (Kirkham, 2007). The same author identified three main phases of the cost planning process; the briefing phase; the design phase and finally the "production and operation" phase.

▪ Stages of cost estimating

Flanagan and Tate (1997, p.48) identified three stages for the cost estimating process: feasibility, scheme design and tender action. In the first two stages estimates are produced using approximate quantities or single rate estimating methods, while in the tender action stage a full bill of quantities is priced. In a different approach, Ashworth, (1999, p. 273-78) divided the cost estimating process into three phases: the preliminary estimate, the preliminary cost plan and the cost plan. The first phase provides an indication of cost before any substantial specifications and quantities are prepared, and is merely perceived as a ballpark figure for guidance. The preliminary cost plan is more correctly described as an 'elemental estimate' that is based on the sketch (outline) design. The cost plan can only be prepared after the detailed design has been completed. In addition, the cost data needed to formulate the cost plan include the information about the project elements, the material to be used, the contractual information and the analysis of previous projects. A sketch of the cost planning process presented by Ashworth (1999, p. 274) is shown in Figure 8.1. Furthermore, Ashworth and Hogg (2007) divided the cost planning and control process into two stages: pre-contract and post contract. In the following discussion there will be more emphasis on the pre-contract cost estimating process. The pre-contract methods for cost estimating identified by Ashworth and Hogg (2007) are shown in Figure 8.1.

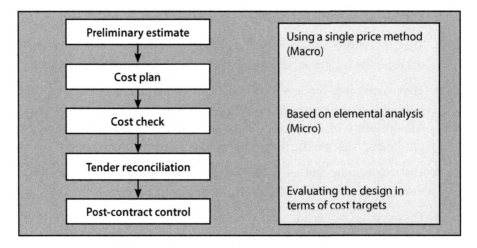

Figure 8.1: Cost planning during the design and execution phases. Source: Ashworth, 1999

The cost estimating process can be divided into five stages: the pre-design estimate, the detailed design estimate, the bid (tender) estimate, the progress estimate and the final estimate/final account (Al-Turki, 2000, p. 56). The client is more concerned with the final cost, which if varied significantly from the tender price, might have detrimental implications on the completion of the project especially in the case of public sector projects in the developing countries. This was emphasised in the work of Kirkham (2007) who stressed that, so far, the clients are not satisfied with the outcome of the cost estimating process and that there is a "major shift in emphasis" towards the final cost rather than the tender figure. The clients are more interested in what they will actually pay for the project on completion.

8.4   Methods of cost estimating

In the project management literature there is variation in the jargon used to name the different cost estimating methods. For example, in addition to the above mentioned, there are other methods such as parametric estimating, trade unit cost, cost per enclosed area, cost per functional unit, factor estimating and range estimating methods. However, by examining these various methods, the underlying assumptions converge so there are hardly any conceptual or technical differences when compared to the methods listed in Figure 8.1. In the following sections some of the most commonly known methods of cost estimating will be briefly discussed. It is worth noting at this stage that the estimates fall into two categories: marco or top-down and micro or bottom-up cost estimates.

■   Expert opinion or conference estimate

A technique that can be used to develop an early price estimate based on the collective view of a group of experts who should have experience in similar projects. This technique is used in special projects when historical data may not be appropriate. Primarily, conference estimates provide a qualitative analysis at an early stage of the cost planning process when quantitative methods might not be feasible.

■   Parametric estimating or the single price rate method

The single price rate method refers to the different methods that depend on a single rate applied to a single parameter at the pre-design stage to produce an approximate estimate given the limited information available at this early stage of the planning phase. Parameters can be size, location, volume or weight to estimate the cost of the project. The cost of the current project is estimated by mathematical modelling of the project based on the cost data. For example:

The current cost of building a 100m², single storey villa in Majorca would be €2,500 per m², based on its size, material and location. Therefore the cost of building a 75m² villa there would be estimated at (€2,500 x 75 m²) = €187,500.

■ Ratio method

This is a quick and simple form of estimating. It uses previous projects to calculate the cost of a current project by applying a ratio. The advantage of the ratio method is that there is a point of reference as to how the cost was generated. For example: The cost of development and installation of a similar IT project was £120,000. The current project is only 60% of the size, therefore would have a cost estimate of (120,000 x 60%) = £72,000.

■ Financial methods

In projects that apply the financial methods, cost limits are fixed, based on the selling price or the rental value. For example, the amount to be spent on the construction of a building by a developer will be the selling price of the built units minus all development costs and profit. The outcome forms an integral component of the feasibility study of the project. This method is used to mitigate the project financial risks by setting a ceiling for the final cost at the feasibility stage of the cost planning process. In addition, any variation during the execution phase beyond the set figure will erode the client's profit, for any given selling price.

■ Bottom-up estimating – elemental estimating

This is quite common in building projects, whereby an element is defined as "a major component common to most buildings which usually fulfils the same function, irrespective of its design, specification or construction" (Flanagan and Tate, 1997, p.101) that is to say the sub-units of the building which should be considered in the cost analysis. Examples of elements are external walls, windows, the roof, etc. An elemental cost analysis provides cost estimators and clients at large with a useful yardstick about the cost of similar projects and how the cost is distributed among the various elements. In this method, unit quantities and unit rates are identified for each element. This helps to pinpoint the source of variation among different projects, whether the variation is due to quantity 'size' or rather due to the quality and price level. Also, this allows a more objective comparison among buildings of "different sizes and uses". It is suggested that the final accounts rather than the tender figures of the previously completed similar projects should be considered in the elemental cost analysis (Flanagan and Tate, 1997, p.102). This method can be applied to various types of projects beyond the specific context of construction, such as product development projects and event management projects among other types.

Elemental cost analysis, further, allows for appropriate remedial actions to be introduced if the bidders request higher values than those produced by the client's cost estimators, by revealing the source of variation. A work breakdown structure (WBS) can form the basis to produce a cost breakdown structure (CBS) than can be utilised in this pursuit. The various elements (boxes) will act as cost centres. By rolling up from one level to the one above, the total cost of the various work packages and subsequently the total cost of the project can be estimated and furthermore monitored and controlled. Though time consuming, bottom-up estimating is the most reliable approach to cost estimating. It involves estimating the individual work packages identified within the WBS and rolling them up to establish a reasonably accurate estimate of the accumulated cost of project activities, as shown in Figure 8.2. The estimated project cost is equal to the sum of all work packages plus any overheads.

The individual estimated work package cost can be determined through a number of sources, including expert opinion, ratio method and parametric estimating. However, within bottom-up estimating these techniques are applied at the micro level, as oppose to the project as a whole.

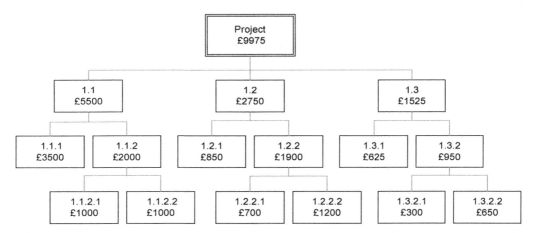

Figure 8.2: Rolling-up of the work packages

The more detailed the cost data, the more accurate the cost estimates, but it has been argued that by identifying the major 100 items of work and pricing them, the produced cost estimate would reach an optimum level of accuracy that could hardly be improved by more detailed pricing (Ashworth, 1999, p. 46). In a bill of quantities (BQ), the Pareto rule, which states that 80% of the total value can be attributed to 20% of the items, seems to be instated. However, Ashworth argued that bills of quantities include a wide variation of rates for items of comparable nature on different projects and that small items on the bills of quantities are not priced carefully. Typically at the early stages of the cost planning phase and before the design reaches the detailed stage, the cost breakdown will yield no more than 40 items which can be described as coarse data rather than refined data (Kirkham, 2007, p. 203).

It can be argued that a good practice is to prepare a cost analysis including supplementary information on market conditions and specifications for every tender (Ashworth and Hogg 2007, p.57). This will enable the client to establish a useful data bank, given the tendency to delay or lay less emphasis on the analysis of final cost records that is perceived by some practitioners as less productive. In order to establish an effective and reliable cost database, the data has to be collected from a large number of similar projects. In practice, the project team usually starts preparing for the next project once they finish the project in hand (Ashworth, 1999, p. 47).

Table 8.1: Sample cost estimate

WBS	Description	Unit	Rate	Qty	Sub-total	Total
1.1.1 Decorator						
	Decorator	Hourly	£ 25.00	16	£ 400.00	
	Wall paper	m^2	£ 15.00	60	£ 900.00	
	Paint	m^2	£ 5.00	10	£ 50.00	
						£ 1,350.00
1.1.2 Floors						
	Carpet fitter	Hourly	£ 28.00	8	£ 224.00	
	Underlay	m^2	£ 5.00	56	£ 280.00	
	Carpet	m^2	£ 15.00	56	£ 840.00	
						£ 1,344.00
1.1.3 Services						
	Electrician	Hourly	£ 18.00	16	£ 288.00	
	Technician	Hourly	£ 30.00	12	£ 360.00	
	Data cables	Item	£ 2,500.00	1	£ 2,500.00	
	Computers	Item	£ 800.00	2	£ 1,600.00	
	Software	Item	£ 450.00	2	£ 900.00	
						£ 5,648.00
Total						£ 8,342.00

Activity based costing is the most common technique to estimate the cost of each work package. The premise of activity based costing is that all projects have activities and all activities consume resources (Maher, 1997). As such, costs are initially assigned to activities and then assigned to projects, based on the projects resource requirement. Activity-based costing consists of four stages:

1 Indentify the resources within each activity or work package and assign costs to them.

2 Identify the cost drivers associated with each work package. In most projects the major cost driver will be labour, but it could also include materials.

3 Compute a cost rate per cost driver unit or transaction. For example, labour could be computed at a cost rate per hour.

4 Assign costs to the project by multiplying the cost driver rate by the volume of cost driver units consumed by the project.

For example, assume the cost of a project manager was £50 per hour and was required to work for 60 hours on a project. The cost to the project would be:

Estimated cost   =   (Cost rate /unit) × time required

=   £50 × 60 hours

=   £3,000

Table 8.1 demonstrates the use of activity based costing in forming a cost estimate.

8.5 Cost modelling

The evolution of research addressing the accuracy of project cost estimating drew the attention to the need for further research to improve the accuracy of the produced estimates. Researchers then embarked on investigating all the factors and variables affecting the cost of projects in more detail, introducing new techniques and in some cases getting too much concerned with details that, albeit they enrich the research and add to the knowledge, have questionable applicability to the real world of practitioners.

Since the late 1950s, modelling has been applied in search for more accurate cost estimates in the construction management research. Cost models can be classified into three generations (Raftery, 1991)

1 The first generation, which began in the late 1950s and continued up to the late 1960s, was characterised by a procedural (elemental costing) approach.

2 The second generation, which began around the mid 1970s, was characterised by intensive use of regression analysis.

3 The third generation began in the early 1980s and was characterised by considering uncertainty through probabilistic estimates, frequently based on Monte Carlo techniques.

In the late 1990s, another generation developed including fuzzy logic, artificial neural network (ANN) (Boussabaine and Kaka, 1998) and neuro-fuzzy (Boussabaine, 1999 and Wanous *et al.* 2004). Also, cost models were classified into the following categories in terms of descriptive primitives (Newton, 1991):

- **Relevance**: whether it relates to a specific design proposal;
- **Units** i.e. the units of measurement.
- **Cost/price**: how the model is intended to be used.
- **Approach**: the level at which modelling is applied.
- **Time point**: when during the design process it is applied.
- **Model**: a general classification of the technique.
- **Technique**: the specific classification.

Cost estimating and price forecasting is still a contentious issue. Simple models have been characterised by being non-specific with implicit assumptions and deterministic outcomes. Other models applying different techniques, such as regression analysis, Monte Carlo simulation, neural network, artificial neural network, fuzzy logic and subjective probability are often beyond the comprehension of practitioners besides the need of adequate recourses to integrate them in the estimating process. Also, cost modelling research has been disadvantaged by having no formal means of describing one cost model relative to another (Skitmore, 1988).

There is a consensus among researchers of the need to communicate the new models and techniques relevant to the industry through training programmes commanded by institutional bodies. The introduction of appropriate techniques as an integral part of new versions of the widely applied software packages may enhance the awareness and reduce the ambiguity in a practical context, especially for small and medium size companies. A large majority of research studies either focus on the methodology, technique or the product variables and attributes, and the consequent relationship with the cost estimates.

8.6   Accuracy of estimates and bidding strategies

For so long, cost estimating was simply the process of calculating the total cost of a project, based on either single unit rate or a relatively more accurate method, by pricing all items of the bill of quantities. The former is an example of macro estimating and mostly used at the initiation phase (feasibility or sketch design) to run a feasibility study whereby an accuracy of up to 25% variation is accepted. The latter, on the other hand, is an example of the micro estimating and is used at a later stage of the planning phase when a detailed design is achieved and an accurate estimate is required before the tendering or the bidding depending on whether the estimate is done by the client or the contractor. Hypothetically, the accuracy at this stage should fall within the range of 5-10%; still in practice and some cases, up to 15% is regarded as acceptable.

In some cases, the variation in cost estimates will be function of the costing strategy, especially by bidders. In many cases, the bidders demonstrate a front-loading strategy when pricing items of the bill of quantities. Thus bid value will have a higher present value compared to the present value of cost estimates under the balanced pricing strategy (applied by most clients) even when the nominal value is apparently the same (asking price is equal to the client's estimate). In general there is tendency by contractors and suppliers towards front-loading rather than back-loading. Even in volatile markets, when the finishing materials and other inputs of the later stages of work items vary significantly with time, back-loading is usually avoided. On the one hand, the back-loading strategy will help to hedge against risks. On the other hand, this will lead to a higher bidding value, which might deter winning the tender, especially in public sector tenders.

Some clients tend to ignore the present value of the bid and rather focus on the total figure; the asking price to complete the project. The argument usually put forward by public sector clients is that the quantities of work items listed in the bill of quantity are subject to change. Once the work is done, the list of actual quantities is produced. This reflects the reality and forms the basis for payments. In some cases there are variations of up to ± 25% in the actual quantities compared to those planned. This last point is sometimes argued as one of the problems identified with the analysis of the bills of quantities (Kirkham 2007, p.208). In addition, different contractors follow different pricing methods with regard to the treatment of preliminaries, overheads and profits. This is conceptually different from front-loading and back-loading. It will still affect the cost of various work packages and activities, but might not affect the total value.

8.7   Factors affecting the accuracy of estimates

During the cost estimating process, project managers should be able to appreciate the significance of cost items, based on their contribution to the total cost (Runeson, 1988). Horner and Zakieh (1996) addressed the effect of 'cost-significant' items by applying the famous Pareto 80-20 rule. That is to say, that 80% of the value of any contract is contained within only 20% of the items in the bill of quantities. By focusing on these significant items and further more aggregating them into quantity-significant work packages, simpler estimating and more effective control procedures can be achieved.

Table 8.2: Factors affecting cost estimates for projects

Influential factors	Sources from the cost estimating and modelling literature
Tough competition	Al-Harbi et al. (1994), Wanous et al. (2004)
Type and size of contract	Al-Harbi et al. (1994), Wanous et al. (2004), Shash and El Khaldi (1992), Bowen and Edwards (1985)
Incomplete specifications	Al-Harbi et al. (1994)
incomplete project scope definition	Al-Harbi et al. (1994) , Flanagan and Norman (1983)
Unforeseeable changes in material prices	Al-Harbi et al. (1994), Raftery (1991), Ashworth (1999)
Changes in owner requirements	Al-Harbi et al. (1994), Al Momani (1996)
Current work load	Al-Harbi et al. (1994) , Wanous et al. (2004)
Errors in judgment by estimators	Al-Harbi et al. (1994) , Runeson (1988)
Inadequate production time data	Al-Harbi et al. (1994), Raftery (1991), Ashworth (1999)
Historical data for similar jobs	Al-Harbi et al. (1994) ,Flanagan and Norman (1983) , Morrison (1984)
Experience of estimators	Al-Harbi et al. (1994) , Wanous et al. (2004), Runeson (1988)
Project cost at awarding the contract	Al Momani (1996)
Variation orders	Al Momani (1996) , Al-Harbi et al. (1994)
Project final area in square metres	Al Momani (1996), Raftery (1991), Ashworth (1999)
Complete drawings and bidding documents	Al Momani (1996), Raftery (1991), Ashworth (1999)
Consistent specifications	Al Momani (1996), Wanous et al. (2004)
Implementation of a project cost system	Al Momani (1996) , Horner and Zakieh (1996)
Size of contractors/suppliers	Wanous et al. (2004), Raftery (1991), Ashworth (1999)
Previous experience of the contractor/supplier on the same type of project	Shash and El Khaldi (1992), Raftery (1991), Ashworth (1999)
Anticipated delays in periodic payments	Shash and El Khaldi (1992)
Type and size of project	Wanous et al. (2004), Shash and El Khaldi (1992), Bowen and Edwards (1985)
Project location	Wanous et al. (2004) , Shash and El Khaldi (1992), Salama et al. (2005)
Anticipated risks	Wanous et al. (2004), Turin (1973), Raftery (1991)

A number of scholars have been investigating the factors affecting the accuracy of the project cost estimates over the past 30 years. Shash and El Khaldi (1992) identified the factors affecting the accuracy of cost estimating. The main factors responsible for accuracy, irrespective of the size of contractors/suppliers were set in the following order: financial issues, bidding situations, project characteristics, the estimating process, previous experience of the contractor/supplier on the type of project, anticipated or frequent delays in periodic payments, type and size of contract and project location. Al-Harbi et al. (1994) studied the major problems facing cost estimators in preparing cost estimates and presented a number of factors in order of importance: tough competition, contract period, incomplete specifications, incomplete project scope definition, unforeseeable changes in material prices, changes in owner requirements, current work load, errors in judgment, inadequate production time data, lack of historical data for similar jobs and lack of experience.

To conclude this section a list was produced that collated the various factors identified in the literature as shown in Table 8.2.

8.8   Project budgeting

Once the project estimates and resource schedules have been finalised, the project budget is able to be developed. The project budget is the costs that the project manager is authorised to incur in fulfilling the project objectives. As shown in Figure 8.3, most of the costs incurred on a project will be during the execution phase when the required materials need to be purchased, equipment needs to be hired and sub-contractors need be employed. In comparison, at the definition phase, project expenditure is relatively minimal, as only a few people are involved in the project. The number of personnel gradually increases during the planning phase as the project team grows and levels off at the closure phase, as the project comes to an end.

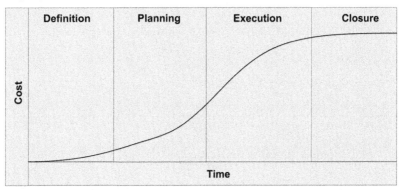

Figure 8.3: Project S-curve

▪ Cost baselines and project life cycle (PLC)

Cost estimating phases are clearly linked to the project life cycle. Typically, cost baselines can be divided into five categories.

1 In the pre-project and the early stages of the inception (initiation) phase, a ballpark figure is required for the strategic decision whether to go ahead with the project as part of the feasibility study. This is known as *order of magnitude* with an acceptable variation of ±25%.

2 Once the initiation phase is completed and an outline design is available an *indicative* cost estimate can be developed with an acceptable variation of ±15%.

3 By the completion of the design phase a *definitive* cost estimate can be produced with an acceptable variation of ±5%.

4 The fourth base line is the *tender price,* since this can vary from the aforementioned estimates, yet this is the actual cost that the owner will incur, in the case of external/extended project management systems.

5 The fifth baseline is a *dynamic* baseline that keeps moving with any variation order or changes in the scope of the project.

Project budgeting involves allocating the project cost estimates to individual activities over the duration of the project. This requires mapping the cost estimates to the project schedule in order to develop a **time phased budget**. The cost baseline is used to measure and monitor cost performance by determining variances between the estimated costs and actual expenditure, as shown in Figure 8.4. Tools for monitoring and control of the project variances are discussed in more detail in the following chapters.

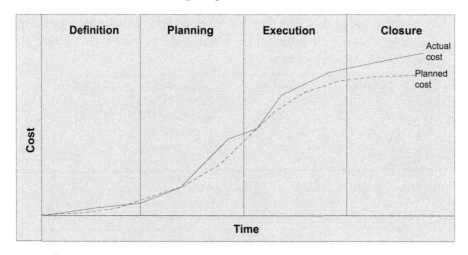

Figure 8.4: Project S-curve with planned and actual costs.

The other benefit of a time phased budget is that it allows the project manager and senior management to know in advance the level of expenditure required during each period of the project. It is unlikely that on projects with a significant sum, project funds will be sitting in an account for the project manager to draw on. Project funds form part of the normal accounting process of the organisation. As such, a project budget showing the cash flow needs to be created in order to ensure monies are available to contractors and suppliers, and to monitor the expenditure over the course of the project.

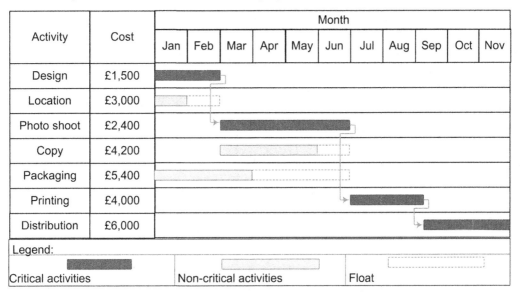

Activity	Cost	Month										
		Jan	Feb	Mar	Apr	May	Jun	Jul	Aug	Sep	Oct	Nov
Design	£1,500											
Location	£3,000											
Photo shoot	£2,400											
Copy	£4,200											
Packaging	£5,400											
Printing	£4,000											
Distribution	£6,000											

Legend:

Critical activities   Non-critical activities   Float

Figure 8.5: Gantt chart showing activity costs

Worked example 8.1: The Calendar project

By estimating the cost of each activity, then allocating costs for each month based on the project schedule, as shown in the Gantt chart in Figure 8.5, the cumulative costs of the activities are presented in the project S-curve, as shown in Figure 8.6, and the generated cash-flow is shown in Figure 8.7.

As demonstrated, the highest monthly expenditure is incurred from January to March. However, by using the slack time of non-critical activities, early expenditure can be reduced, whilst maintaining the project budget. Figure 8.8 shows the cash-flow when late finish (LF) of the Packaging activity is exploited.

8

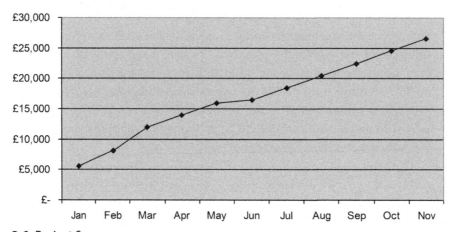

Figure 8.6: Project S-curve

Activity	Jan	Feb	Mar	Apr	May	Jun	Jul	Aug	Sep	Oct	Nov	Act. cost	Cum. Cost
Design	.75	.75										1.5	1.5
Location	3											3	4.5
Photo shoot			.6	.6	.6	.6						2.4	6.9
Copy			1.4	1.4	1.4							4.2	11.1
Packaging	1.8	1.8	1.8									5.4	16.5
Printing							2	2				4	20.5
Distribution									2	2	2	6	26.5
Total	5.55	2.55	3.8	2	2	.6	2	2	2	2	2		
Cumulative Cost	5.55	8.1	11.9	13.9	15.9	16.5	18.5	20.5	22.5	24.5	2.65		£26.5

Figure 8.7: Time-phased budget (000)

Activity	Jan	Feb	Mar	Apr	May	Jun	Jul	Aug	Sep	Oct	Nov	Act cost	Cum. cost
Design	0.75	0.75										1.50	1.50
Location	3.00											3.00	4.50
Photo shoot			0.60	0.60	0.60	0.60						2.40	6.90
Copy			1.40	1.40	1.40							4.20	11.10
Packaging			1.80	1.80	1.80							5.40	16.50
Printing							2.00	2.00				4.00	20.50
Distribution									2.00	2.00	2.00	6.00	26.50
Total	3.75	0.75	2.00	3.80	3.80	2.40	2.00	2.00	2.00	2.00	2.00		
Cumulative Cost	3.75	0.45	6.5	10.3	14.1	16.5	18.5	20.5	22.5	24.5	26.5		26.50

Figure 8.8: Time-phased budget exploiting the LF of activity "Packaging"

■ Budget provisions and contingencies

No matter how accurate we aim to be in our estimates, they are just estimates. These should include provisions for *risk* and *uncertainties*. The difference between the two terms lies in the ability to assign probability and impact in the case of risk events, whereas this is not possible in the case of uncertainties.

Budget provisions consider the risk events and other similar cost items where there is a possibility, but not a certainty, of occurrence. An example would be risk reserves which are typically produced during the risk response analysis whereby, in most cases the selected response strategy will be associated with costs.

Budget contingencies, on the other hand, take into consideration inadequate information, unknowns or unforeseen circumstances that could impact on the initial estimate. It is therefore prudent to allocate extra funds to the budget to pay for any uncertainties.

While there are no strict guidelines as to the amount required for the budget contingency, it should take into consideration the amount of exposure of the project, the accuracy of the information that has been provided in creating the budget and the trade-offs the project manager is expected to make. For, example a low risk project with a reasonable level of accurate information may have a contingency budget of 5%. Conversely, a high risk project, with a great deal of uncertainty should have a contingency budget of 10-15%. What must be made certain is that this budget is used for contingency, and is not an excuse for poor estimating and poor project control. If the funds budgeted for provisions or contingencies were not used, then by the closing of the project these are added to the project overall profit or surplus.

Summary

In this chapter the key concepts of project cost estimating and budgeting were presented and discussed using examples. The various stages of cost estimating, including a comparison between the macro and micro approaches, have been discussed. The chapter provided a brief discussion on the different cost items and various methods used in estimating project cost, in the context of enhancing the accuracy of the project cost estimates. In addition, the section on budgeting illustrates how to construct a time phased project budget taking into consideration the relevant provisions and contingencies, and draw the S-Curve based on the given resource constraints that will guide the project time scheduling. Finally, the different bidding strategies are discussed with emphasis on the impact on project final cost.

End of chapter review questions

Choose the most suitable answer. Only one should be selected. (Answers on page 177.)

1 Macro-level estimates refers to

　a) The cost estimates for major projects that typically large in size

　b) The estimates produced for strategic national projects

　c) Those produced in a top-down approach at the conception phase

　d) Estimates produced during the planning phase using WBS

2 Micro-level cost estimates refer to

　a) The cost estimates for major projects that are typically large in size

　b) The estimates produced for strategic national projects

　c) Those produced in a top-down approach at the conception phase

　d) Estimates produced during the planning phase using WBS

3 The magnitude of variation in project cost will not depend on

　a) The size of the project

　b) The work breakdown structure

　c) The duration of the project

　d) The estimating approach used

4 In a project budget, the term risk reserves refers to

　a) Any contingencies within the project

　b) The cost required to respond to any contingencies

　c) A provision for whatever may go wrong

　d) The provision for the planned risk responses

5 Which of the following factors is least likely to jeopardize the bidder's chances?

　a) The bidding strategy of competitors

　b) The cost estimates produced by the client

　c) If the bidder is following a back-loading strategy

　d) If the bidder is following a front-loading strategy

6 Produced by the end of the planning phase, the term S- curve refers to

　a) The project expenditure curve

　b) The project net cash flow curve

　c) The project actual cost curve

　d) All of the above

References

Al-Harbi, K. M., Johnston, D. W., & Fayadh, H. (1994). Building Construction detailed estimating practices in Saudi Arabia. *Journal of Construction Engineering and Management*, ASCE, **120** (4).

Al-Momani, A. (1996). Construction Cost Prediction for Pubic School Buildings in Jordan. *Construction Management and Economics*, **14** (4), 311-17.

Akintoye, A. (2000). Analysis of factors influencing project cost estimating practice. *Construction Mangement and Economics*, **18**, 77-89.

Akintoye, A., & Fitzgerald, E. (2000). A survey of current cost estimating practices in the UK. *Construction Mangement and Economics*, **18**, 161-172.

Ashworth, A., & Hogg, K. (2007). *Willis's Practice and Procedure for the Quantity Surveyor* (12th ed.). Oxford: Blackwell.

Ashworth, A. (1983). *Building Economics and Cost Control*. London: Butterworths.

Ashworth, A. (1994). *Cost Studies of Buildings* (2nd ed.). Longman Scientific & Technical.

Ashworth, A., & Skitmore, R. M. (1983). *Accuracy in Estimating*. CIOB Occasional, paper No. 27 .

Ashworth, A., Neale, R. H., & Trimble, E. G. (1980). An analysis of some builders' estimating. *The Quantity Surveyor*, **36** (4), pp. 65, 70.

Boussabaine, A. H. (1996). The use of artificial neural networks in construction management: A review. *Construction Mangement and Economics*, **14**, 427-436.

Boussabaine, H. A., & Kaka, A. P. (1998). A neura network approach for cost-flow forecasting. *Construction Management and Economics*, **16** (4), 471-9.

Bowen, P. A., & Edwards, P. A. (1985). Cost modelling and price forecasting: practice and theory in perspective. *Construction Mangement and Economics*, **3**, 199-215.

Bowen, P. (1982). Problems in econometric cost modelling. *The Quantity Surveyor*

Brandon, P. S. (1982). *Building Cost Research*. London: E&FN Spon.

Brandon, P. S., & Newton, S. (1986). Improving the forecast. *Chartered Quantity Surveyor*, **14**, 26.

Flanagan, R., & Norman, G. (1983). The accuracy and monitoring of quantity surveyors' price forecasts in building work. *Construction Mangement and Economics*, **1** (2), 157-80.

Flanagan, R., & Tate, B. (1997). *Cost Control in Building Design*. Oxford: Blackwell Science

8

Gray, C. F. & Larson, E. W. (2008) *Project Management: The Managerial Process*, New York, McGraw-Hill Irwin

Horner, M., & Zakieh, R. (1996). Characteristic items, a new approach to pricing and controlling construction projects. *Construction Mangement and Economics* , **14**, 241, 252.

Kirkham, R. (2007). *Ferry and Brandon's Cost Planning of Buildings* (8th ed.). Blackwell Publishing.

Maher, M. (1997) *Cost Accounting: Creating Value for Management* Chicago, Irwin.

Morrison, N. (1984). The accuracy of the quantity surveyors' cost estimating. *Construction Mangement and Economics*, **2**, 57-75.

Newton, S. (1991). Agenda for cost modelling. *Construction Mangement and Economics*, **9**, 97-112.

Pinto, J. K. (2007) *Project Management: Achieving Competitive Advantage*, New Jersey Pearson Education Ltd.

Raftery, J. (1998). From Ptolemy to Heisenberg: quantitative models and reality. *Construction Management and Economics*, **16**, 295-302.

Raftery, J. (1991). Models for Construction Cost and Price Forecasting. Proceedings of the first RICS National Research Conference. E & FN Spon, Chapman Hall.

Raftery, J. (1991). *Principles of Building Economics*. Oxford: BSP.

Raftery, J., McGeorge, D., & Walters, M. (1997). Breaking up methological monopolies. *Construction Mangement and Economics*, **15** (3), 291-7.

Runeson, K. G. (1988). Methodology and method for price level forecasting in the building industry. *Construction Management and Economics*, **6** (1), 49-55.

Salama, M, Kaka, A and Leishman, C (2005) The relationship between the performance of the economy and the cost of construction of educational buildings in Egypt: a preliminary study. In: Khosrowshahi, F (Ed.), 21st Annual ARCOM Conference, 7-9 September, SOAS, University of London. Association of Researchers in Construction Management, Vol. 2, 731-40.

Salama, M, Kaka, A and Leishman, C (2006) Investigating the effect of macroeconomic variables on the cost of construction of schools in Egypt In: Amaratunga et al (ed), 6th International post graduate research conference, 6-7 April Delft, Netherlands

Salama, M, AL Sharif, F, Kaka, A and Leishman, C (2006) Cost modelling for standardised design projects. In: Boyd, D (Ed.), 22nd Annual ARCOM Conference, 4-6 September 2006, Birmingham, UK. Association of Researchers in Construction Management, Vol. 1, 531-40.

Shash, A. A., & AL-Khaldi, Z. S. (1992). The production of accurate cost estimates in Saudi Arabia. *Cost Engineering*, **34** (2), 15-24.

Skitmore, M., & Gunner, J. (1999). Comparative analysis of pre-bid forecasting of building price based on Singapore data. *Construction Mangement and Economics*, **17**, 635-646.

Skitmore, M., & Ng, T. (2001). Australian time-cost analysis: Statistical analysis of intertemporal trends. *Construction Management and Economics*, **19** (3), 455-58.

Standish (2004) *CHAOS report*. West Yarmouth, MA, Standish Group.

Wanous, M., Boussabaine, H., & Lewis, J. (2004). A Neurofuzzy decision support model for mark-up estimation. 20thAnnual ARCOM Conference 1-3 September 2004 Heriot Watt University , pp. 153-62

Answers to end of chapter review questions

1 c), 2 d), 3 b), 4 d), 5 c), 6 a)

8

9   Project Scheduling

Mohamed Salama and Amos Haniff

Learning objectives

By the time you have completed this chapter you should be able to:

- ☐ Understand the concept of project time planning and scheduling.
- ☐ Compare and contrast logic driven and resource driven scheduling.
- ☐ Draw a network and a Gantt chart to illustrate a simple work package.
- ☐ Understand the concept of Critical Path Method (CPM).
- ☐ Identify the critical activities, critical path and total duration of the network.
- ☐ Calculate the early and late times for each activity.
- ☐ Compare and contrast deterministic and probabilistic scheduling.
- ☐ Appreciate the need for rescheduling at different stages of the PLC
- ☐ Apply the concept of Crashing as an example of trade-off analysis
- ☐ Understand the difference between concurrent engineering and fast track.

Introduction

Delivering the project by the imposed deadline is a primary objective in many projects and is typically one of the project constraints. Therefore, the ability to develop and manage the project schedule is a critical competence for any project manager. Scheduling projects involves defining the duration of activities, determining the optimum start and completion date of activities and calculating the cost of accelerating projects in a traditional manner. In some cases, in order to reduce the calculated total duration of the project, it is imperative to explore different options such as phased concurrent engineering and fast tracking. This chapter explains the stages in developing a project schedule, from developing and analysing a project network to creating the Gantt charts required for the project plan. The chapter also discusses the concept of project crashing as an example of trade-off analysis between time and cost.

9.1   Project scheduling

The statement of work which is derived from the scope statement is the first building block in project scheduling. The statement of work includes the details of the project deliverables that can be divided into phases, elements and work packages, by breaking down the bigger chunks of work into simpler forms.

■ Work breakdown structure (WBS)

The work breakdown structure is a useful technique that can be applied to any complex structure take it into its simplest form. This can be applied to all types of work including, but not limited to, projects. Typically, in projects the WBS is deliverable based and should have a list of tasks or activities in order to facilitate more accurate time and cost estimates. In addition, the WBS can be a very useful tool in risk management during the risk identification stage. Ideally, the WBS should reach five to seven levels. At the higher levels of the WBS, projects can be broken down into phases, then elements then work packages. The lowest level will reflect the activities which will feed into building the project schedule. At the activity level, the WBS should reflect deliverables rather than processes, which might be acceptable at higher level. So for example, at the work package level, 'design' can be an appropriate title, but at the lowest level of this work package, the deliverables should be the output of this design process such as drawings, specifications and quantities. An example of a WBS for a software project is shown in Figure 9.1.

Project scheduling includes all the processes required to accomplish timely completion of a project. Scheduling processes include:

- **Activity definition:** Determining the list of activities needed to accomplish each project deliverable.

- **Activity sequencing:** Determining the order in which each activity should be executed and identifying the dependences among the activities.

- **Activity timing:** Calculating the duration of each activity

- **Resource allocation:** Determining the level of resources required to execute each activity.

■ **Schedule control:** Controlling changes to the project schedule. These are the timetables and charts required to monitor and control the project activities. There are two types of project schedules: Project network diagrams and Gantt Charts

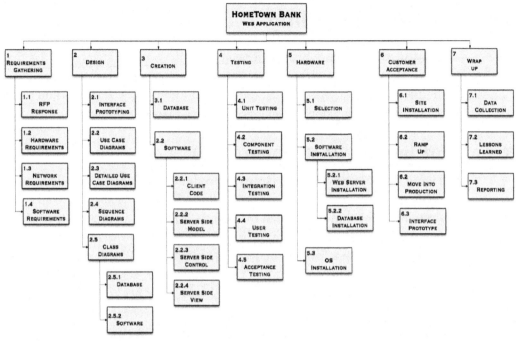

Figure 9.1: WBS for a software project. Source : Emily Wadsworth, (2016) http://diagram.cf/w/wbs-example-software-project.html

9.2 Project network diagrams

A project network diagram is a schematic representation of the project, developed from the WBS. It identifies all the activities within the project, the start and completion time of each activity, the logical sequence in which activities should be performed, the dependent activities and the critical activities that define the project duration.

Activities within the network diagram are those tasks that must be performed to complete the project. They usually refer to the work packages at the lowest level of the WBS, as these are the first level of deliverables that are individually planned, resourced and priced. However, as the WBS is only broken down to work package level, the network diagram is the perfect tool for identifying the activities within each work package and determining the logical sequence in which they should be performed.

■ Types of network diagrams

A network diagram is created from a series of **nodes** and **arrows.** Arrows identify the flow of the network, whereas the nodes are the connecting points for each arrow.

There are two types of network diagram:

- **Activity on the Arrow (AOA):** Within this type of network, the activity is represented by the arrow and node represents the start and end-point of each activity.

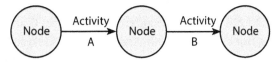

Figure 9.2: Activities on the Arrow

- **Activity on the Node (AON):** In this method the arrows identify the sequence of activities and each node represent an individual activity, as shown in Figure 9.3.

Figure 9.3: Activities on the Node

While AOA is still used by some project managers, AON is the preferred modern method of drawing the network. This is because AON identifies all the attributes of an activity enabling transition of the network to a **Gantt chart.** Moreover, it is the AON method that is the common type of network used in project management software and therefore demonstrated in this text book.

■ Activity relationships

There are two basic types of activity relationships in any project network diagram.

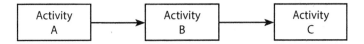

Figure 9.4: Activities in series

- **Activities in series:** When the project activities are executed one after the other. The example in Figure 9.4 shows that Activity C can not start until Activity B has been completed and Activity B can not start until Activity A is complete. In other words, Activity C is **dependent** on Activity B being complete and Activity B is **dependent** on Activity C being complete.

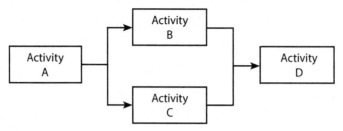

Figure 9.5: Activities in parallel

- **Activities in parallel:** When the project activities are executed simultaneously. This method saves time on the project. The example in Figure 9.5 shows that Activity D is dependent on Activities C and B being complete. Activity D can not start until both Activity B and C have been complete. Activity B and C can be performed at the same, but are both dependent on Activity A being complete before they can start.

■ Estimating activity durations

The value of a project network is highly dependent on the accuracy of the activity duration estimates. High quality in the duration estimates is essential, as most project management tools are dependent on this. For example, project scheduling, project costing, resource schedules and project control all use activity durations as a variable. Pinto (2007) and Hill et al (2000) identify a number of methods for estimating the duration of an activity within a project network:

- **Past experience:** Historical data derived from previous projects is always an ideal source for gaining knowledge. However, this does have its limitations as processes change through developments and we now have faster methods of working.

- **Expert opinion:** Expert judgement can be very accurate, especially from someone who has performed a similar or the same task on numerous occasions. However, it fails to provide a quantitative and objective analysis of the factors that effect duration and through experience experts become faster at performing a task.

- **Pilot testing:** An expensive method of determining project duration, but still used on major technology and research projects.

- **Parametric approaches:** Sophisticated mathematical models, such as the COCOMO model proposed by Boehm (1981) computes the effort and durations of the total project, using regression formula. Developed for software development, this is far too complex to be used on average projects.

■ **Statistical analysis:** A less sophisticated, but highly effective approach is to use probability analysis. This the preferred approach for dealing with uncertainty and minimising risk within the duration estimating process. It can also be used to complement other methods, such as past experience, expert opinion and pilot testing.

Logic driven versus resource driven scheduling

Once the activity duration is estimated, project managers would typically start planning activities as early as possible, which is a logic driven approach. Adding a logic sequence to the list of activities will yield a dependency table that includes activity duration and dependencies. This table is used to draw a network diagram and a Gantt chart. The latter can be used to project the required resources at any point in time. Comparing the required routes to the available resources will help to identify the peaks where the required exceeds the available resources. Resource levelling and resource shuffling techniques can be used to reconcile the required with the available resources. This can change the start and finish dates of some activities and in some cases may lead to some changes in the sequences (dependencies). The modified schedule will be resource driven rather than logic driven.

Constructing the network diagram

There are five basic rules for constructing a network diagram that must be followed, (Gray and Larson, 2008):

1 Network schedules typically flow from left to right.

2 An activity cannot start until all the preceding connected activities have been finished.

3 Arrows on a network indicate precedence and flow. As a rule, they should not cross over each other.

4 Each activity should have a unique identification number, which should be a larger number than the activities that precede it.

5 Each activity is only considered once within the network.

The starting point for creating the network is to list all the activities required for the project in a logical order. This is normally done in the format of a **logic table**, which identifies the dependent activities and the duration of each activity.

Example 9.1

Let us consider the work package of producing a simple marketing brochure. The brochure must first be designed. Whilst the content of the brochure is being written, the photo shoot can be performed. Once the publisher has a copy of the photographs and content, the layout of the brochure can be produced. Finally this is sent for publication.

Table 9.1: Brochure logic table

Activity ID	Activity	Dependency	Duration (days)
A	Design brochure	None	2
B	Write copy	A	3
C	Photo shoot	A	2
D	Layout brochure	B,C	2
E	Print brochure	D	4

The network diagram will therefore be as follows:

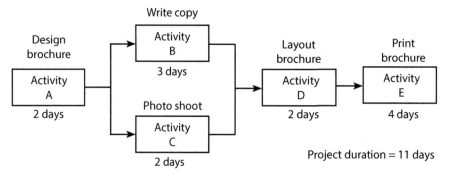

Figure 9.6: Brochure network diagram

Note that Activity B and Activity C are performed in parallel, thus saving time on the project. If these activities were performed in series, the time it taken to complete the 'Photo shoot' would be add a further 2 days to the project duration. The project duration is calculated by the sum of all the activity durations along the longest path through the network, which in this example is Activities A,B,D and E. The total project duration is therefore 11 days.

The path through the network with the longest duration is termed the **'critical path'.** Activities on the critical path determine the project duration. Critical activities have no **float** (or slack) time, in that any delay in the critical activities will delay the project as a whole.

Class discussion:

What would be the impact on the project duration if the photo shoot took 1 day to complete?

What would be the impact on the duration if the photo shoot took 5 days to complete?

The critical path method

The critical path method (CPM) calculates the shortest time in which a project can be completed, by identifying those activities on the critical path. This enables the project manager to control and manipulate the project duration by recognising which activities can be delayed without impacting on the project duration and which activities will effect the duration if they are delayed. To do this the node is labelled as follows:

- **Earliest start (ES):** The earliest time an activity can start, assuming all preceding activities have been complete.

- **Earliest finish (EF):** The earliest time an activity can be complete, assuming all preceding activities have been complete.

- **Duration:** The length of time an activity will take to complete

- **Latest start (LS):** The latest time an activity can start to start in order to meet the project deadline

- **Latest finish time (LF):** The latest time an activity can finish in order to meet the project deadline

- **Float:** The amount of time an activity can be delayed without affecting the project deadline

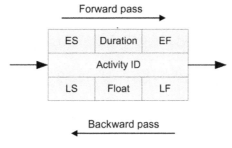

Figure 9.7: Activity node

There are two stages to the critical path method:

- **Forward pass:** Concerns the top level of the activity node. The forward pass calculates the overall project duration by determining the EST and EFT for each activity. Within this stage the following equation is used:

    EF = ES + Duration

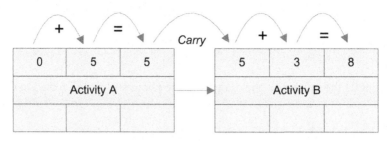

Figure 9.8: The forward pass

Note in Figure 9.8, the EF for Activity B is the same as ES for Activity B. This is because Activity B can not start before Activity A is complete.

■ **Backward pass**: Concerns the bottom level of the activity node. The backward pass identifies the activities on the critical path by determining the LS and the LF of each activity. Activities on the critical path are those activities with a zero float. Within this stage the following equations are used:

LS = LF – Duration

Float = EF – LF

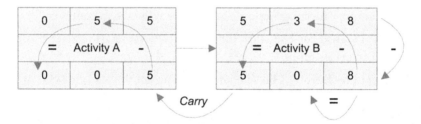

Figure 9.9: The backward pass

Example 9.2

Draw an AON network diagram using the following logic table.

Table 9.2: Example 9.2 Logic table

Activity	Dependency	Duration (weeks)
A	-	3
B	A	2
C	A	3
D	C, B	5
E	B	7
F	E, D	5

The first step in creating the network diagram is to sequence the project activities according to the dependences identifies in the logic table set out in 9.2. In this example activities B, E and C, D are parallel activities. Also activities D and F have more than one dependency, which result in a three paths through the network, as shown in Figure 9.10.

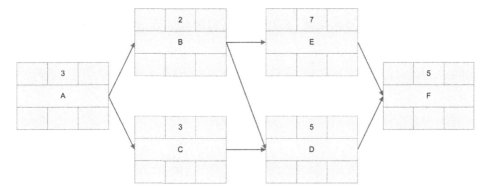

Figure 9.10: Activity sequence

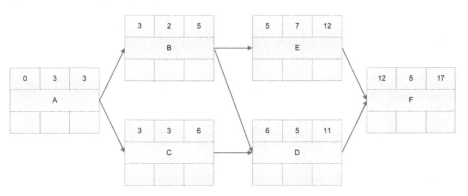

Figure 9.11: Forward pass

The forward pass, shown in Figure 9.11, begins with the earliest starting time of the project. This must be 0 weeks, as a project can not start any earlier. As the duration of activity A is 3 weeks, the earliest time the activity can finish (EF) will be week 3. As activities B and C can not start until activity A is complete, the earliest start time (ES) for these activities will be week 3. Note that activity D is dependent on both activity B and activity C. As the activity can not start until both these activities are complete, the ES for D will be determined by the longer of the early finish times, which in this case is 6 weeks. Similarly, activity F can not start until both D and E are complete. As the longer of the early finish times is E, the EF for activity F will be week 12. The total project duration will therefore be 17 weeks.

The backward pass starts with the last activity on the network, which in Figure 9.12 is activity F. The latest time the project can finish must be same as the project duration.

Therefore the LF for activity F will be 17 weeks. By deducting the activity duration of 5 weeks, the latest time activity F can start (LS) will be week 12 (17 – 5 = 12). As activities E and D can not finish after activity F starts, the latest time both these activities can finish (LF) will be week 12. Deducting the durations from the latest finish times will result in the latest start times (LS) for D as being week 6 and E as being week 5.

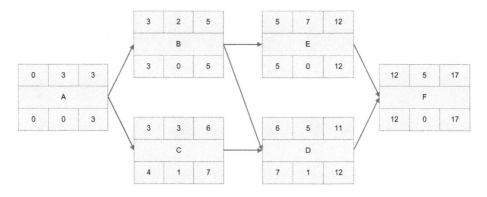

Figure 9.12: The backward pass

Note that activities D and E are both dependent on activity B. As activity B can not finish after D and E starts, the LF for B is determined by the shorter of the latest finish times, which in this case is week 5. Similarly, activity A can not finish after both B and C are start. As the shorter of the early finish times is B, the LF for activity A will be week 3. If drawn correctly, the LS for the starting activity will be equal to 0 weeks.

The critical path is computed by identifying those activities with a zero float. This is calculated by deducting the earliest finish time (EF) from the latest finish time (LF) time, or when ES = ES and EF = LF. In Figure 9.12 the critical activities will are A, B, E and F. These activities have no flexibility and any delays on these will delay the project as a whole.

■ Project Evaluation and Review Technique (PERT)

In project management, the use of probability analysis to determine the duration of an activity is referred to as **Project Evaluation and Review Technique** (PERT). In modern project management the terms CPM and PERT appear to be used interchangeably, with both referring to drawing an AON network. PERT uses three estimates of the project duration to determine the average project duration:

1 **The optimistic time (a):** The estimated activity duration if all factors that determine the project duration goes well.

2 **The pessimistic time (b):** The estimated activity duration if all factors that determine the project duration goes badly.

3 The most likely time (m): The estimated activity duration if all factors that determine the project duration are normal.

If we assume that the optimistic time (a) and the pessimistic time (b) were evenly distributed around the most likely time (m), a normal distribution would occur, as shown if Figure 9.13.

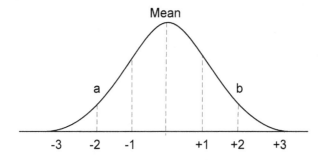

Figure 9.13: The Normal distribution

However, it is very unlikely that the optimistic time and the pessimistic time will be symmetrical around the mean. Instead the distribution will be asymmetrical or 'beta' as it is commonly called.

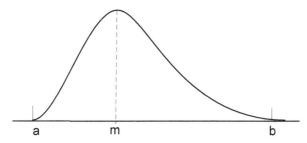

Figure 9.14: Beta distribution

The difference between the most optimistic time (a) and the most pessimistic time (b) will be six standard deviations, with three standard deviations either side of the mean (m). In a beta distribution, a weighting of one-third is applied to (a) and (b), with two-thirds being applied to the most-likely time. The estimated time for the activity (Te) is therefore calculated as:

$$Te = \frac{a + 4m + b}{6}$$

Example 9.3

Calculate the mean duration (d) for the following activities and draw an AON network diagram using the following logic table.

Table 9.3: Example 9.3 logic table

Activity	Dependency	Optimistic time (a)	Pessimistic time (b)	Most likely time (m)
A	-	7	9	8
B	A	2	8	5
C	A	3	9	6
D	B, C	1	3	2
E	D	7	15	8

To calculate the estimated time for each activity (Te)

Te activity A	$= (7 + (4\times8) + 9)/6$	$= \mathbf{8}$
Te activity B	$= (2 + (4\times5) + 8)/6$	$= \mathbf{5}$
Te activity C	$= (3 + (4\times6) + 9)/6$	$= \mathbf{6}$
Te activity D	$= (1 + (4\times2) + 3)/6$	$= \mathbf{2}$
Te activity E	$= (7 + (4\times8) + 15)/6$	$= \mathbf{9}$

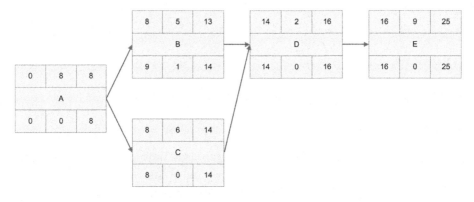

Figure 9.15: Network diagram

9.3 Gantt charts

Designed by Henry Gantt (Gantt, 1916) at the beginning of the twentieth century, the Gantt chart was originally used to monitor progress in the production of shipbuilding. Since then the Gantt chart has become the standard method of presenting project scheduling and is used daily within project management.

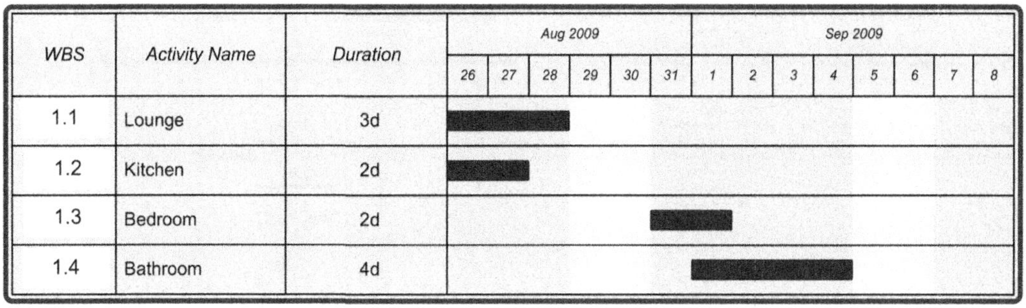

WBS	Activity Name	Duration	Aug 2009						Sep 2009							
			26	27	28	29	30	31	1	2	3	4	5	6	7	8
1.1	Lounge	3d	███	███	███											
1.2	Kitchen	2d	███	███												
1.3	Bedroom	2d							███	███						
1.4	Bathroom	4d									███	███	███	███			

Figure 9.16: Typical Gantt chart

A Gantt chart is basically a bar chart, with a horizontal timescale, that lists the activities down one side of the sheet, and has bars drawn to represent the activities from start to finish. Each activity within the Gantt chart is a deliverable of the WBS and therefore uses the WBS code for cross referencing. Activity names and durations are also presented for clarity, as are the actual dates of when an activity is to be complete. The simple nature of the Gantt chart makes it a useful tool for discussing the project schedules, as most people can understand them. The Gantt chart is therefore the main document referred to within the project plan when describing scheduling issues.

However, despite the widespread use, there are a number of limitations in the use of Gantt charts. In the first instance Gantt charts do not allow for the detailed analysis and manipulation of a project in the same way as network diagrams. They tend to lack the creative flexibility that the network offers. Furthermore, showing interdependencies and identifying the critical path on a Gantt chart do present difficulties. The biggest drawback of Gantt charts is that they require their software and subsequently specialist training. Despite this, software programmes such as Microsoft Project is relatively easy to use, and attempt to take into account the dependences between activities, as shown in Figure 9.17.

9

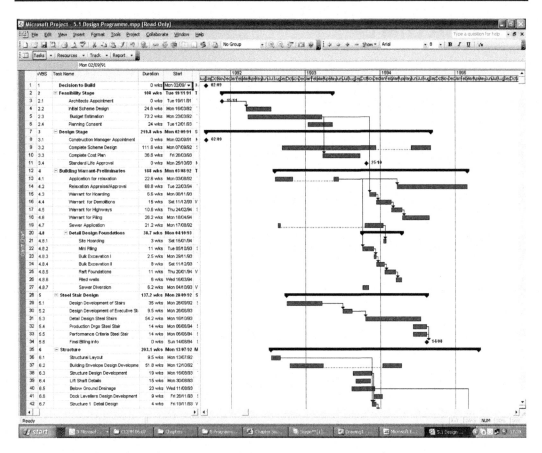

Figure 9.17: Screenshot of MS Project

■ Network to Gantt chart

Project managers who prefer to maintain control of the project tend to use the network diagram for calculating the project duration on each work package and for identifying the most efficient sequence for executing each work package. The Gantt is used to control each work package within the project and present the schedule to the project team.

Figure 9.18 demonstrates how the network diagram is translated into a Gantt Chart. The solid bars in the Gantt chart represent the earliest start times within the network. These are the activities on the top level of the node. The dotted bars represent the float of the non-critical activities. These are the activities on the bottom level of the node. It is useful to show the float times within the Gantt chart as the amount of flexibility can be clearly demonstrated.

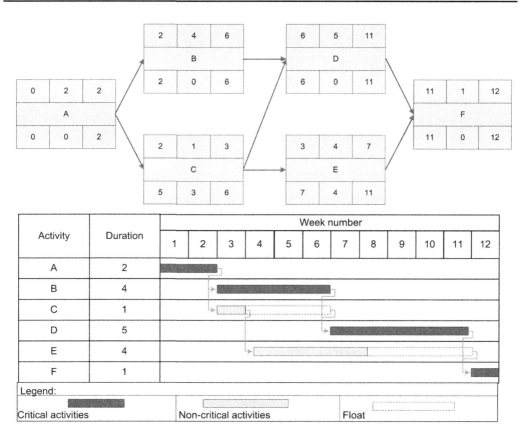

Figure 9.18: Network to Gantt chart

Milestones

Another feature of the Gantt chart is the milestone. This is represented by a diamond, as shown in activities D and G of Figure 9.19 and has a zero duration.

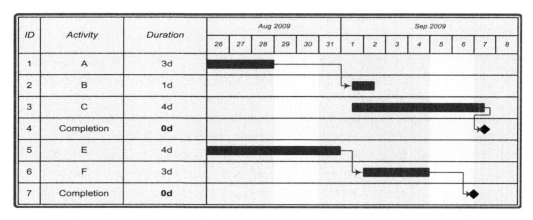

Figure 9.19: Milestones

A milestone is a predefined scheduled event in the project that signifies the completion of major deliverable. For example, the achievement of each deliverable at the second level of the WBS could be considered a milestone. A milestone therefore has no effort associated to it, although attaining a milestone does involve the completion of a number of activities. The purpose of the milestone is to mark key progress on the project. As a milestone represents a fixed point on the schedule, there can be no doubt at to whether the deliverable that the milestone represents has been completed or not. A benefit of defining millstones is that they allow for a summary of the project schedule, as shown in Table 9.4.

Table 9.4: Milestone schedule

Milestone Schedule		
WBS	Milestone	Scheduled date
1.1	Reception	11.03.09
2.1	Front office East	22.04.09
3.1	Front office West	12.06.09
4.1	Central Galley	08.08.09
5.1	Executive Office	06.11.09

Case study: Heriot-Watt Project Management Conference

Project scheduling tools and techniques are applicable to all types of project, including service projects such as events. Event management is a growing niche in the context of project management. A typical example of events is exhibitions, seminars and conferences. Heriot-Watt University - Dubai Campus has decided to organize a research one day conference in project management in March 2017. The conference is planned to take place on a Saturday. However, in March the teaching activities for the second semester are still on-going, and there are some classes running on Saturdays. The scope of the conference includes presentations of academic peer-reviewed papers, a plenary session and a keynote speaker-led session.

The day starts at 8:30am with registration, followed at 9:30am by an hour keynote speaker session. At 11am the paper presentation sessions spanning five different tracks start in parallel in different rooms. After lunch, participants attend a plenary session from 2:00pm till 3:30pm. The rest of the afternoon and early evening is dedicated to presentation of papers till 6:00pm. In addition, the catering service includes tea, coffee and soft drinks at 8:30am for an hour during registration then another coffee break at 10:30am, lunch at 1:00pm then another coffee break at 3:30pm and finally dinner at 6:30 pm. This year the conference has attracted a significant number of good papers. The total number of presentations to be scheduled has reached 100 papers.

In groups of four, making reasonable suggestions, produce a time schedule for the programme of the conference. Draw a Gantt chart a network diagram for the programme. Discuss the main constraints that need to be considered while scheduling the conference in general and the programme in particular. Discuss, providing reasonable justification, whether the produced schedule is logic driven or resource driven.

9.4 Project rescheduling

Sometime it is necessary to achieve an earlier completion date for the project than originally scheduled. There could be a number of reasons for this:

- Market forces, such as increased competition or market demand, has resulted in the project being required earlier than anticipated.

- The project start date has been delayed, but the completion date remains the same.

- Slippage in the project during execution, resulting in the project potentially missing the deadline

- The original project duration not achieving the desired completion date.

The project manager therefore needs to adopt appropriate tools to achieve an earlier completion time for the project. There are two methods the project manager can use to accelerate a project: fast-tracking and crashing

■ Project fast-tracking

Fast-tracking is a scheduling approach whereby the project is accelerated by overlapping activities that would normally be executed consecutively. Instead of waiting for a dependent activity to be complete before starting the next one, the successor activity starts at the same time as the dependent activity or part-way through.

For example, consider a project where the full design of a component is followed by manufacture of the component. If the duration of each activity takes five weeks, the total project duration will be 10 weeks as shown in Figure 9.20.

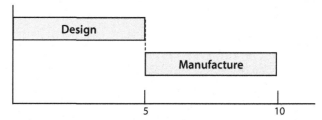

Figure 9.20: Consecutive activities

By splitting the design activity into phases, the manufacture of the component can start earlier. This way the design and manufacture are being partly performed in parallel, as shown in Figure 9.21.

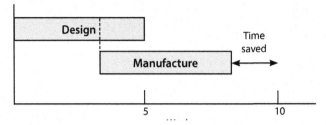

Figure 9.21: Project fast tracking

Despite the process of fast tracking being used frequently on projects with a short duration, it does carry significant risks. In the first instance, overlapping activities in this manner removes the slack from within the project and delays will impact on the project completion time. Second, it requires very close coordination as the predecessors of dependent activities must be complete to a sufficient stage before the dependent activities can begin. This is a common problem when fast tracking and often results in projects running into problems and will inevitably have an effect on the quality of the project outcome.

■   Project crashing

Sometimes it is necessary to make a trade-off between the project objectives. As discussed in Chapter 1, a trade-off or compromise can be made between cost and quality, time and quality or cost and time. This final trade-off is referred to as project crashing.

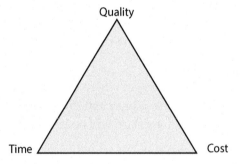

Figure 9.22: Trade-off between objectives

Project crashing involves reducing the duration of certain activities in order to reduce the overall project duration. There are two methods in which the activity durations can be reduced, which both incur additional costs:

1 **Extend the working day:** In this case additional costs will be incurred through overtime.

2 **Employ additional resources:** In this case additional costs will be incurred through the additional people, equipment or materials required to execute the activity in a shorter timeframe.

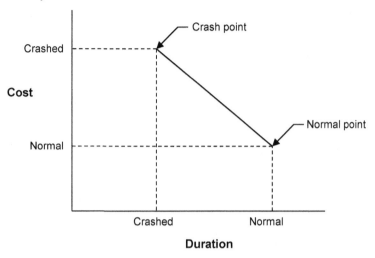

Figure 9.23: Crash slope

Before we can start to crash the project, we must first determine which activities within the project to crash, the sequence in which the crashing exercise should be performed and the additional cost of each activity as a result of the crashing process.

Figure 9.23 illustrates the relationship between the normal point of an activity and the crash point. Note how the cost increases as the duration of the activity is reduced. The crash point represents the minimum time in which an activity can be executed and the maximum cost of the activity.

Analysis of the crash slope enables the project manager to draw comparisons across each project activity. A shallow angle of the cost slope would suggest a relatively low cost per unit of time. Whereas a sharp rise in the cost slope would suggest a relatively expensive cost per unit of time.

In general, those activities with the lowest cost per unit of time are the activities that are crashed first. This is because project crashing should be performed in the most economical sequence. The cost per unit of time is determined by the following calculation:

$$\text{Crash slope} = \frac{\text{Crash cost} - \text{Normal cost}}{\text{Normal duration} - \text{Crash duration}}$$

Example 9.4

From the following logic table, reduce the project duration by 4 weeks in the most economical method and determine the project cost after each crash.

Table 9.4: Example 9.4 Logic table

Activity	Dependency	Normal Duration (weeks)	Normal Cost (£)	Crash Duration (weeks)	Crash Cost (£)
A	-	2	20	1	50
B	A	4	30	1	60
C	A	3	10	2	20
D	A	2	10	1	40
E	B, D, C	3	10	1	20
F	E	4	10	3	40
			90		

To calculate the cost of crashing each activity, the crash cost equation is applied:

Activity A $= £40$ per week $= \dfrac{60 - 20}{2 - 1}$ $= \dfrac{£40}{1}$

Activity B $= £10$ per week $= \dfrac{60 - 30}{4 - 1}$ $= \dfrac{£30}{3}$

Activity C $= £10$ per week $= \dfrac{20 - 10}{3 - 2}$ $= \dfrac{£10}{1}$

Activity D $= £30$ per week $= \dfrac{40 - 10}{2 - 1}$ $= \dfrac{£30}{1}$

Activity E $= £5$ per week $= \dfrac{20 - 10}{3 - 1}$ $= \dfrac{£10}{2}$

Activity F $= £30$ per week $= \dfrac{40 - 10}{4 - 3}$ $= \dfrac{£30}{1}$

Table 9.5: Cost of crashing each activity

Activity	Crash cost per week (£)
A	40
B	10
C	10
D	30
E	5
F	30

The calculation suggest that the least expensive activity to crash would be activity E at £5 per week, followed by activities B and C at £10 per week. Activity D and F are the next least expensive activities at £30 per week, followed by activity A at £40 per week.

However, there is little point in crashing non-critical activities as this would make no difference to the project duration. The next stage therefore to draw an AON network in order to determine the critical activities.

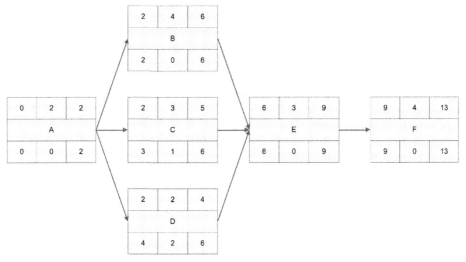

Figure 9.24: Network at the normal point

Normal Point: Project Duration = 13 weeks

Project Cost   = £90.00

From the network diagram it can be determined that activities A, B, E and F are the critical activities. The lowest cost of these activities is Activity E, which can be crashed by a maximum of 2 weeks.

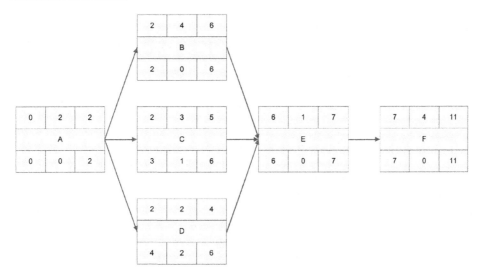

Figure 9.25: Network at Crash 1

The duration of activity E now becomes 1 week, with the project duration being reduced by 2 weeks. The additional cost of the project will be £10. Thus:

Crash 1: Crash activity E by 2 weeks at cost of £5 per week
    Revised Project Duration   = 11 weeks
    Revised Project Cost   = £100.00

The next critical activity with the least cost is activity B, which can be reduced by a maximum of 3 weeks. However, as Activity E is dependent on activities B, C and D we should only crash activity B by 1 week in this stage.

The duration of activity B now becomes 3 weeks, with the project duration being reduced by 1 week. The additional cost of the project will be £10. Thus:

Crash 2: Crash activity B by 1 week at cost of £10
    Revised Project Duration   = 10 weeks
    Revised Project Cots   = £110.00

Note the network now has two critical paths: A,B,E,F and A,C,E,F. As a result of crashing activity B, activity C has now become critical. The cost of crashing activity A or F will be £30 per week each, whereas, the cost of crashing B and C together will be £20 per week. This is therefore the cheapest option.

The duration of activity B and activity C now becomes 2 weeks, with the project duration being reduced by 1 week. The additional cost of the project will be £20. Thus:

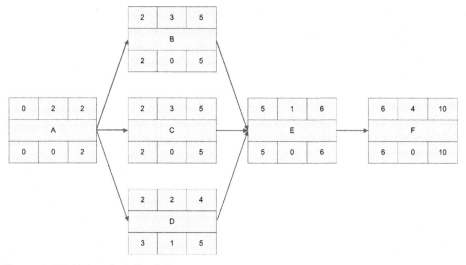

Figure 9.26: Network at Crash 2

Crash 3: Crash activity B by 1 week at cost of £10
    and   Crash activity C by 1 week at cost of £10
        Revised Project Duration   = 9 weeks
        Revised Project Cost   = £130.00

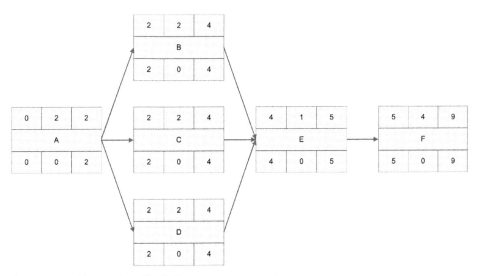

Figure 9.27: Network at Crash 3

Note that all activities are now critical. Activity D can not be crashed as activity C has been crashed to its maximum. The next lowest cost activity will therefore be activity F, which can be crashed by a maximum of 1 week.

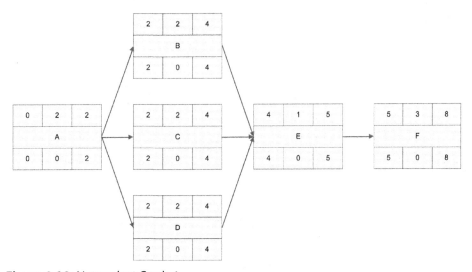

Figure 9.28: Network at Crash 4

The duration of activity F now becomes 3 weeks, with the project duration being reduced by 1 week. The additional cost of the project will be £30. Thus:

Crash 4: Crash activity F by 1 week at cost of £30
              Revised Project Duration   = 8 weeks
              Revised Project Cost   = £160.00

Finally activity A is reduced by 1 week at a cost of £40.

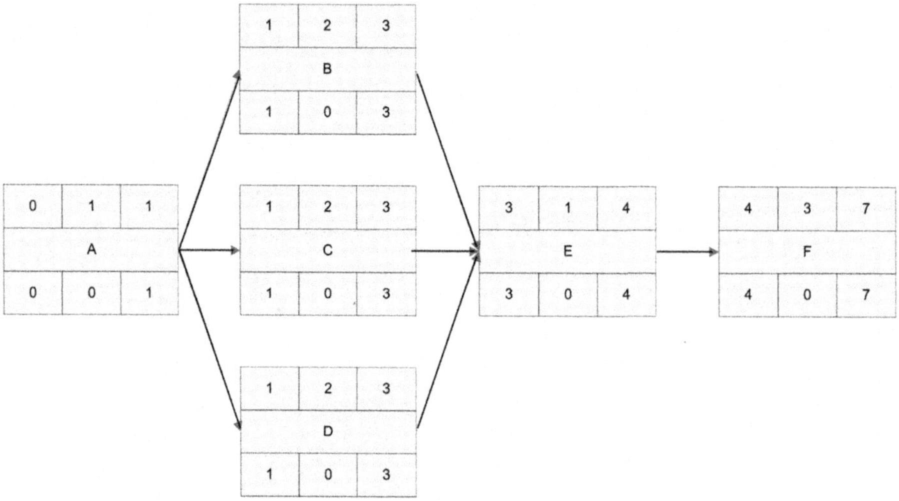

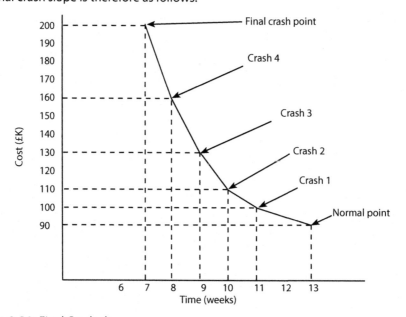

Figure 9.29: Final Crash sequence

The duration of activity A now becomes 1 week, with the project duration being reduced by 1 week. The additional cost of the project will be £40. Thus:

Final Crash: Crash activity A by 1 week at cost of £40

        Revised Project Duration   = 7 weeks

        Revised Project Cost   = £200.00

The final crash slope is therefore as follows:

Figure 9.30: Final Crash slope

The advantage of presenting the final crash slope is that it allows the project manager to assess by how much the project can be economically reduced. In this example the normal project duration of 13 weeks would incur a cost of £90, whereas reducing the project to 7 weeks would increase the cost to £200. The amount of time by which the project can be reduced is dependent on the expense the project can afford.

Summary

- Project scheduling includes all the processes required to accomplish timely completion of a project. These processes are activity definition, activity sequencing, activity timing, resource allocation and schedule control.

- A project network diagram is a schematic representation of the project. It identifies all the activities within the project, the logical sequence in which activities should be performed, the dependent activities and the critical activities that define the project duration.

- The critical path is the longest duration through the network. Activities on the critical path determine the project duration. Critical activities have no float time, in that any delay in the critical activities will delay the project as a whole.

- The duration of an activity may be estimated by either past experience, expert opinion, pilot testing, parametric approaches or statistical analysis. PERT is a statistical method that uses probability analysis to determine the duration.

- Gantt charts are bar charts that list the activities down one side of the sheet and use a horizontal timescale to represent the activities from start to finish. Gantt charts use the earliest start times of the network, with the float shown in a dotted line.

- A milestone is a predefined scheduled event in the project that signifies the completion of major deliverable. A milestone has no effort associated to it, although attaining a milestone does involve the completion of a number of activities. It is represented on the Gantt chart by a diamond.

- Project fast-tracking is a scheduling approach whereby the project is accelerated by overlapping activities that would normally be executed consecutively.

- Project crashing involves reducing the duration of certain activities in order to reduce the overall project duration. As the project is reduced, the cost of the project will increase. Project crashing should be performed in the most economical sequence. The calculation for cost per unit of time is as follows:

$$\text{Crash slope} = \frac{\text{Crash cost} - \text{Normal cost}}{\text{Normal duration} - \text{Crash duration}}$$

9

End of chapter review questions

Choose the most suitable answer. Only one should be selected. (Answers on page 206.)

1 The project scheduling process starts by

   a) Assigning duration to the project activities

   b) Activity sequencing and dependency table

   c) The statement of work

   d) Checking the availability of required resources.

2 The project manager typically starts the scheduling project activities applying

   a) All acquired expertise and experience from past projects

   b) A logic driven approach

   c) Resource driven approach

   d) All of the above

3 The concept of shuffling is more likely to be associated with

   a) Project crashing

   b) Trade off analysis

   c) the case of lack of resources, utilizing the existing float in the network

   d) When the resource distribution is uneven; with high peaks.

4 By definition the critical path in CPM is

   a) The longest path in the network

   b) The shortest path in the network

   c) The path with the highest cost

   d) The path with the highest risk in the network

5 To calculate the total duration of the project

   a) Add the duration of all critical activities within the network.

   b) Calculate the duration of the critical path

   c) Add the duration of all non critical actives then add the float

   d) a and b

6 An alternative approach when trade-off analysis does not suffice would be

   a) Crashing

   b) Shuffling

   c) Fast tracking

   d) Scope management.

Practice numerical questions

1 From the following logic table draw an **AON** network diagram to calculate the normal project duration of the project and identify the critical path.

Activity	Dependency	Normal Duration (weeks)	Normal cost (£)	Crash Duration (Weeks)	Crash cost (£)
A	-	5	60	3	380
B	A	6	60	5	80
C	B	8	120	6	180
D	B	5	40	3	70
E	B	1	70	1	70
F	D,E	5	40	3	120
G	C,F	2	50	1	220

2 Draw a Gantt Chart of network distinguishing the critical and non-critical activities and the float times.

3 Your projects director has asked you to calculate the *most economical method* to reduce the project duration by 5 weeks and report on the increased cost.

Perform a crashing exercise on the project, clearly stating the order in which the activities should be crashed, the project duration and project cost after each crash.

4 Draw a final crash slope, illustrating the financial consequences of each crash.

References

Boehm, B. W. (1981) *Software Engineering Economics,* Englewood, Cliffs, Prentice Hall.

Gantt, H. L. (1916) *Work, Wages and Profit,* New York, NY, Engineering Magazine Co.

Gray, C. F. & Larson, E. W. (2008) *Project Management: The Managerial Process,* New York, McGraw-Hill Irwin

Hill, J., Thomas, L. C. & Allen, D. E. (2000) Experts' estimates of task durations in software development projects. *International Journal of Project Management,* 18, 13-21.

Pinto, J. K. (2007) *Project Management: Achieving Competitive Advantage,* New Jersey, Pearson Education Inc.

Wadsworth, E. (2016) http://diagram.cf/w/wbs-example-software-project.html

Answers to end of chapter review questions

1 c), 2 b), 3 c), 4 a), 5 b), 6 c)

Answers to practice numerical questions

1 Network Diagram: Project duration = 23 weeks; Critical path = A ,B, D, F & G.

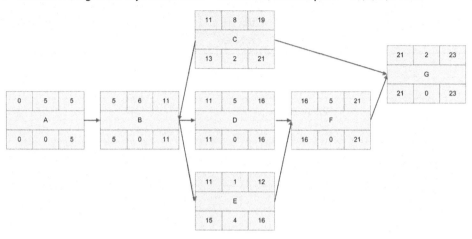

2 Gantt Chart

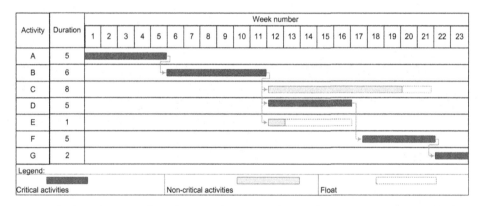

3 To calculate the cost of crashing each activity, the crash cost equation is applied:

Activity A	$= \dfrac{380 - 60}{5 - 3}$	$= \dfrac{£320}{2}$	= £160 per week
Activity B	$= \dfrac{80 - 60}{6 - 5}$	$= \dfrac{£20}{1}$	= £20 per week
Activity C	$= \dfrac{180 - 120}{8 - 6}$	$= \dfrac{£60}{2}$	= £30 per week
Activity D	$= \dfrac{70 - 40}{5 - 3}$	$= \dfrac{£30}{2}$	= £15 per week
Activity E	$= \dfrac{70 - 70}{1 - 1}$	$= \dfrac{£0}{0}$	= £0 per week

Activity F $= \dfrac{120-40}{5-3}$ $= \dfrac{£80}{2}$ $= £40$ per week

Activity G $= \dfrac{220-50}{2-1}$ $= \dfrac{£170}{1}$ $= £170$ per week

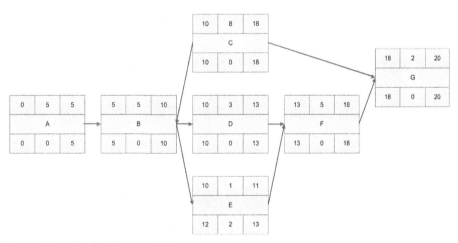

Figure A3.1: Crash 1 Network Diagram

Crash 1: Crash D by 2 weeks @ £15 per week.
Revised Cost = £470. Revised Schedule = 21 weeks

Crash 2: Crash B by 1 week @ £20 per week
Revised Cost = £490. Revised Schedule = 20 weeks

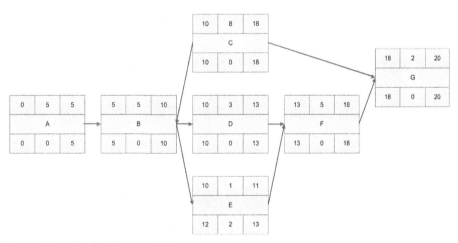

Figure A3.2: Crash 2 Network Diagram

Crash 3: Crash C by 2 weeks @ £30 per week
Revised Cost = £550.
Crash F by 2 weeks @ £40 per week
Revised Cost = £630. Revised Schedule = 18 weeks

9

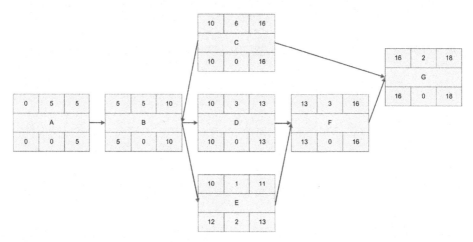

Figure A3.3: Crash 3 Network Diagram

4. The final crash slope is therefore as follows:

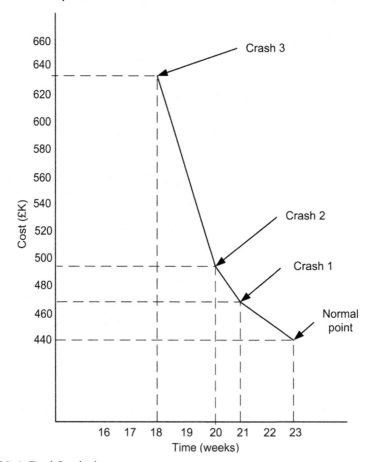

Figure A3.4: Final Crash slope

10 Project Resource Management

Gowrie Vinayan and Mohamed Salama

Learning objectives

By the time you have completed this chapter you should be able to:

☐ Understand the types of resources

☐ Estimate the resource needs

☐ Design the project staffing plan

☐ Develop a schedule constrained by time

☐ Develop a schedule constrained by resources

☐ Construct a multi-project resource schedules

Introduction

The project schedules cannot be finalised until the resources have been allocated to them. A resource can be any entity required to accomplish a project. This includes all the people working on the project, equipment required to perform tasks within the project and any materials required to achieve the project deliverables. All resources have costs associated with them which determine if the project is viable in the first instance. It is the project manager's responsibility to estimate the level of resources required for the project. However, certain constraints maybe outside the project manager's control. This includes the availability of resources, time constraints of the project and the availability of project funds. This chapter begins by discussing the different approaches to resource management, before investigating the resource constraints imposed on a project.

10.1 Types of required resources

Project resource scheduling involves determining the type of resource required for each work package, in terms of people, equipment and material; determining the quantity of resources required for each work package; and identifying when utilisation of each resource is required. Project resource scheduling must therefore be closely co-coordinated with project cost estimating.

When preparing a schedule, we generally make a mistake by assuming that all resources will be available when required, that there is an unlimited supply of resources and that the required resources are affordable. In reality, resources are limited in supply and availability. A particular problem for project managers is the need for specialist resources. These tend to be scarce, expensive and availability rarely coincides with the preferred schedule. When faced with the challenges and constraints of scheduling resources, it may be necessary to schedule activities not at the earliest start date, but rather at a time that suits the availability of resources or the maximises efficiency of resource usage. Otherwise projects may fail to achieve the project deadline schedule, as illustrated in the following example:

Example 10.1

Consider the example of three friends planning a huge party to celebrate their graduation and award of degree. With all three resources available to work on the project, the earliest day the party can occur will be day 3, as shown in figure 10.1.

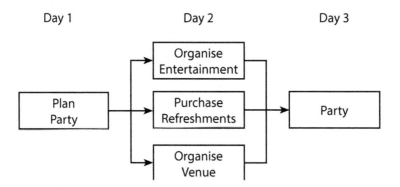

Figure 10.1: Three available resources

Now let us assume that one of the friends decide to have an alternative arrangement for his celebrations. This would result in only two available resources and the completion date of the party extending to four days.

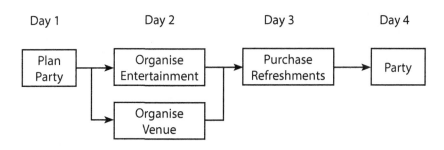

Figure 10.2: Two available resources

Finally let us assume that a second friend chooses not be involved in the party. This would result in only one available resource and all activities being performed in a series. As a consequence the project would now take five days to complete.

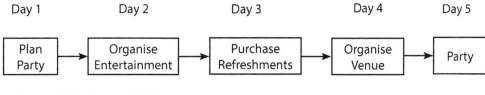

Figure 10.3: One available resource

10.2 Estimating resource needs

The action that the project manager takes to manage the constraints imposed by a resource is dependent on the schedule constraints of the project. In terms of scheduling there exist two types of project constraints: time constrained projects and resource constrained projects

■ Time constrained projects

Projects that are constrained by time must be completed by a fixed date. It may be necessary to acquire additional resources in order to achieve the deadline, although this does increase the risk of cost overrun. Time constrained projects have three objectives:

1 To maintain the project completion date.

2 To determine the resource requirements so that they will be available at the right time.

3 To schedule each activity so that the resource usage is as smooth as possible.

10

■   Resource constrained projects

Despite the assumption that resources are unlimited in a time constrained project, it is inefficient to schedule the work with erratic peaks and troughs in the resource usage, as shown in Figure 10.4.

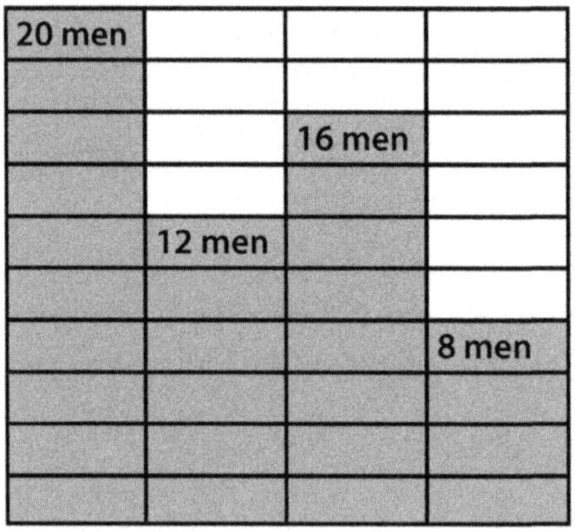

Figure 10.4: Inefficient resource utilisation

Not only is it expensive to move resources back and forth from the project, but it also consumes valuable effort in managing the resource variance. A more efficient utilisation would be where the resource usage is levelled across the project life cycle. Thus ensuring peak resource demands are reduced and fluctuations in resource demand is minimized, as shown in Figure 10.5.

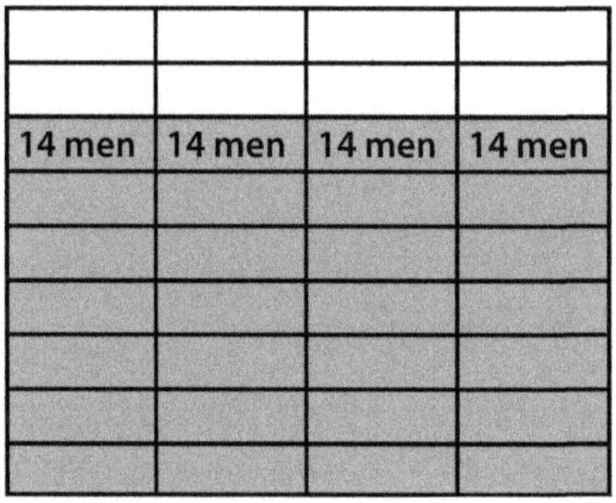

Figure 10.5: Efficient resource utilisation

10.3 Project staffing plan

Time constrained projects seek to maximise the efficient use of resources through **resource levelling**, which is sometimes referred to as **resource smoothing.** The objective of resource levelling is to reduce the fluctuation in the resource demand without extending the project duration. It does this by using the flexibility of non-critical activities. Rather than scheduling an activity at the earliest start time, a start time is used that maximises efficiency in resource usage. Consider the following gardening project which involves labour as a resource (adapted from Gray and Larson, 2011).

Example 10.2

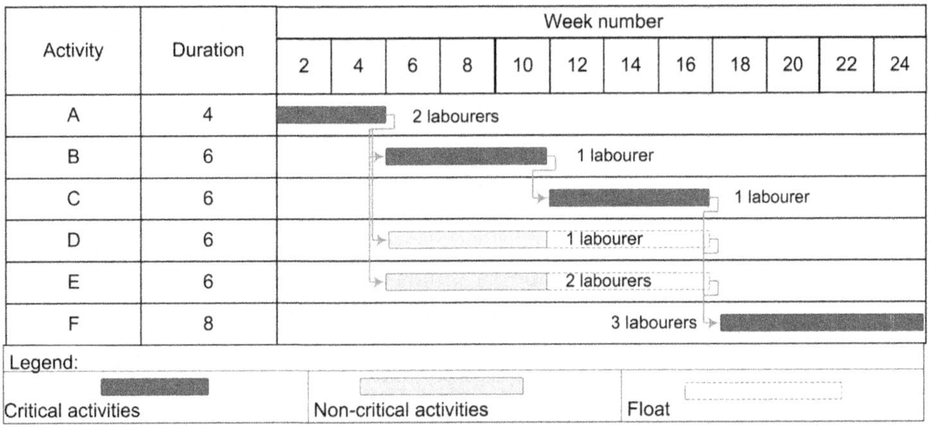

Activity	Duration	Week number											
		2	4	6	8	10	12	14	16	18	20	22	24
A	4	■■■ 2 labourers											
B	6			■■■ 1 labourer									
C	6					■■■ 1 labourer							
D	6		1 labourer										
E	6		2 labourers										
F	8					3 labourers ■■■							

Legend:

Critical activities ■■■   Non-critical activities ▭   Float ▭

Figure 10.6: Gantt chart

The following project has six activities, A,B,C,D,E, and F and must be completed by week 24. It utilises a single type of resource which is a gardener. As shown in Figure 10.6, the critical activities are A, B, C and F.

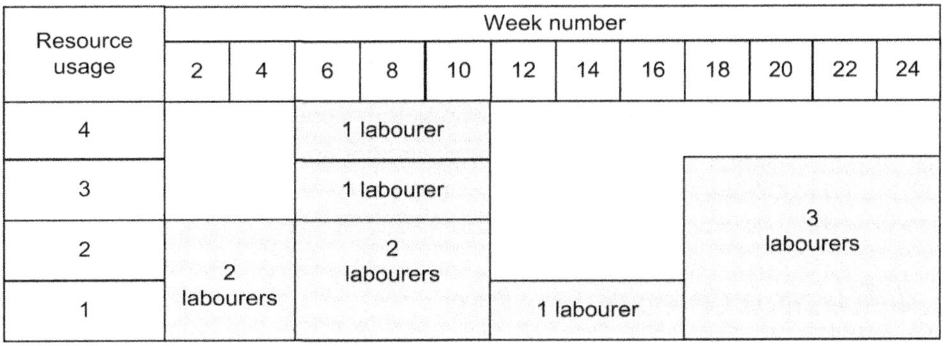

Resource usage	Week number											
	2	4	6	8	10	12	14	16	18	20	22	24
4			1 labourer									
3			1 labourer						3 labourers			
2	2 labourers		2 labourers									
1						1 labourer						

Figure 10.7: Resource histogram

The resource histogram in Figure 10.7 demonstrates an inefficient use of the resources. In the first four weeks only 2 labourers are required to dig the garden. As activities B, D and E are being executed in parallel, resource usage increases to 4 labourers from weeks 4 to 10. Demand reduces to only one resource for the next 6 weeks then increases to 3 labourers for the final weeks.

10

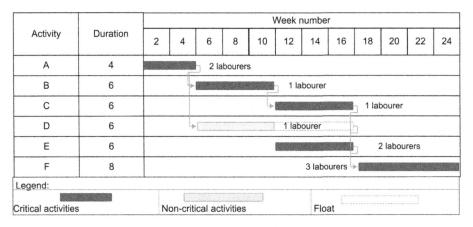

Activity	Duration	Week number											
		2	4	6	8	10	12	14	16	18	20	22	24
A	4	2 labourers											
B	6	1 labourer											
C	6	1 labourer											
D	6	1 labourer											
E	6	2 labourers											
F	8	3 labourers											

Legend:

Critical activities   Non-critical activities   Float

Figure 10.8: Gantt chart utilising slack of non critical activities

Because the project is time constrained, the goal will be to reduce the peak requirements without extending the project duration. By simply using the slack time of activity E, fluctuations in demand are minimised, whilst the project duration remains at 24 weeks.

Resource usage	Week number											
	2	4	6	8	10	12	14	16	18	20	22	24
4												
3						2 labourers			3 labourers			
2	2 labourers		1 labourer									
1			1 labourer			1 labourer						

Figure 10.9: Resource histogram showing efficient use of resources

Despite the improvement in resource utilisation, it should be noted that resource leveling does have the disadvantage of removing the flexibility from activities, whilst increasing its criticality.

10.4 Resource constraints

On a resource constrained project the level of available resources cannot be exceeded. This could be for a number of reasons such as limited availability of resources, maximum capacity levels or a strict resource allocation policy within the organisation. The biggest problem for the project manager comes when resource availability is below the required resource demand. Under these constraints it would be permissible to delay the project completion, although the extent of delay should be kept to a minimum.

Resource scheduling methods

The challenge for the project manager would therefore be in allocating available resources to activities, whilst minimizing the impact on the project duration. This requires decisions on which project activities to prioritise and which to delay. In considering the number of activities involved in a typical project, there could be numerous permutations and options available to the project manager. For simplicity, Gray and Larson (2011) suggest the use of heuristics to allocate resources. Whereas heuristics may not provide the optimum solution for prioritisation of resource allocation to activities, it does provide us with some basic rules. Working from left to right through the network, they should be applied as follows:

1   Prioritise those activities with least amount of slack

2   Prioritise activities with the least duration

3   Prioritise activities with the lowest activity identification number

The nature of heuristics is that these rules are flexible. The project manager's knowledge and experience take precedence over the rules, as do the project objectives. Consider the following example, which, Gray and Larson (2011) use to demonstrate the use of heuristics.

Example 10.3

The following project is constrained by a maximum resource availability of only 3 persons throughout. Consider the network diagram in Figure 10.10 and the Gantt chart in Figure 10.11. It can be clearly seen that from week 3 to week 8, the resource constraint has meant that there are inadequate resources to execute activities during this period.

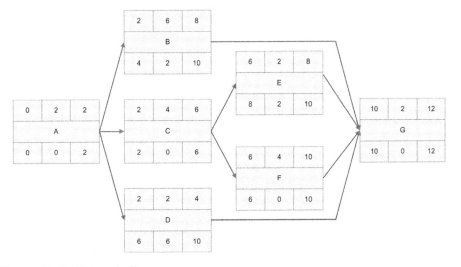

Figure 10.10: Network diagram

10

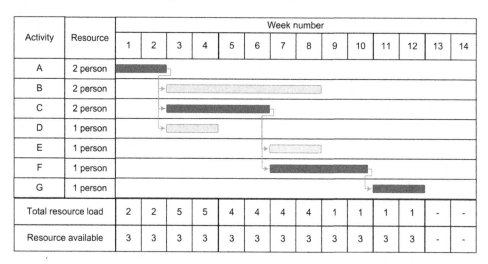

Figure 10.11: Resource schedule showing constraint from weeks 3 to 8

The first rule is to prioritise those activities with the minimum slack time. These are activities B and E, which both have a float of 2 weeks. Using their available slack time, they are rescheduled to start at the latest finish time (LF). The impact on the schedule is shown in Figure 10.12. Now only weeks 5 to 8 are under resourced, but activities B and E are critical.

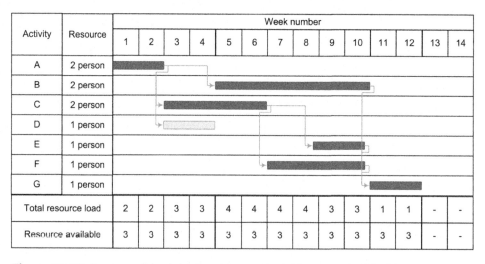

Figure 10.12: Resource schedule showing constraint from weeks 5 to 8

The next stage would be to prioritise activities with the least duration. Those concerned with resource constraint are activities B, C and F. There is no need to reschedule activity C as weeks 2 and 3 are adequately resourced. The activity with the least duration is activity F, but this can not be rescheduled as activity G is the dependency. We will therefore need to reschedule activity G by two weeks, thus, extending the project duration.

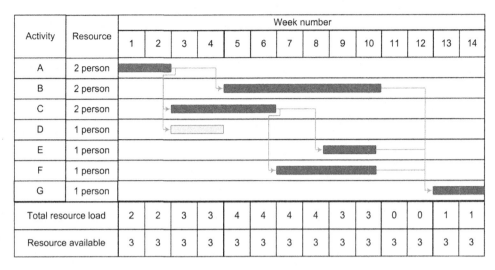

Activity	Resource	1	2	3	4	5	6	7	8	9	10	11	12	13	14
A	2 person														
B	2 person														
C	2 person														
D	1 person														
E	1 person														
F	1 person														
G	1 person														
Total resource load		2	2	3	3	4	4	4	4	3	3	0	0	1	1
Resource available		3	3	3	3	3	3	3	3	3	3	3	3	3	3

Figure 10.13: Resource schedule showing the impact of extended duration

We can now apply the third rule of prioritisation, which is the activity with the lowest identification number. We therefore reschedule activity B first, followed by activity E as shown in Figure 10.13. Although the project duration has been extended by two weeks and most activities have become critical, there are now adequate resources to execute the activities, though in some instances the sequence of activities may need to change.

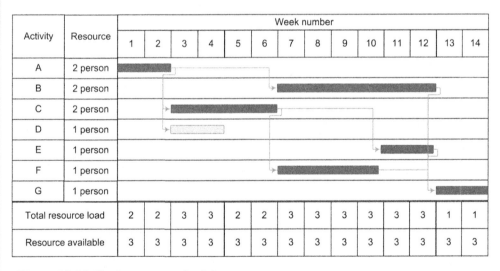

Activity	Resource	1	2	3	4	5	6	7	8	9	10	11	12	13	14
A	2 person														
B	2 person														
C	2 person														
D	1 person														
E	1 person														
F	1 person														
G	1 person														
Total resource load		2	2	3	3	2	2	3	3	3	3	3	3	1	1
Resource available		3	3	3	3	3	3	3	3	3	3	3	3	3	3

Figure 10.14: Final resource schedule.

10

10.5 Dealing with multi–project resource schedules

The project management office (PMO) helps to develop and nurture expertise in the management of multiple projects, and to assist in the evaluation of the inter-relationships between projects, which may differ in resource and skill requirements. The PMO will also ensure that the objectives of its portfolio of projects are related and are consistent with the overall goals of the organization.

The scheduling and resource allocation issues for multiple projects are more complicated than for a single project. One way to eliminate this complexity, would be to treat the projects as if they were elements of a single large project. Another method would be to consider each project in the portfolio of projects as dependent on one another. Though, in concept they are the same, the results from these two approaches would provide different schedules and resource allocation.

In a portfolio of projects, each project would have its own unique tasks, completion dates, and differing resource requirements. This issue is compounded further by different penalty costs incurred for not meeting time, cost, and scope specification for several different projects. As such, this scenario calls for the design and development of a dynamic multi-project scheduling system.

The multi-project scheduling system which is not static but dynamic in nature, must take into account three important standards which can monitor project scheduling effectiveness. They are i) *schedule slippage*, ii) *resource utilization*, and iii) *in-process inventory*. The project manager must pick the criterion which is most appropriate in managing his portfolio of projects.

■ Schedule slippage

A project may slip when it exceeds its delivery date. This is considered an important criteria in the management of multi-projects, because schedule slippage will attract penalty costs and the loss of goodwill. The monetary loss, coupled with loss of reputation will affect the long term sustainability of the company. Schedule slippage in one project may also cause other projects to slip thus having a disastrous 'domino effect'. The problem will be further prolonged, if new projects are added to the existing portfolio of projects.

■ Resource utilization

In reality, different projects require different resources in terms of money, labour, and capital equipment, to name a few. Though it would be easy to compute the costs of less than optimal scheduling due to excess resource utilization, the costs incurred in uncoordinated management of multiple projects can be difficult and exhorbitant. This is true in service industries, such as information technology, where one project may have to wait, because of resource scarcity. Potential clients will not wait but seek out your competitors in the industry. This leads to a decline in revenue, profits and customer satisfaction.

■ In-process inventory

This anomaly is due to the amount of work that needs to be processed, but has to wait, because there is a shortage of some resource. This is evident in a production shopfloor, where work-in-process is the uncompleted percentage of the product, which has to wait, and is in the intermediary position between raw material at the input stage and finished good at the output stage. This will result in stock holding cost which will increase the inventory costs and affect the profit margin of the finished item.

It is not possible to eliminate the three criteria at the same time and reach optimization. As usual, a firm has to decide which criterion is the most appropriate to implement in a given situation. The project manager must analyse and evaluate the various scheduling and resource allocation options and pick the one which is most critical to project success.

■ Heuristic techniques

Mathematical programming techniques, like Linear Programming (LP), could be used in project scheduling and resource allocation. The advent of information technology and the processing speed of powerful mathematical simulation tools have made it possible for project managers to conduct 'what if' analyses. However, it must be noted, that the use of LP in multi–project scheduling and resource allocation can be cumbersome and complex.

The use of heuristics approaches, on the other hand, are popular in practice. They are the only approach for projects which are large, nonlinear, and complex, and that occur in the real world. The availability of many software solutions by different vendors have given the project manager a wide choice from which to pick the solution which best fits his priority rules and decision criteria. The additional priority rules that the project manager needs to examine are:

Resource scheduling method

In project scheduling, the project manager must give priority to the activity that consumes the minimum time in project duration. This comparison is made on a 'pair-wise' basis among activities which are in conflict with one another in terms of completion time.

Minimum late finish time

This approach prioritises activities based on finish times. The activity which is the earliest late finisher is scheduled first.

Greatest resource demand

The resource with the highest demand in terms of dollar value will be given preference over other resources, whose dollar values may be lower or insignificant. This will eliminate possible resource bottleneck activities.

Greatest resource utilization

This would eliminate project slippage by giving priority to an aggregation of activities that would result in maximum resource utilization. This would lead to a minimum occurrence of idle resources during each project scheduling period.

Most possible jobs

This will give importance to a group of activities that would spur a combination of many activities in any scheduling period.

In conclusion, we can state that the heuristic approach to multi-project scheduling and resource allocation is a practical solution to mega-projects associated with complex multi-project issues encountered in the real world of project management.

Summary

Project schedules cannot be finalised until the resources have been allocated to them. A resource can be any entity required to accomplish a project. Project resource scheduling involves determining the type of resource required for each work package, in terms of people, equipment and material; determining the quantity of resources required for each work package; and identifying when utilisation of each resource is required.

In terms of scheduling there exist two types of project constraints: Time constrained projects and Resource constrained projects. Time constrained projects seek to maximise the efficient use of resources through **resource levelling,** which is sometimes referred to as **resource smoothing.**

The scheduling and resource allocation issues for multiple projects are more complicated than for a single project. It can be claimed that the heuristic approach to multi-project scheduling and resource allocation is a practical solution to mega-projects.

End of chapter review questions

1   Discuss the difference between time constrained projects and resource constrained projects.

2   Explain using examples the term 'resource levelling' in the context of project management.

3   Discuss the three standards applied to multi-project scheduling.

4   Critically evaluate the advantages of heuristic approach in the case of mega projects

References

Erik W. Larson, and Clifford F. Gray (2011). *Project Management – The Managerial Process*, 5th Ed., McGraw – Hill International Edition.

Jack R. Meredith, and Samuel J. Mantel (2012). *Project Management – A Managerial Approach*, 8th Ed., John Wiley & Sons, Inc.

11 Project Evaluation and Control

Mohamed Salama and Amos Haniff

Learning objectives

By the time you have completed this chapter you should be able to:

- ☐ Understand the concept of Project Performance Measurement.
- ☐ Identify and explain Project Performance Measurement Baselines.
- ☐ Describe the change management process
- ☐ Differentiate between change management and configuration management.
- ☐ Identify the types and causes of change within a project
- ☐ Develop a robust system for requesting change within a project
- ☐ Monitor and analyse performance using Milestone Tracking
- ☐ Monitor and analyse performance using Earned Value Analysis

Introduction

This chapter begins to look at the execution phase of the project. During this phase it is assumed that most of the project planning activities have been completed. Therefore most of the project management efforts will be on ensuring that the project will be realised as planned and taking corrective action for any deviations from the plan. This chapter begins by discussing project performance measurement, leading to change management and configuration management, before showing two effective methods of monitoring and controlling the performance of the project.

11.1 **Project performance measurement**

In projects in general, monitoring and control procedures use the **project base-lines** as the point of measurement. The project baselines comprise the planned cost and schedule recorded in the time phased budget. These reflect the agreed upon specifications and other parameters such as health and safety, besides any special customer requirements as per the defined scope of the project. At the end of the day, project success will be measured against the realisation of the benefits sought through the deliverables of the project, and in this context customer satisfaction is the overarching envelope. At any specific point on the project timeline, the project estimated expenditure is given. However, we have to accept that change will occur and will have an impact on the project baselines. It is the project manager's responsibility to control change, record the change, take corrective action for deviation from the project baseline and amend the project baseline accordingly.

It is necessary to establish a system to measure the performance of the project, and of the project manager. If there is no baseline or benchmark, then it will be difficult to make any objective evaluation of project performance. There are two levels: the micro level and the macro level. The former is concerned with the project scope, cost and time parameters which will be discussed in the later sections of this chapter under *earned value analysis* (EVA). It is worth noting that the approved detailed project scope statement and its associated WBS and WBS dictionary are the scope baseline for the project. The scope baseline is a component of the project management plan.

The latter on the other hand is concerned with the macro (strategic level) which is more grounded in the benefit realisation management concepts, as part of the strategic project management theory. In brief, this refers to the benefits sought through the implementation of this project and its contribution to the strategic objectives of the organisation as a whole. How can this be measured, especially if it includes a mix of tangible and intangible benefits? This can be an interesting topic for class discussion.

11

11.2 **Change management**

Despite the effort that goes into project planning, most elements of the detailed plans will not be fully realised as expected. This is because projects are unique and have a high degree of uncertainty. As a consequence, projects are highly susceptible to deviation from the original plans.

However, implementing changes to the project quite often impacts on the project objectives. Changes to the project involve re-design, re-planning and re-working, which consume time, resources and costs. The impact on the project is at it greatest during the execution phase, when the client has committed to expenditure on contractors and suppliers. It is therefore essential that an effective change management process is employed on the project, which will prevent any ad hoc and unauthorised amendments to the project, whilst maintaining control of any changes that needs to be made.

Sources of change

Change comes from many sources within a project. This includes the client, the project team, the participating organisation or external sources. Typical sources of change include:

- **Scope changes:** The most common form of changes in a project are those imposed by the client. This includes 'scope creep' when small constant incremental changes occur on the project scope, that when presented as whole have a significant impact. Scope changes could include additional elements of the project or redesign. It may be a request to improve the quality or change features of the project, or it may be to remove specific deliverables.

- **Baseline changes:** It is not uncommon for a client to seek improvement of the project baseline, by either reducing the budget costs or the master schedule.

- **Risks:** As discussed in Chapter 7, identification of risks or implementation of contingency plans may force the project to take a different course of action. This inevitably represents a change in the baseline costs and schedules.

- **Failure:** Risks that are not identified in the risk management process, such as contactor or supplier failure result in failure. These will also incur change.

- **Improvements:** Change is not always negative. Change can also come from improvements to the project process, such as those recommended by the project team.

The change management process

The purpose of the change management is to ensure that formal procedures exist to record, monitor and control changes to the project baseline. A typical process may include the following stages:

1 **Identify the proposed changes to the project:** The process must include a procedure for identifying change issues, which are the actions or circumstances that cause change. This includes routine assessments, reviews, meetings and inspection.

2 **Evaluate the effect of the proposed change on the project baseline:** Before a change can be authorised, analysis must be conducted to quantify the impact on the master schedule and budget, as a result of the change occurring.

3 **Formally approve (or reject) the proposed changes:** Following analysis of the change the proposal is either approved or rejected for refinement. Most decisions are made by the project manager, but when the change involves cost or schedule overrun, the authorisation of the change needs to be escalated to the project sponsor.

4 **Communicate the changes to all affected stakeholders:** Communication of the change is critical. The process must include a plan for communicating the change to the client, management, project team members and other relevant parties. The responsibility of ensuring that details of the change are disseminated in an effective manner lies with the project manager.

5 **Assign responsibility for implementing the change:** Once the change has been authorised it needs to be implemented effectively, normally within the constraints of time and cost. The project manager will therefore need to allocate responsibility for execution of the change to either a work package manager or another project team member. As change is often unwelcome by certain stakeholders, this role includes negotiation and resolving with those opposed to the change.

6 **Amend the master schedule and budget:** Once the changes have been implemented, the master schedule and budgets will need to be revised and endorsed by the client.

7 **Monitor the changes that have been implemented:** As with all activities on the project, the consequences of the change will need to be monitored for deviation from the revised schedule and budget baseline.

◼ Change management documentation

Most of the request for changes emerges at the execution phase of the project. This is the most expensive time to implement modifications to the project, as previously discussed. It is therefore necessary to have all the information regarding the change prior to consideration. This ensures that only necessary changes are considered for implementation and avoids ad hoc, unauthorised change decisions. Furthermore there needs to be clear evidence that the change has been subject to the change management process and has been fully approved. A standardised change request form, as shown in Figure 11.1, demonstrates justification for any change and ensures that approvals are agreed at the appropriate level.

11

Change request					
Project Title:					
Project Sponsor:			Request No.		
Originator:			Date:		
Change Requested by:					

Change Details

Change category	Scope	Schedule	Cost	Quality	Technology

Reasons for change: (Briefly describe why the change is required)

Description of Change: (Briefly describe the change to be implemented)

Risk of implementing Change: (Identify the risks of implementing the change, including do nothing)

Date of implementation		Priority level			

Authorization

Project manager			
Project Sponsor			
Client			
Other			

Figure 11.1: Sample change request form

11.3 Configuration management

Configuration management focuses on the specifications of both the project deliverables and the processes. This should be distinguished from change management which is focused on identifying, documenting and controlling changes to the project as whole with emphasis on the project baselines (*PMBOK Guide*, Fifth Edition). A *change management plan* is a generic plan that guides the project manager in terms of making any kind of change on the project, especially the ones that can impact the baselines (scope, time, cost baselines). As discussed in the previous section, a change management plan documents the process for managing change to the project as a whole and how it will be will be monitored and controlled. A *configuration management plan* on the other hand documents how configuration will be performed and guides on making changes which are specific to the product configuration. It defines those items that are configurable, those that require formal change control, and the process for controlling changes to such items.

In construction projects, changes are inevitable, and they involve changes in drawings and in specifications of different elements and deliverables of the project. It is not unusual to hear that unfortunately, the set of drawings sent to the site were not the latest version approved by the client. Or that the project manager was provided with an out-dated version of the specifications agreed by the client for a key deliverable in the project. Configuration management is the solution to this type of problem. It tracks the different revisions to the design, blueprints, technical specifications, and clearly identifies the latest version, when it was released, approved and shared with relevant parties.

The key elements of configuration management:

1 **Version control:** The ability to check the work into a common repository, retrieve it at any time to see any changes done by anyone, and maintain full version history.

2 **Baseline and release information:** When was the last version released, what did it contain, and having a baseline version to deploy at any time.

3 **Audits and review:** Audit of the process to ensure that people are actually following the configuration management and versioning system properly, correctly, consistently.

4 **Documented process:** A process agreed upon by all team members to ensure compliance in actual implementation. No point having a great system that no one uses or uses at random.

11

5 **Build, integrate and deploy scripts:** Common, standard scripts that automate the work of building, testing, integrating, deploying, and removing manual errors from the process. Standardization of the processes and its implementation is the key here.

Configuration management is a generic umbrella term for all the activities that reduce the risk of integration failure due to component changes on the project.

11.4 The project control process

It is not only changes that impact on the schedule and budget; activities can incur schedule and cost overruns if the performance on them does not match the anticipated performance at the time of creating the project baseline. When such an event happens, it is the responsibility of the project manager to take corrective action, in terms of allocating resources, exploiting slack time, extending the project duration or even drawing on contingency funds.

Project control is the process of monitoring and comparing actual performance with the estimated, planned performance. This involved identifying deviations in costs, deviations in the schedule, taking appropriate corrective action and amending the schedule and budget baseline accordingly. Pinto (2007) identifies a four step process for measuring and evaluating project performance (Figure 11.2). The salient issue within this process is that it is cyclic. Once the baseline has been set with the revised budget and schedule, performance measurement will continue, resulting in the baseline being revised numerous times throughout the execution phase.

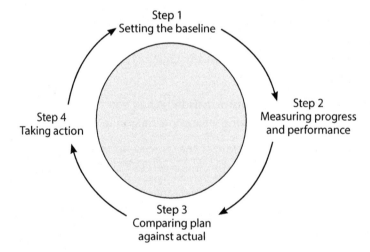

Figure 11.2: The project control cycle

Step 1: Setting the baseline

The baseline plan provides the basis of measurement performance. It is derived from the estimated cost and duration of each work package found in the WBS.

Step 2: Measuring progress and performance

Within projects progress and performance are mostly measured quantitatively through time and budgets. This involves collecting data through inspection or reports and drawing comparison with the baseline. However, qualitative measurement could include client satisfaction and meeting technical requirements.

Step 3: Comparing plan against actual

The project manager must identify any deviations from the baseline. This involves periodic monitoring and measurement of the project status and drawing comparison against the expected plans within the baseline.

Step 4: Taking action

If deviations are significant corrective action will be needed to bring the project back in line with the ordinal or revised plan. In some cases conditions to the scope may change which in turn will require changes to the project baseline.

11.5 Milestone tracking

Milestone tracking is a simple method of monitoring and recording progress on a project. This is commonly used when there is no requirement for detail of how progress has been achieved. Rather the purpose of the monitoring process is to provide an overview of the present status of the project. Despite the lack of detail, milestone tracking does have the advantage of consuming little management effort to set up and maintain.

As discussed in Chapter 6, a milestone is a predefined scheduled event in the project that signifies the completion of a major deliverable. The term 'milestone' actually derives from the use of medieval stone road obelisks that marked the distance to towns. Travellers would use the 'milestone' as point of progress within their journey. Similarly in projects a milestone represents a fixed deliverable within the schedule and there can be no doubt as to whether the milestone been achieved or not.

Milestones therefore must be **clear and well defined**. There must be a target completion date as to when the milestone must be achieved and the milestone deliverable must be delivered in its entirety. Partial completion of a deliverable

11

does not represent achievement of the milestone. Drawing on the time-phased budget it is also possible to associate a budget cost for each deliverable represented by the milestone. This is calculated by the estimated cost of the total number of work packages that form the deliverable. However, monitoring costs using milestone tracking tends to ignore the non-direct costs associated with the project. The following example demonstrates the use of milestone tracking.

Worked example

Table 11.1 compares the planned performance on product development project with the actual performance at week 18. The project was scheduled to be complete by week 16 at a budget cost of £16,000.

Code	Activity	Planned		Actual	
		Week	Cum. cost (£)	Week	Cum. cost (£)
A	Brief	2	3,000	2	3,000
B	Feasibility	5	5,000	5	6,000
C	Phase 1 Design	7	10,000	7	12,000
D	Phase 2 Design	8	12,000	9	20,000
E	Detail Design	10	18,000	11	25,000
F	Prototype	13	24,000	14	28,000
G	Build	16	26,000	18	30,000

Table 11.1: Record of planned and actual performance

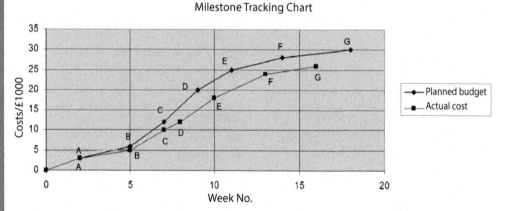

Figure 11.3: Milestone tracking chart

The milestone tracking chart in Figure 11.3 shows that the project began as planned with activity A achieving the cost and schedule target. However, by the completion of activity B, the project had a cost overrun of £1,000 and by completion of activity C there was a cost overrun of £2,000. This is despite the schedule being maintained. By activity D the project was also behind schedule by one week with cumulative costs at £8,000 over budget. Whilst the project managed to claw back the costs in the remaining activities, it still finished 2 weeks late and £4,000 over budget.

Class discussion

Comment on the activities in the milestone tracking chart (Figure 11.3). Suggest some reasons as to why the project has not managed to achieve its performance targets.

11.6 Earned value analysis

A more detailed use of monitoring performance is **earned value analysis (EVA)**. Sometimes referred to as **earned value management (EVM)** or **earned value technique (EVT)** (PMI 2004), EVA was originally developed by the US Government in the 1960s as a method of ensuring that contractors accurately track their costs along the lifespan of projects. Consequently, in 1967 the US Department of Defence imposed thirty-five Cost/Schedule Systems Criteria that all future defence projects must satisfy (DoD 1967); among these was earned value. Despite its intended use on major contacts, it was found that EVA could be applied to any contact within any industry. In fact, the concept is seen to be so effective that it is now deemed as best practice for monitoring project performance within most project management bodies of knowledge (APM 2006; PMI 2004).

EVA is based on the concept of value for money. It seeks to determine the value of work that has been completed on a project at any given time. It does this by drawing comparison between the planned schedule and costs with the current schedule and cumulative costs, similar to milestone tracking. However, the use of EVA has the significant advantage of enabling the project manager to calculate the revised completion time, the revised cost estimate and the additional cost required to complete the project. It also identifies those activities which are performing well and those activities which are not. This allows the project manager to take corrective action in order to either bring the project back within schedule and budget or to amend the project baseline accordingly.

EVA variables

Earned value analysis can be conducted at any level of the project, although it is most beneficial at the work package level. The process involves drawing comparison across three variables. It compares the cumulative value of actual work performed (earned value) with the planned progress and expenditure as determined in the project base-line, and the actual cost of the work performed, as shown in Figure 11.4.

11

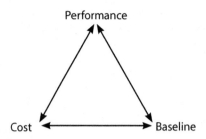

Figure 11.4: The EVA relationship

In order to calculate the current and future status of a project, EVA uses acronyms to describe each variable. In the past these were described as the budget cost of work performed (BCWP), budget cost of work scheduled (BCWS) and actual cost of work performed (ACWP). However, in recent years the acronyms have been shortened to be more phonetically friendly (Gray & Larson 2008; Pinto 2007; PMI 2004).

- **Planned value (PV):** The planned time-phased baseline of the value of work scheduled. The PV is the estimated value (for money) that is scheduled to be complete at a given point in time.

- **Earned value (EV):** The percentage of the cost budget that has been earned by actual work performed. The EV is the budgeted value (for money) of work completed to date.

- **Actual cost (AC):** The actual cost incurred in accomplishing the actual work performed. This figure derives from the project reports, request for payment and cost control data.

- **Cost variance (CV):** The difference in cost between the work content actually performed (EV) and the actual cost of the work scheduled (AC). Therefore:

$$CV = EV - AC$$

- **Schedule variance (SV):** The difference between the work content actually performed (EV) and the work content scheduled to be performed (PV). Therefore:

$$SV = EV - PV$$

However it should be noted that in EVA, schedule is measured in monitory terms.

- **Cost performance index (CPI):** The ratio cost between the work content actually performed (EV) and the actual cost of the work scheduled (AC). Therefore:

$$CPI = EV / AC$$

This index enables calculation of the budget to completion.

- **Schedule performance index (SPI):** The ratio between the work content actually performed (EV) and the work content scheduled to be performed (PV). Therefore:

$$SPI = EV / PV$$

This index enables calculation of the project schedule of the project to completion.

- **Budget at completion (BAC):** The current cost estimate of the total project as stated in the project budget.

- **Estimate at completion (EAC):** This is the estimated costs at completion, which includes the revised cost estimate based on the current cost performance of the project (CPI). Therefore:

$$EAC = BAC / CPI$$

- **Variance at completion (VAC):** The forecast of the final cost variance between the original budget and the revised estimated cost to completion. Therefore:

$$VAC = BAC - EAC$$

- **Estimate to complete (ETC):** The revised schedule at completion, based on the current schedule performance (SPI). Therefore:

$$ETC = Original\ estimated\ duration / SPI$$

■ Planned value (PV) and earned value (EV)

Table 11.2 shows the schedule and planned costs of all the activities within a particular work package at week 6 of its life cycle.

Activity	Planned		Percentage Complete (%)
	week	Cum. cost (£)	
A	1	1000	100
B	2	2000	100
C	3	3000	100
D	4	4000	100
E	5	5000	100
F	6	6000	58
G	7	7000	0
H	8	8000	0
I	8	9000	0
J	10	10000	0

Table 11.2: Progress record of activities

11

These figures derive from the time-phased budget. The work package is scheduled for completion at week 10 at a budget cost of £10,000. In reviewing the work package progress report for each activity, it has been recorded that at week 6 activities A, B, C, D, E are complete, but activity F is only 58% complete and activities G, H, I and J have not started yet. What the project manager needs to know is the earned value of actual work completed to date. In other words, what is the current status of the project in terms of cost, schedule and performance?

By week 6, it is estimated that all activities up to activity F should have been complete and the current spend on the work package is £6,000. The planned value (PV) at week 6 is therefore £6,000. This is represented as the PV in Figure 11.5.

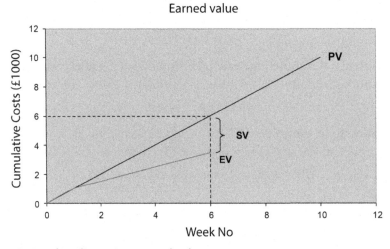

Figure 11.5: Project baseline using earned value

To calculate the earned value for each activity, the planned budget for each activity is multiplied by the percentage complete. Therefore by week 6, the earned value (EV) of the work package is 6000 x 58% = £3,500. This is represented as the EV in Figure 11.5.

■ Schedule variance (SV)

The schedule variance is the difference between earned value and the planned value. Therefore:

$$SV \quad = \quad EV - PV$$
$$= \quad £3,500 - £6,000$$
$$= \quad \underline{- £2,500}$$

A negative variance shows that the value of work complete is less than scheduled and the work package is currently under performing in terms of project duration. By the end of week 6 the planned budget estimated that £6,000 worth of work should have been complete. The negative schedule variance calculates that only £3,500 worth of work has been achieved to date and the work package is unlikely to achieve its completion date.

■ Schedule performance index (SPI)

To calculate the shortfall in project duration, we must first calculate the schedule performance index (SPI).

$$SPI = EV / PV$$
$$= £3,500 / £6,000$$
$$= 0.58$$

Calculating the SPI also has the added benefit of enabling at quick glance the current status of the work package. An SPI equal to 1 indicates that the work package is on schedule. An SPI less than 1 indicates that the work package is behind schedule. An SPI greater than 1 indicates that the work package is ahead of schedule. At week 6, it can be determined that the work package is significantly behind schedule.

■ Estimate time to completion (ETC)

In order to establish when the work package will now be complete, based on the current performance, the ETC is calculated by dividing the original estimate to completion by the SPI.

$$ETC = \text{Original estimated buration} / SPI$$
$$= 10 \text{ weeks} / 0.58$$
$$= 17.24 \text{ weeks}$$

We can therefore determine that based on current performance, the work package will be complete 7.24 weeks later than scheduled.

■ Actual costs (AC)

It cannot be assumed that the cost of work content for each activity will be as estimated. Activities may require more resources, equipment, materials or time to complete, than originally planned. The actual cumulative cost of each activity therefore needs to be compared against the work content actually performed. The figures for actual costs derive from the updated project cost estimate, project team or the contactors request for payment. They are represented in Table 11.3 as the *Actual Cum. Costs* (AC).

11

■ Cost variance (CV)

Table 11.3: Record of planned and actual costs at week 6

Activity	Planned		Actual Cum
	week	Cum. cost (£)	Costs (£)
A	1	1000	1000
B	2	2000	2500
C	3	3000	4000
D	4	4000	5000
E	5	5000	7000
F	6	6000	8000
G	7	7000	
H	8	8000	
I	8	9000	
J	10	10000	

Table 11.3 shows that at week 6, the work package has incurred a cumulative cost of £8000, whereas it was only scheduled to have spent £6000 by this date. A £2000 difference between the planned and actual cost is meaningless unless the amount of actual work complete is taken into consideration. For Pinto (2007) the cost variance is one of the key benefits to EVA when compared to other techniques, as EVA does not only show the money spent on a project, but also in terms of value created (performance).

Cost variance (CV) is the difference between earned value and the actual costs. Therefore:

$$CV = EV - PV$$
$$= £3,500 - £8,000$$
$$= -£4,500$$

The negative cost variance shows that only £3,500 value of work has been complete and the actual cost for this is currently £8,000. In other words we are predicting a significant cost shortfall at completion.

■ Cost performance index (CPI)

To calculate the cost shortfall, we must first calculate the cost performance index (CPI).

$$CPI = EV / AC$$
$$= £3,500 / £8,000$$
$$= 0.44$$

The CPI of 0.44 shows that for £6,000 worth of work planned to date, only £3,500 worth of work completed and has cost £8,000, which a very unfavourable position indeed.

The CPI is the most accepted and used index. It has been tested over time and is found to be the most accurate, reliable and stable. As with the SPI, calculating the SPI also of enables instant assessment of the current project cost status. A CPI equal to 1 indicates that the work package is on budget. A CPI less than 1 indicates that the work package has a cost overrun. A CPI greater than 1 indicates that the work package is currently performing under schedule. At week 6, it can be determined that the work package has a significant cost overrun.

■ Estimate at completion (EAC)

In order to calculate the revised cost estimate for the work package, based on the current performance, the EAC is calculated by dividing the original budget at completion by the CPI.

$$
\begin{aligned}
\text{EAC} \quad &= \quad \text{BAC} / \text{CPI} \\
&= \quad 10{,}000 / 0.44 \\
&= \quad \underline{£22{,}727}
\end{aligned}
$$

We can therefore determine that the work package is not performing well at all. Based on current performance the work package will be complete 7.24 weeks later than scheduled at a cost of £12,727 over budget.

■ Analysing performance

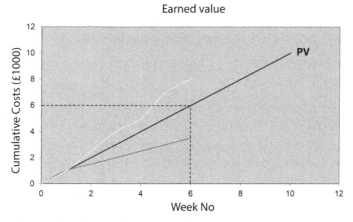

Earned value

Figure 11.6: Final earned value analysis

As shown in Figure 11.6, the work package has been underperforming since week 1. The schedule has slipped dramatically with only activity A being complete as planned. This has produced a cumulative effect on all the other dependent activities within the work package. In order to meet the planned schedule, extra resources have been employed. However, it would appear that this has been unsuccessful, as costs have risen dramatically and the schedule has still not been maintained. Based on the analysis the project manager can take corrective action to mitigate the situation and amended the project base line accordingly.

The clear advantage of using EVA is that it allows detailed analysis of each activity within a work package, which other techniques such as milestone tracking fail to do. But most importantly it enables calculation, at any time, of the cost to complete the project and the time of completion.

■ Disadvantages to EVA

As with any metric system there are disadvantages to the use of EVA. The main problem is that the performance measurement used in EVA is calculated on the percentage complete. This means that EVA is only as accurate as the information provided. Measuring the percentage complete on an activity requires subjective judgement, unless it is a linear activity such as laying railway track. More often the percentage figure is agreed based on round figures (25%, 50%, 75%), and this reduces the accuracy of the analysis.

It must be accepted that EVA is subject to human factors, and in many cases, bias. It is therefore the responsibility of the project manager to develop and enforce an efficient reporting system. Monitoring of work activities and work packages needs to be conducted on a regular basis and percentage measurements need to be as realistic and honest as possible.

Case Study: Heriot Watt Project Management Conference

Refer to the conference Case Study in Chapter 9 under section 9.3 and consider the following changes:

Due to the current global economic situation and the drop in oil prices that has affected many sectors, two key sponsors and 30 of the accepted papers and hence scheduled presenters have withdrawn. The registration deadline is not yet over but the deadline for submitting full papers is past. The review of full papers has now been completed and the feedback was communicated to authors two weeks ago. The submission of the final version of accepted papers is due in 4 weeks. There is a need for an effective change management plan to address these changes.

Questions

1 Develop an effective change management plan for this case. Discuss with your group the key items you need to consider. You can make any reasonable assumptions.

2 Develop an effective configuration management plan for this change. Identify and explain the main components and key inputs required for the proposed plan

Summary

- Changes to the project involve re-design, re-planning and re-working, which consumes time, resources and costs. The impact on the project is at it greatest during the execution phase, when the client has committed to expenditure on contractors and suppliers.

- The change management process has seven stages. These are: identify the proposed changes to the project; evaluate the effect of the proposed change on the project baseline; formally approve (or reject) the proposed changes; communicate the changes to all affected stakeholders; assign responsibility for implementing the change; amend the master schedule and budget; monitor the changes that have been implemented.

- A configuration management plan documents how configuration will be performed and guides on making changes which are specific to the product configuration. It defines those items that are configurable, those that require formal change control, and the process for controlling changes to such items.

- The project control process is a four step cycle: 1) setting the baseline; 2) measuring progress and performance; 3) comparing plan against actual; 4) taking corrective action

- Milestone tracking is a simple method of comparing planned with actual performance on a project. Is used when there is no requirement for detail of how progress has been achieved.

- Earned value analysis is a sophisticated and accurate technique for comparing cost, schedule and performance. It draws on three key variables: The value of work performed (EV); the value of worked planned (PV) and the actual cost of work performed (AC). It also beneficial in that EVA can determine the revised completion time (ETC); the revised estimated cost at completion (EAC) and the variance in cost from planned (VAC).

11

End of chapter review questions

Choose the most suitable answer. Only one should be selected. (Answers on page 242.)

1 The scope baseline includes:

a) The risk management plan

b) The communication management plan

c) The change management plan

d) The work breakdown structure

2 The change management plan is mainly concerned with

a) The project as a whole

b) The key deliverables of the project

c) The specifications of the project deliverables.

d) How to manage the changes that impact the project baselines.

3 The configurations management system is primarily focused on

a) The project as a whole

b) The key deliverables of the project

c) The change in the specifications of the project deliverables.

d) How to manage the changes that impact the project baselines

4 The cost baseline at the very early start of the execution phase in external projects is the

a) Tender price

b) Schedule performance index

c) Earned value

d) Cost performance index

5 Ideally, project managers have fewer concerns when rescheduling occurs:

a) During the planning phase

b) During the planning phase or for the future activities during the implementation.

c) Any time during the PLC if adequate financial resources are available.

d) All the above.

6 Project evaluation should be based on

a) Project success criteria

b) Project performance measurement.

c) Project critical success factors

d) Project team spirit

Typical examination questions

1   From the following data prepare an earned value analysis showing the current status of the project and make brief comment of each activity.

Activity	A	B	C	D	E	F	G
AC	£900	£700	£825	£500	£720	£1000	£700
EV	£600	£700	£525	£400	£720	£850	£700
PV	£900	£1000	£625	£250	£400	£500	£250

Make comment on the performance of each activity

2   The project is scheduled to be complete by the end of week 12 at a budget cost of £6000. Using the information provided estimate:

a) The estimated cost at completion (EAC)

b) The variance at completion (VAC)

c) The revised completion time. (ETC)

References

APM (2006) *APM Body of Knowledge* Bucks, Association of Project Management.

Department of Defence (DoD) (1967), *Performance measurement for selected acquisitions"*, *Department of Defence Instruction 7000.2*, Department of Defence, Washington, DC

Gray, C. F. & Larson, E. W. (2008) *Project Management: The Managerial Process,* New York, McGraw-Hill Irwin

Pinto, J. K. (2007) *Project Management: Achieving Competitive Advantage,* New Jersey, Pearson Education Inc.

PMI (2004) *A Guide to the Project Management Body of Knowledge: PMBOK guide,* Pennsylvania Project Management Institute Inc.

11

Answers to end of chapter review questions

1 d), 2 d), 3 c), 4 a), 5 a), 6 a)

Solutions to typical examination questions

1 In order to conduct the analysis an EVA will be performed as follows

Activity	AC	EV	PV	CV	SV	SPI	CPI
A	900	600	900	-300	-300	0.67	0.67
B	700	700	1000	0	-300	0.7	1
C	825	525	625	-300	-100	0.84	0.64
D	500	400	250	-100	150	1.6	0.8
E	720	720	400	0	320	1.8	1
F	1000	850	500	-150	350	1.7	0.85
G	700	700	250	0	450	2.8	1
Project:	5345	4495	3925	-850	570	1.15	0.84

2 Comments will be as follows:

Activity A: Is behind schedule and has a cost over run

Activity B: Is behind schedule but is under budget

Activity C: Is behind schedule and has a cost over run

Activity D: Is ahead of schedule but has a cost over run

Activity E: Is ahead of schedule and under budget

Activity F: Is ahead of schedule but has a cost over run

Activity G: Is ahead of schedule and under budget

3 The calculations will be as follows:

a)   Estimate at completion = BAC/ CPI

              = £6,000 / 0.84

              = £7135

b)   VAC   = £1135

c)   ETC   = Original estimated duration / SPI

            = 12/1.15

            = 10.43 weeks

12 Project Closure

Amos Haniff and Mohamed Salama

Learning objectives

By the time you have completed this chapter you should be able to:

☐ Recognise the conditions for closure of a project

☐ Implement a project closure process

☐ Conduct a post-project review

☐ Understand the problems inherent with project closure

Introduction

As introduced in Chapter 1, project closure, or **termination,** is the final phase of the project life-cycle. This phase commences upon completion of all the project deliverables in the scope statement. However, despite being successful through the earlier stages of planning and execution, a number of project managers have difficulties at the closure phase. This is because closure of a project requires both strong technical and personal skills. The greatest challenge to the project manager at termination is showing understanding of the people issues and compassion towards a team that may feel demotivated as the project draws to a close.

It is possibly this reason that Spire and Hamburger (1988) propose that 'project termination' should be treated as a project itself. Indeed the task of project closure does fit the classical definition of a project, as a unique undertaking with specific recourse constraints. Spire and Hamburger have produced a very useful WBS for closure, shown in Figure 12.1. This identifies a number of potential problems at the closure phase. These are divided into the intellectual and emotional elements that management should address when the project begins the process of termination.

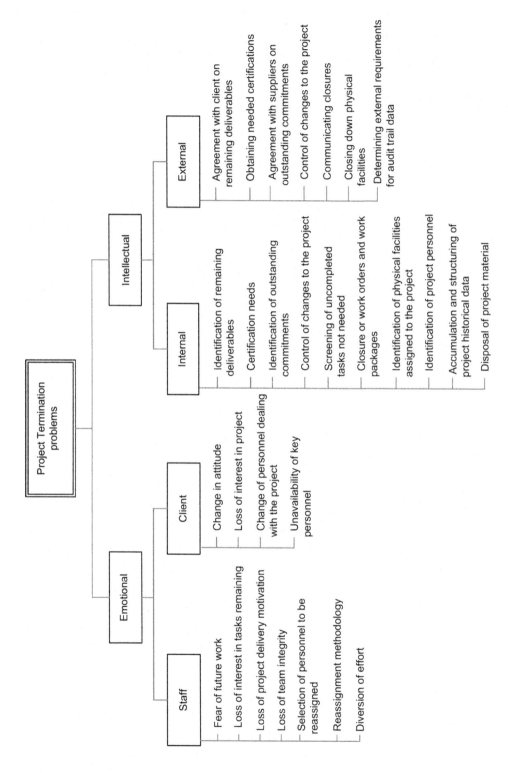

Figure 12.1: Issues for Project Termination. Source: (Spirer and Hamburger, 1988)

- **Intellectual components**: Activities that need to be complete in order to formally handover and close the project.

- **Emotional components**: Potential issues encountered by personnel involved in the project.

12.1 Conditions for project closure

As we have discussed in Chapter 1, projects are temporary and therefore must come to an end. When planning a project we schedule for project completion and plan closure accordingly. However, a project may close for variety of reasons. Gray and Larson (2008) identify five circumstances for project closure:

1 **Normal closure:** The common condition of project closure is when the project is completed as planned. This is when the project objectives are achieved, the client accepts the project and normal project closure commences.

2 **Premature closure:** Many projects do not achieve all their deliverables or are not given the opportunity to so. Instead, they are closed prematurely by eliminating elements of the project originally identified in the project scope. This could be for the reason of costs, where the client reduces funds on the project or the project has already consumed the budget. Premature closure also occurs when the project is of strategic importance and must be delivered earlier than expected, such as a new product launch. Delaying the product until the original completion date may result in opportunity lost for the client.

3 **Perpetual projects:** Conversely, some projects never seem to end. These are projects that have had numerous delays, set backs and problems. Perpetual projects also suffer from endless scope creep, add-ons and changes, as discussed in Chapter 6. The problem with these types of projects is that they never achieve their goals or objectives, due to the changes and consistent scope screep. This becomes highly frustrating for the project manager and the project team. It will also be highly frustrating for the client as they do not see the objectives of the project being achieved, despite the consistent request for changes. At some point the project manager needs to fix the scope and plan for closure. Redefining the project scope so project closure is forced, limiting budget or resources, or setting a time limit can do this. As a result, any additions that the client requests can be viewed as a second phase of the project, rather than the project being perpetual

4 **Failed projects:** Far too often projects close because they have failed. There are a number of causes for project failure. It is not uncommon for the client to run out of funds, thus permanently killing the project. Another common

12

reason for failure is where the original design for the project deliverable is unworkable or needs to be abandoned due to unacceptability from the end user. There are also reasons,beyond the control of the client and project team, such as changes in government policy forcing projects to terminate, changes in social and economic conditions, or even 'Acts of God', such as extreme weather conditions, that can force the project to be abandoned. The client may also choose to terminate the project if the progressing costs of the project exceed the business benefits, deadlines are continually missed or the client simply loses trust in the project and the project team.

5 **Changed priority:** Some projects close because the original objectives of the projects are no longer aligned to the organisation's strategy. This is probably the most frustrating situation for the project management as it does not matter how well the project or the project teams are performing. If the project no longer contributes to the strategy of the organisation, investment should be withdrawn. Far too often, rather than killing the project, many organisations choose to wind-down the project by starving it of necessary resources or shifting resources to projects with higher priority. This cause great stress and difficulty to the project manager, as despite its impeding doom, there is loyalty to the project and the remaining project team.

12.2 The project closure process

As the project moves towards natural completion, a number of activities are necessary to formally close it. This is referred to as the **closure process** and should be presented as a formal closure plan. As with other phases in the project life cycle, management of the closure process requires careful attention by the project manager. However, as the project nears completion it is often difficult to ensure high performance from the project team. In the first instance the adjournment process, discussed in Chapter 5, may have already begun, with some team members already leaving the team, as their responsibilities are complete. Second, existing team members will be considering their next assignment. As such, they will find it difficult to remain focused on the current project. The challenge for the project manager at the closure phase is to keep the project team motivated throughout the closure process. Figure 12.2 illustrates the typical activities to be complete.

Completing the work	Client acceptance	Project documentation	Project handover	Post-project review
Disbanding the project team				

Figure 12.2: The project closure process

■ Completing the work

Before handover of the project to the client, all work must be complete, in accordance with the agreed specification. Whereas most deliverables at this stage will be 'practically complete', in terms of being useable, they may still need final finishes or modifications. For example IT projects may require debugging; new product development projects may require minor amendments to handbooks, and construction projects may need to repair minor defects in the building.

It is the responsibility of the project manager to generate a control document in the form of a checklist, such as that shown in Figure 12.3. This identifies those items that need to be modified or complete for satisfactory handover. Similar to a responsibility matrix, the checklist should also identify which team member is responsible for ensuring that the final tasks take place. It is strongly recommended that conducting an inspection of the project, preferably with a client representative, is the best method of generating the list of activities for the checklist. When considering the activities, the current project status should be checked against the scope statement and WBS. It also needs to be checked against updated schedules and change documentation to ensure that the completed project meets the client's expectations.

Project Closure Checklist				
Project Details				
Project name:				
Prepared by			Date	
Closure phase begins		Closure phase ends		
Item No.	Activity Description	Due date	Person Responsible	Notes

Figure 12.3: Sample project closure checklist

12

■   # Client acceptance

The project manager needs to obtain formal acceptance of the project deliverable by the client in order to close the project. However, the client reserves the right to refuse acceptance if the project does not meet the specification defined in the scope. It is therefore beneficial to review the project objectives before formal acceptance. The project manager needs to anticipate any objections the client may have to accepting the project and develop a plan for overcoming those objections. However, there is very little reason for the client to refuse the project if the following conditions apply:

- The project is delivered in accordance with the scope statement and revised change documents.

- The quality of the project is delivered as specified.

- The cost of the project accurately reflects the work content.

Client acceptance involves comparison of the scope statement with the final deliverable. The client will expect to be taken through the project and test various elements for suitability. It should be noted that client acceptance my not necessarily be final. The client may accept the project with 'conditions'. These are items that still need to be complete in accordance with the specification on quality and should be documented in a revised checklist. Any outstanding items identified by the client should be complete by a specific date and checked again by the client.

■   # Project documentation

Prior to formal handover of the project all project documentation relating to the project must be complete. Unfortunately, projects involve an abundance of paperwork, generated at each phase. At the closure phase all project documentation needs to be reviewed in order to check they are current and accurate. Project documentation must also be archived and referenced in a traceable manner. This is for future reference and lessons learned for future projects. Typical project documentation at the closure phase should include:

- **Schedule and planning documents:** These include the scope statement, project plans, Gantt charts, monitoring and control documents, resource usage, customer change requests and the updated specification.

- **Costs accounts:** The project is not complete until the project costs have been paid. All cost accounts related to the project must be closed prior to handover. Any unused project funds will be reverted back to the organisation's financial department. Documentation includes cost accounting records for materials, purchases, rebates and any other budgetary items. Invoices and payments need to be checked and all receipts must be in order. The costs and charges for the all personnel contributing to the project must either be charged against the project or a departmental budget. As all spending on the project needs to be accounted for, the project manager must check the actual works against the costs in the EVA before recommending formal handover. Finally, the contactors and external consultant fees accounts must be closed. This includes any additional expense claims and other verified extra costs.

- **Legal documents:** These include all the contractual documents, guarantees, warrantees and conditions of service. As many projects have an indemnity period, in which defects that appear in the project after handover must be repaired by the appropriate contactor, it is critical to that all legal documentation are archived. On some projects it is common to retain a percentage of the amount payable to a contactor over a defined warranty period. This is to ensure the contactor returns to repair any defects under the warranty.

Project handover

Project handover involves officially transferring the project to its intended user, in accordance with the contractual terms of the project. It is expected, by this stage, that all items will be complete and any outstanding 'reservations' will be only minor and scheduled for completion. However, Pinto (2013) advises that project handover often involves more than straightforward transfer of project ownership. It may also include training programmes for end users, production of maintenance manuals, demonstrations and transition periods in which the project contactor must first demonstrate viability of the project, as in **build, operate and transfer** (BOT) or **build, own, operate and transfer** (BOOT) agreements. This is when the contactor operates or takes ownership of the project for specified period of time, usually until all contractual problems have been resolved.

At handover there should be a through formal 'walkthrough' of the project with the client and client representatives. Quite often handover is a formal affair and is marked by a presentation and demonstration of the deliverable to the end users and key stakeholders. This may be the first opportunity they have at seeing the project and may raise a number of questions. This should be of no concern on a successful project, rather project handover should be a time of celebration and an opportunity to thank the project team for their efforts.

12

■   Post-project review

Unless there is a thorough review exercise at completion, 'lessons learnt' on the project will be lost. Leaning from past projects is invaluable for organisations conducting projects. Not only can the organisation avoid common mistakes on projects, but they also allow inexperienced project managers to gain access to and learn from closure reports provided by previous project managers. Despite this, few project managers actually conduct project evaluations effectively. Instead, the project review becomes a vehicle for apportioning blame for mistakes and errors on the project, rather than being productive.

The underlying purpose of the review is to identify areas for improvement and methods of achieving this. Improvements could range from minor modifications, to standard practice, to a radical redesign of the project management processes. The review should also identify those elements of the project that went extremely well. Projects are unique and it is not uncommon for project teams to find new innovative ways of problem solving. These need to be captured, documented and advised as 'best practice' for future application.

Whereas the project review may take a variety of forms, Boyle (2003) proposes a three stage process for the review.

Stage 1: Define strategic objectives and resources

- **Appoint a chairperson:** In order to ensure objectivity, it is recommended that someone from the client board, who has not had direct involvement in the project, chair the review process.

- **Define the objectives of the post project review process from the client organisation's perspective:** Feedback from the review not only provides opportunity to assess how well the project was implemented, but also how well the brief was developed, the management issues involved in the process and the part played by the client representatives. It should also consider more specific issues, such as budget overspend, missed deadline or other particular problems that have impacted on the strategic objectives of the project.

- **Define resources that can be made available for the review:** The client needs to identify the management and staff that will conduct the review on behalf of the participating organisation. There also needs to be a budget available to carry out the review with deadlines set as to when the review will be complete. Specific issues that cause legal concerns may need to be complete by specific dates; for example, the end of the financial year.

Stage 2: Select and prioritise the specific objectives

- **Assess the result of the final project to the project brief:** This requires comparison of each of the major deliverables against the project charter and project scope.

- **Assessment of objectives:** The review should identify how the final project outcome compares with the strategic objectives identified in the project charter. This includes the business case, justification for the project and return on investment.

- **Project initiation:** The review must also access the quality of the initial project documentation. Were the project objectives clear in the project charter and were these interpreted correctly to the scope statement? How comprehensive was the documentation provided to the project team?

- **Project performance:** How did the actual project performance compare against planned performance? These include measurement against the project constraints of time, cost and quality. Where objectives have not been met, the obstacles that have prevented this must be identified.

- **Performance of contributors:** This is probably the most sensitive part of the review process. Evaluation of the project team, in terms of achieving the performance, needs to be assessed. However, the evaluation will also go beyond time, cost and quality specifications. It may also review common purpose, teamwork and respect within the project. This stage must also review the reward system employed. Were the team rewards adequate? Did they motivate the team to perform?

Stage 3: Design a simple and realistic review post project review process

This final stage of the review process involves dissemination of the findings of the review. In the first instance, information from the review needs to be circulated. The findings should be discussed at senior level, with recommendations made for future projects. On conclusion of the review, a final report must be written with suggested improvement measures and best practice guidelines.

■ Disbanding the project team

The final and probably most uncomfortable stage of the project closure process is disbanding the project team. This is the emotional component of the closure process.

As the project draws to completion, project team members will be concerned about future employment, starting other projects and joining other teams. This may result in the prolonging of tasks, as team members will be reluctant for the

12

project to end. However, the biggest challenge at closure stage is motivating the project team to complete the remaining tasks. Most of the tasks at this stage may appear tedious in comparison to the interesting activities at the earlier stages of the project. As a consequence, there is a risk of poor performance at the final stages. Another effect on the team is the gradual reduction of the team, as members are redeployed onto other projects or back to their functional department. This can be difficult for the remaining team members, as the dynamics of the team change and motivation diminishes.

During the final stages the project manager must remain the key motivator. The team must be encouraged to complete any outstanding works, whilst being supported in their transition to other projects. The project manager should also host some form of celebration with the project team to mark the closure of the project, even if it is only lunch time pizza.

Exercise 1

Consider being part of a project team that has been working intensely together for some time in order to deliver a successful project.

☐ How would you feel when the team is about to disband?

12.3 Difficulties in the closure process

As previously emphasised, an effective closure process is essential for improvement of future projects. Despite this, many organisations rarely conduct an effective closure process. Given the time constraints imposed on projects, pressures on project teams and the need to focus on project goals, it is hardly surprising that project closure becomes secondary. However, the same mistakes appear to be repeated on varied projects. Too often, critical lessons learned during a project become lost in documentation and dissemination of valuable information for future projects is often vague (Haniff and Kaka, 2001).

It is often the case that projects become perpetual in that they never appear to end. Minor contractual issues take a long time to be resolved and the project closure is prolonged. Getting project personnel to complete the outstanding work is a common problem for the project manager at the closure phase. Once the client has indicated acceptance of the project, it becomes difficult to motivate the team to complete minor activities.

Furthermore, when contactors, suppliers and consultations have been paid for their efforts, there is little motivation for them to return and repair or modify outstanding items. It is for this reason that retention sums are included in the contacts. The closure of a project also creates a paradoxical situation for the project team. If they complete all the outstanding activities and close the project, the team will disband or become unemployed. Conversely, if they do not complete the project, the performance review of the project will be negative, which could affect future employment opportunities.

It is not only the project team who are responsible for poor closure. The participating organisation also creates difficulties towards the end of projects. Organisations that implement numerous projects will no longer see the current project as a priority, as the deliverables of the project will have already been realised by the closure phase. As a result, the organisation will focus on new projects and shift project personnel and project managers to the new undertakings. Not only does this send a message to the existing project staff that the project is now of low priority, but junior and inexperienced project managers are often left to complete the closure process.

Pinto (2013) advises that developing a natural process for project closure offers the project organisation a number of advantages. First, it allows the project office to create a database of lessons learned for future projects. Second, it provides a structure for project closure that changes it from a secondary, ad hoc exercise, into a rigorous project process. Third, when handled correctly, project closure can serve an important source of information and motivation for project team members. Not only can the team gain knowledge from the project, but it can also take this new knowledge onto future projects when the team disbands.

Summary

- Effective project closure is notoriously difficult. The project team may not be motivated to complete the final elements of the project. It is for this reason that closure should be viewed as a project itself.

- At the closure stage there are two types of problems that need to be dealt with: Technical issues that require project management skills and emotional issues that require empathy and human interaction by the project manager.

- There various reasons why a project terminates. These include normal closure, premature closure, perpetual projects, failed projects and changed priorities.

- The project closure process involves completing outstanding works; gaining client acceptance; completing and archiving all project documentation; conducting a project review and disbanding the team.

12

End of chapter review questions

- ☐ Discuss the reasons why a project may be terminated before it has had the opportunity to achieve its stated objectives.
- ☐ Outline the stages of the project closure process.
- ☐ Evaluate the importance of the project review process
- ☐ Consider the emotional problems involved in project closure. How would you support the project team?

References

Boyle, G. (2003) *Design Project Management* Aldershot, Ashgate Publishing.

Gray, C. F. & Larson, E. W. (2008) *Project Management: The Managerial Process,* New York, McGraw-Hill Irwin

Haniff, A. P. & Kaka, A. P. (2001) A framework for development of a knowledge database for use within the construction industry, *ARCOM 17th Annual Conference.* University of Salford, UK, ARCOM.

Pinto, J. K. (2013) *Project Management: Achieving a Competitive Advantage,* Harlow, Essex, Pearson Education Limited.

Spirer, H. F. & Hamburger, D. H. (1988) Phasing out the project, In Cleland, D. I. & King, W. R. (eds) *Project Management Handbook.* New York, John Wiley & Sons.

Index

Printed in the United States
By Bookmasters